SINO-AMERICAN ECONOMIC EXCHANGES

SINO-AMERICAN ECONOMIC EXCHANGES

The Legal Contributions

by Guiguo Wang

PRAEGER

PRAEGER SPECIAL STUDIES • PRAEGER SCIENTIFIC

New York • Philadelphia • Eastbourne, UK
Toronto • Hong Kong • Tokyo • Sydney

Library of Congress Cataloging in Publication Data

Wang, Guiguo.
Sino-American economic exchanges.

Bibliography: p.
Includes index.
1. Foreign trade regulation—United States.
2. Foreign trade regulation—China. 3. United States—Foreign economic relations—China. 4. China—Foreign economic relations—United States. I. Title.
KF6668.C6W36 1985 343.73'087 84-18108
ISBN 0-03-001659-2 (alk. paper) 347.30387

Published in 1985 by Praeger Publishers
CBS Educational and Professional Publishing
a Division of CBS Inc.
521 Fifth Avenue, New York, NY 10175 USA

56789 052 987654321

Printed in the United States of America
on acid-free paper

PREFACE

Since World War II, international economic relations have undergone great changes. For one thing, diversified economic systems have been established, especially in newly independent countries. Today there exist traditional market economies, mixed economies, and centrally planned or state-controlled economies. Indeed, another change is the increasing interdependence between countries of different social and political systems, and between countries at different stages of economic development. This interdependence is represented largely by the complementary roles played by developed and developing countries in each other's economic development. In order to further develop their economies, the developed countries need new markets and raw materials and want labor-intensive goods at lower prices, which the developing countries have the potential to meet. Cheap labor, which the developing countries possess, is crucial for the developed countries to strengthen their competitiveness in the world market. At the same time, the developed countries can play an important part in the economic development of developing countries by providing advanced technology and machinery, management finance and marketing organization, and techniques as well as capital, all of which are crucial for industrialization.

Owing to this interdependent nature of the world economy, the economic situation in one country may unavoidably affect economies in other countries. For instance, in 1982, when an economic crisis in the West was developing, an unprecedented and profound debt crisis in the developing world eventually broke out. The possible default of developing countries that may be unable to repay their debt may in turn provoke a serious banking crisis in the developed world and aggravate the economic crisis in the world as a whole.

It is urgent to identify and study the issues in the international economic exchanges common among countries of different social systems and at different stages of industrialization to seek an understanding of the difficulties and potentialities of cooperation between them and to devise means to facilitate it. This study examines major issues in the bilateral economic relations between China and the United States. It will illustrate potential cooperation between countries of different social systems and levels of development. The United States is the quintessential developed capitalist country; China is both a socialist and a developing country. This work analyses the political and legal systems as well as laws relating to the foreign economic exchanges of both countries. Economic and legal issues that are crucial to the development of bilateral relations will be discussed to the extent possible. Political issues, such as Taiwan, are not remediable at the technical trade level and will not be discussed at length. Finally, some proposals will be recommended for enhancing bilateral relationships.

Owing to the short history of Sino-American relations and the novel nature of the subject, parts of this study must be rather descriptive. Foreigners can hardly be expected to be familiar with the rapidly changed legal and administrative structures of China; very few Chinese know the US laws and the operation of the political-legal system of the United States. Issues concerning the bilateral relationship will be illustrated by examining relevant cases. Chapter 1 serves as a brief introduction of the bilateral economic relations. Chapters 2 and 3 describe the political and legal systems relating to the foreign economic relations of both countries. Both chapters, however, are radically abbreviated; a comprehensive discussion would require volumes. It is the intention of the author that Chapter 2 be for non-Chinese readers and Chapter 3 be for non-US readers. Therefore, Chinese readers may skip Chapter 2, while US readers may skip Chapter 3. Case studies on finance, US export control laws, US antidumping and countervailing duty laws, and textile trade will be explored in Chapters 4 to 7, respectively. In the last chapter, Chapter 8, suggestions that this author deems necessary and realistic will be put forward as alternatives for the better growth of bilateral relations.

ACKNOWLEDGMENTS

This book was developed from a doctoral dissertation presented to the Yale Law School in May, 1984. I wish to express my thanks to the Yale Law School for providing me with the necessary facilities to complete the study.

My intellectual debt goes to W. Michael Reisman, which is evident throughout the book. Starting from the preparation to the completion of the book, Professor Reisman read every version of the manuscript, and was very generous in criticisms and suggestions. Professors E. Donald Elliott, Jr. and Geoffrey C. Hazard, Jr. read and commented on the manuscript and made valuable suggestions. I am also fortunate to benefit from Gary N. Horlick's professional and practical experience. Mr. Horlick read the earlier version of the manuscript and made valuable comments on it. Professor Myres S. McDougal was tireless in giving his advice and suggestions. He read part of the manuscript and, unsurprisingly, made valuable contributions to the book. In addition, I wish to express my gratitudes to Professor Richard N. Gardner of Columbia Law School for his intellectual input. Professor Gardner supervised a term paper I did at Columbia which was built into this book. Of course, none of them is responsible for what is said here.

I was particularly fortunate in having the benefit of the editorial expertise and taste of the Praeger Publishers; I owe the editorial board there a special debt. The index was prepared by the Praeger Publishers.

CONTENTS

PREFACE v
ACKNOWLEDGMENTS vii
LIST OF ACRONYMS xi

CHAPTER 1: LEGAL FRAMEWORK OF BILATERAL RELATIONS 1
Relationship Prior to Normalization 2
Legal Framework for the Bilateral Relationship 5
Recent Development of Commercial Exchanges 9
Perspectives on the Bilateral Relationship 13
Notes 17

CHAPTER 2: CHINA'S POLITICAL AND LEGAL SYSTEMS PERTAINING TO FOREIGN ECONOMIC RELATIONS 22
The State Power 23
Other State Organs and the Party 28
The Special Economic Zones 33
Laws Related to Foreign Investment 38
Notes 47

CHAPTER 3: POLITICAL AND LEGAL SYSTEMS OF THE UNITED STATES PERTAINING TO FOREIGN RELATIONS 53
Structure of the US Democracy 54
Congress and the Committee System 57
The Federal Bureaucracy and the Administrative Process 63
Political Parties and Election Campaigns 69
Pressure Groups and Lobbying 73
The Monetary and Financial System 77
Notes 81

CHAPTER 4: FINANCIAL ISSUES OF THE BILATERAL EXCHANGE 87
China's Utilization of Foreign Funds 88
The US Financial Facilities 96
Implications of World Bank Membership 104
Notes 108

CHAPTER 5: HIGH-TECHNOLOGY SALES TO CHINA 115
Evolution of Export Controls 116
Administrative Structure of Export Controls 125
Export Administration Regulations 127
Policy Versus Law 132
Notes 137

CHAPTER 6: ANTIDUMPING LAWS AND MUSHROOMS UNDER 406 140
Institutional Scheme Relating to Dumping 142
Determinations of Agencies 147
Escape Clause 152
Chinese Mushrooms Under Section 406 156
Efforts to Reform Trade Law 163
Notes 167

CHAPTER 7: TEXTILE TRADE 174
Historical Background 175
Difficulties of the Textile Trade 181
Prospects of the Textile Trade 186
Notes 190

CHAPTER 8: ALTERNATIVES 193
Notes 200

BIBLIOGRAPHY 201

INDEX 213

ABOUT THE AUTHOR 221

LIST OF ACRONYMS

ACEP, Advisory Committee for Export Policy
ADB, Asian Development Bank
CCC, Commodity Credit Corporation
CCL, commodity control list
CEROILS, China National Cereals, Oil, and Foodstuff Import and Export Corporation
CHINCOM, China Committee
CITIC, China International Trust and Investment Corporation
COCOM, Coordinating Committee
EEC, European Economic Community
Ex-Im, Export-Import (Bank)
GATT, General Agreement on Trade and Tariffs
GNP, gross national product
HITIC, Hainan International Trust and Investment Corporation
IDA, International Development Association
IMF, International Monetary Fund
ITC, International Trade Commission
MFA, Multi-Fiber Arrangement
MFN, most-favored-nation (adj.)
NATO, North Atlantic Treaty Organization
OEA, Office of Export Administration
OPIC, Overseas Private Investment Corporation
PAC, political action committee
RMB, Renminbi, Chinese currency

SINO-AMERICAN ECONOMIC EXCHANGES

Chapter 1 Legal Framework of Bilateral Relations

China and the United States differ in social systems. Yet, they have quite a few points in common in the present international situation. To further promote the Sino-American relationship is not only in conformity with the fundamental interests of the two countries, but also significant for maintaining world peace and stability.

– Huang Hua (1982)

On December 15, 1978, Premier Hua Guofeng and President Jimmy Carter announced that the People's Republic of China and the United States had agreed to "recognize each other and to establish diplomatic relations as of January 1, 1979."[1] Thus, the process of normalizing diplomatic relations between the two countries was substantially completed.[2] Weeks later, then Chinese Vice-Premier Deng Xiaoping visited Washington to celebrate the completion of the process of normalization. Working with equally good faith and commitment, China and the United States in short order established the framework for extensive economic, cultural, and scientific relations. By January 31, 1979, a Consulate Agreement, a Cultural Relations Agreement, and a Scientific Relations Agreement had all been signed by China and the United States.

On August 28, 1979, Vice-President Walter Mondale became the first US official since 1949 to give a public address in China. He spoke at the campus of Peking University and greatly impressed his Chinese audience when he said, "Any nation which seeks to weaken or isolate China in world affairs assumes a stance counter to American interest." He made it clear that the United States "must take the position we [the United States] have always taken – that anyone who violates the integrity of China is the enemy of China and is acting contrary to our interest."[3]

With the signing of the Claims and Assets Settlement Agreement and the Trade Relations Agreement, full Sino-American relations came to fruition in 1980.

This chapter will survey the growth of Sino-American trade and the development of the legal framework regulating the bilateral economic relations. Primary impediments still remaining in the bilateral relationship and areas for future cooperation will be identified as well.

RELATIONSHIP PRIOR TO NORMALIZATION

The China-US economic relationship can be traced back to 1899 when the so-called "open-door" policy was imposed on China. Following the establishment of the People's Republic of China and the outbreak of the Korean War, the political relations and economic exchanges between the two countries disintegrated rapidly. On December 17, 1950, the United States imposed an embargo on exports to and imports from China. Thus, the bilateral relationship came to a standstill. This situation prevailed into the 1970s.

In early 1971, the United States removed the embargo against China. As a result, China was placed in the same category with the Soviet Union and certain Eastern European countries. On February 21, 1972, President Richard M. Nixon visited China, marking the resumption of the bilateral relationship. The president and his party conducted seven days of private discussions with the leaders of China, after which he asserted that this was "a week that changed the world."[4] Efforts were made by the leaders of the two countries toward restoration of friendly relations between their respective countries. As a result, the Shanghai Joint Communique was promulgated on February 28, 1972. It in turn helped to establish the bilateral subdiplomatic relationship and to eliminate the differential treatment of China by the United States. Commercial exchanges amounted to $804.2 million in 1973.[5]

In 1975, commercial delegations from foreign trade corporations of China and the China Council for Promotion of International Trade made their first visits to the United States. By 1976, a few US trade groups had been invited to China. As of the beginning of 1978, more than 27 US delegations planned to travel to China, and 12 Chinese teams had scheduled trips to the United States.[6] Thus, the total number of delegations between the two countries was more than in any other year since 1972 when the bilateral relationship was renewed.

More frequent contacts resulted in increased bilateral trade. In 1975, the United States exported $303.6 million to, and imported $158.3 million from, China. The total trade amounted to $461.9 million.[7] Led by the rapid growth of trade, US exports to China increased enormously. In 1978, the total bilateral trade amounted to $1.1 billion.[8]

Several factors accounted for this steady growth in trade. The Shanghai Communique paved the way for and defined the character of the relationship between the two countries. Another factor was China's tolerance of a highly imbalanced trade. From China's perspective, a two-way trade is supposed to be more or less in balance. Since the US market for Chinese goods was quite restricted,[9] this situation would limit not only US imports from China, but US exports as well, for China prefers a trade balance with the United States. China, however, managed to absorb its trade deficits with the United States.

Since there were poor harvests in China in the 1970s, about 80 percent of US exports to China were agricultural goods, while the remainder consisted of industrial and transport equipment and products. About 4 of the 7.7 million tons of grain China imported in 1973 was from the United States. In October 1978, the Department of Agriculture announced that China had purchased 276,000 metric tons (about 10.9 million bushels) of US corn that year.[10] It was worth about $26.2 million.[11] Sales of other agricultural commodities also grew at a significant speed. US cotton exports to China were estimated to be 131,000 metric tons (577,579 running bales) in 1978, worth some $163.5 million.[12] Soybean oil exports, as of August 1978, amounted to about 41,200 tons, worth $24.7 million.

The foreign economic policies of the two countries helped the US exports of agricultural commodities. In October 1978, the US Congress overwhelmingly approved the Agricultural Trade Act of 1978.[13] This statute makes China eligible for both buyer and supplier credits of up to three years financed by the Agricultural Department through the Commodity Credit Corporation (CCC). The CCC credit was normally available to countries enjoying most-favored-nation (MFN) status. Nevertheless, it provides that "in order to expand and develop markets for United States agricultural commodities, the Commodity Credit Corporation may provide financing for commercial sales of agricultural commodities out of private stocks on terms of not to exceed three years to the People's Republic of China."[14] Under the provisions of the statute, credits can be extended through either the short-term export credit sales program or the deferred payment sales program conducted by the CCC.[15]

Under the export credit sales program, the exporters, after making their sales, register with the CCC. If the sale conforms to CCC regulations, the exporter asks the buyer to post a letter of credit with the CCC. After the commodities are shipped, the exporter presents the CCC with an onboard bill of lading, an invoice for the value of the goods, and an assignment of accounts receivable from the exporter at the port value. If the buyer wants to spread payment out over the maximum three-year period, the CCC then bills the buyer for one-third of the principal plus interest each year. Repayment must be in US dollars.

In addition to the direct financing program, a supplier's credits or deferred payment program has been established by the CCC. Under this program, the CCC may extend credits to the exporter, who in turn allows the foreign buyer to spread payments out over 36 months. Interest rates under this program would be the same as in direct financing by the CCC. This kind of credit, however, may not be "provided by the Corporation until the applicant's export sales plan has been approved by the corporation and the applicant has established to the satisfaction of the Corporation that exports have been made in accordance with the approved plan."[16] Repayment to the CCC must be in US dollars as well.

Having been provided with CCC credits, China made new major purchases of grain from the United States in October and November 1978. Thus, the total US export of agricultural commodities to China was brought to over 6.6 million tons.[17] It constituted about 60 percent of China's imports of grain that year.[18]

On the other hand, the growth of China's exports to the United States was comparatively slow, though on a continuous basis. China's exports comprised textiles, raw materials, minor consumer items, and some luxury products. Since China was not familiar with the US market and since it takes time to adapt goods to a new market, Chinese products were very uncompetitive on the US market in the initial years. As a result, none of these imports from China could count on large mass markets in the United States.

The growing trade deficit that China suffered limited the growth of bilateral economic exchanges. New institutional changes became necessary in order to further develop the economic relationship.

LEGAL FRAMEWORK FOR THE BILATERAL RELATIONSHIP

While the diplomatic normalization process was completed in 1979, economic relations remained incomplete. Full economic exchanges could not come about before such barriers as frozen assets, blocked claims, and MFN status were agreed upon by the two countries.

The Claims and Assets Settlement Agreement,[19] which was signed on May 11, 1979, opened the door to direct shipping and banking relations between the two countries. The claims and assets issue arose during the Korean War when the United States blocked and froze Chinese assets, while the Chinese government seized US-owned property in China. After the start of economic relations between the two countries, the immediate effect of this issue was that Chinese exhibitions could not come to the United States, nor could Chinese deposit any funds in a US bank, for fear of attachment by US claimants.

In light of this issue, the Claims and Assets Settlement Agreement provides that the Chinese government pay to the United States $80.5 million for the settlement of the claims by US nationals.[20] The United States was required to unblock by October 1, 1979, all assets that were blocked because of an interest, direct or indirect, in those assets of China.[21] The lump sum of $80.5 million to be paid by the Chinese government was divided as follows: $30 million was paid on October 1, 1979, and the remaining $50.5 million should be paid in five annual installments of $10.1 million on each October 1, with the first installment due on October 1, 1980.[22]

Under the terms of the agreement, the United States agreed to notify the holders of China's blocked assets.[23] At the same time, it undertook to assist the Chinese government in recovering unblocked assets.

As far as the distribution of the payments made by China to US claimants is concerned, the US government has exclusive responsibility. After the first $30 million payment was made by China on October 1, 1979, the Treasury's Bureau of Government Financial Operations began the process of distributing payments to recognized claimants.

Although the assets and claims issue was largely technical in nature, further promotion of bilateral economic exchanges could not be achieved without solving the problem. Almost simultaneously with the signing of the Claims and Assets Settlement Agreement, negotiation of another legal document, the Trade Relations Agreement, started.

The Trade Relations Agreement,[24] which was signed on July 7, 1979, provided the infrastructure for the bilateral economic relationship between China and the United States. Becoming effective on February 1, 1980, the agreement represents a shift of US policy toward China. Before 1979, the US government pursued, at least officially, a policy toward China and the Soviet Union that treated them alike. With the establishment of a diplomatic relationship, a policy of favorable treatment for China was formulated that removed the barrier to granting MFN status for it.

Section 402 of the Trade Act of 1974 of the United States mandates that before MFN status is extended to any nonmarket economy country, the president must report to Congress that the country in question does not: deny its citizens the right or opportunity to emigrate; impose more than a nominal tax on emigration or on the visas or other documents required for emigration, for any purpose or cause whatsoever; or impose more than a nominal tax, levy, fine, fee, or other charge on any citizen as a consequence of the desire of such citizen to emigrate to the country of his or her choice.[25]

The president may, however, temporarily waive this restriction, if: it is determined that such waiver will substantially promote the objectives of the purpose of the statute; and assurances are received that the emigration practices of that country will henceforth lead substantially to the achievement of the objectives of the statute.[26] Assured by the Chinese government's commitment that the freedom of emigration would be enjoyed by the nationals of China, President Carter used his waiver authority set out in the Trade Act of 1974 to make China eligible for MFN treatment in the United States.

The MFN status is important to bilateral economic relations. First, although to grant MFN status seems a technical matter, it has political implications, especially between countries of different systems. The agreement on MFN treatment shows that both China and the United States are willing to treat each other as friends. Second, MFN status affects customs duties, procedures in customs transit and clearance, taxes on goods or services, regulations on sale, and export and import licenses.[27] Third, the securing of MFN status puts US companies investing in China on the same footing with investors from Japan and Western European countries, regarding cooperation of China in such areas as service and labor. The agreement provides that the MFN treatment must be accorded in the same way that each party applies it to its other trading partners.[28]

In order to promote bilateral trade and to reduce imposed tariff restrictions, the contracting parties have agreed that in handling the bilateral trade, consideration should be taken that "at its current state of economic development, China is a developing country."[29]

The immediate effect of MFN status for China was that Chinese exports to the United States were no longer subject to the high tariff rates of the 1930 Hawley-Smoot Act, or the "least-favored-nation" tariff treatment. In other words, since the Trade Relations Agreement came into effect, Chinese exports to the United States have, at least in law, been treated on an equal basis with exports from other countries.[30]

The agreement is of great significance. It established the overall framework of trade relations between the two countries. In addition to the MFN treatment, it addresses such issues as the establishment of business offices, the stationing of business representatives, and the improvement of conditions under which these offices operate. Other provisions concern visits by economic trade and industrial groups and undertakings to assist the operation of government trade offices.[31] It also contains provisions regarding international payments and facilities for international financing, currency, and banking transactions. In addition, the parties have agreed to facilitate the availability of official export credits in accordance with applicable laws.[32]

Since no industrial rights law was in existence in China when the agreement was negotiated, it provides for reciprocal and equivalent protection of patents, trademarks, and copyrights. It also includes provisions for protecting other industrial rights and processes.[33]

During the last several years, China has moved steadily toward a policy to open emigration. US Foreign Service posts in China issued over 6,920 emigrant visas in fiscal year 1980 alone, and over 15,293 nonimmigrant visas for business, study, and family visits.[34] At present, the problem is not so much the restrictions imposed by the Chinese government on immigration, but US policy and annual immigration quota. Thus, President Reagan decided to extend the waiver on June 2, 1982.[35]

In July 1980, the US Congress passed legislation to allow the Overseas Private Investment Corporation (OPIC) to support US businesses investing in China. On October 30, 1980, an investment guarantees agreement was signed between the Chinese government and the OPIC.[36] This agreement provides US private investors with protection from the political risks of investment in China. It mandates that if the OPIC or its successor makes payment to US investors under an insurance or reinsurance policy against political risks, the Chinese government must recognize the transfer to the OPIC of any currency, credits, assets, or investment on account of which payment is made.[37] OPIC's rights of succession to any right, title, claim, or cause of action existing in relation to the payment are recognized by the Chinese government as well.[38]

The availability of OPIC facilities was important for companies intending to invest in China in the initial years after the normalization process. Despite the Chinese government's assurances of the protection of foreign investors' interests, some US companies were very much concerned with the nationalization issue. Owing to their lack of experience in dealing with China, those companies were concerned with other investment risks, too. OPIC has played a role to fill the gap. Its insurance policy may be issued for a maximum period of 20 years and covers inconvertibility of currency, expropriation, and losses caused by war, revolution, or insurrection.

On January 24, 1980, the China-US Joint Committee on Scientific and Technological Cooperation held its first session in Beijing to review the previous year's achievements in bilateral cooperation and to offer suggestions regarding future activities. The joint committee is a mechanism through which the two countries try to manage the various areas of government involvement. Both China and the United States look upon it as a very useful mechanism and devote the time of cabinet ministers to its annual meetings, with a lot of preparation and follow-up in between.

The committee consists of representatives of all the major government agencies of both countries, which have economic contacts with one another. For instance, the US group comprises the Treasury, Commerce, State, USTR, National Security Council, OPIC, trade and development program, Export-Import (Ex-Im) Bank, and other interested agencies. The Chinese group is organized in a similar way.

The momentum behind the committee is a series of annual meetings held between the Chinese group and a counterpart group from the United States with cochairpersons.[39] Between annual meetings, each side holds a series of sessions, whereby the coordination of various agencies is managed. This mechanism is particularly significant for the United States. It serves as a centralized agency in which different sectors exchange information and negotiate coordination.

Both China and the United States attach considerable importance to the bilateral relationship. In 1984, Premier Zhao Ziyang became the first Chinese premier ever to visit the United States, whereas President

Ronald Reagan was the first incumbent US President to visit China. They conducted "constructive, sincere, and friendly" discussions on issues at both bilateral and international levels.[40] In addition, a bilateral tax treaty was signed and industrial cooperation and nuclear cooperation agreements were initialed during their visits.[41] The nuclear cooperation agreement opens new opportunities for US companies to participate in China's energy program. When the agreement goes into effect (after the Congress approves), US companies will be able to compete directly with other foreign suppliers, such as Japanese, German, and French companies, in the new market – "a market which some in the industry have estimated at $10 billion worth of imports over the next 15 years."[42] The agreement also helps to build mutual trust and confidence and to enhance stable cooperation.

These various agreements and arrangements not only provide a guarantee for the continuing development of China-US economic relations, but also place future development on a planned and long-term basis. They serve as the institutional framework of China-US economic and political relations.

RECENT DEVELOPMENT OF COMMERCIAL EXCHANGES

The establishment of the institutional framework of the bilateral relationship coupled with China's policy of opening to the outside world resulted in the rapid development of economic exchanges between the two countries. Chinese and US companies have in recent years signed more than 100 contracts and agreements.[43] Commercial exchanges, which were nonexistent a decade earlier, have grown to over $5 billion per year. By 1981, the total trade between China and the United States amounted to $5.64 billion.[44] This amount constituted 12.4 percent of China's trade in 1981.[45] The two-way trade turnover in 1982 topped $5 billion,[46] with the United States having a $628.4 million surplus.[47]

Led by the rapid growth of trade, US exports to China increased enormously, from $171.3 million in 1977 to $3.749 billion in 1980.[48] The total US exports declined slightly in 1981, however, down 4 percent to $3.6 billion,[49] and down 19 percent in 1982 to $2.9 billion.[50] The only significant decline was in cotton imports by China. Owing to the success of its agricultural policies to encourage free farming and cash crops, China's output of cotton increased greatly in 1981 and succeeding years. Thus, the domestic demand in cotton was met largely by Chinese production instead of imports. China ranks behind Japan and South Korea as the largest export market in Asia and is among the top 15 export markets for the United States worldwide. On the other hand, although Japan continues to be China's leading trading partner by a large margin, the United States moved into third place behind Hong Kong and ahead of West Germany and is China's second largest foreign supplier. The US share of the China market has increased from about 4 percent in the mid-1970s to about 20 percent of total Chinese imports in 1980.[51] With Chinese imports reduced by 12.8 percent in 1982 to $17 billion, the US share of Chinese imports decreased to 17 percent.[52]

China continues to represent a major market for US primary commodities, such as grain, soybeans, lumber, cotton, synthetic resins, and paperboard. It is estimated that nearly 30 percent of the US sales to China were wheat shipments. Under the Grain Trade Agreement signed on October 22, 1980, in Beijing,[53] a total quantity of at least 6 to 8 million metric tons of US wheat and corn would be exported to China.[54] In 1982, China bought 2.4 million tons of grain more than that provided in the Grain Trade Agreement.[55] At the same time, the growth rates of manufactured goods are impressive, although the sales themselves still do not add up to a large proportion of the bilateral trade. For instance, US exports of office machinery and computers for the January-to-October 1982 period were up 66 percent from the previous year.[56] For coal-cutting, oil-drilling, and other mining equipment, the increase was 48 percent.[57]

On the other hand, US imports from China continue to grow in volume and diversity. Some of the Chinese products have entered the mainstream of the US market. Although the bulk of the imports from China comprises light industrial products and agricultural commodities, Chinese hydroelectric generators and beam pumps for extracting oil have been imported to the United States. In October 1983, a US company signed a contract with China to purchase Chinese-made planes. According to the contract, 1,000 superlight multipurpose planes will be shipped to the United States in three years from the signing.[58] China also exports oil products to the United States. The exportation of gasoline amounted to about $400 million in 1982.[59]

In the past, China-US economic exchanges were in the form of pure purchases and the sale of commercial goods. Today, the United States has become an active participant in China's economic development program, doing business in a variety of forms, such as compensation trade, joint ventures, wholly foreign-owned enterprises, and other commercial arrangements used in international commercial exchanges. For instance, in October 1981, the Tianjin Elevator Company of Tianjin, China, signed a preliminary accord exchanging marketing rights with Otis Elevator Company of the United States.[60] Under the pact, Tianjin Elevator would sell the Otis line of automated elevators for high-rise buildings in China. Otis would sell Tianjin elevators for small- and medium-sized buildings in countries other than China. Otis also agreed to progressively introduce its advanced technology into the Tianjin Elevator Company.[61]

In addition to the bilateral trade growth, the development of other economic exchanges has also made progress. For instance, in 1981 alone, nearly 50 major contracts were signed between enterprises of the two countries.[62] They cover such areas as agricultural commodities, agricultural technology, construction materials and plants, consumer goods, electronics, food processing and packaging, machinery, scientific instruments, electric generating equipment and technology, shipping, textile products, tourism, and transportation.[63] In September 1982, an agreement was signed by China and the United States, giving US engineering firms the exclusive right to bid for feasibility studies on part of a ten-dam Hongshui River development plan.[64] The project could cost more than $7 billion by the time it is completed at the turn of the century. The agreement is in fact an addition to a China-US hydropower protocol, one of 17 science and technology compacts between the two countries. In the summer of 1983, the largest high-technology transaction in the history of China's foreign trade was announced. The $250 million joint venture between International Telephone and Telegraph's Belgian subsidiary and China's telecommunication industry involved the first sales to China of US software and semiconductor technology.[65]

The United States has become a major partner in China's coal development plan. On March 8, 1983, China and the Occidental Petroleum Corporation signed an interim agreement to develop a huge coal mine that would become China's largest joint venture with a US company. The signing of the agreement followed the completion of a feasibility study begun the year before.[66] The venture involves the Pingshuo mine in Shanxi province, China's major coal-producing region. The project, which includes a $230 million investment by Occidental, is to produce 15 million metric tons of coal annually by 1986.[67] The mine will be developed by Occidental's Island Creek subsidiary. In order to buy equipment while continuing talks on certain details, the two parties signed an interim agreement in early 1983.[68]

Another US company involved in China's coal mining is Fluor. At the beginning of May 1982, China National Coal, a unit of the Ministry of Coal Industry, and Fluor Mining and Metals Inc., a subsidiary of Fluor, signed a contract to modernize and expand the Fushun West Open-Pit Mine in Liaoning province, China.[69] The Fushun mine began production in 1914 and today is the world's largest operating oil shale mine and a major coal producer. It is also one of the largest open-pit mines in the world. The contract, the first of its kind for China's coal industry, calls for increasing production to five million tons per year of coal and eight million tons per year of oil shale. Fluor Mining has agreed, under contract, to provide engineering and design services for mine planning, equipment selection, and modernization of materials handling.[70]

Another area of intensive bilateral cooperation is offshore oil. By the end of January 1983, 33 Western companies submitted bids for offshore oil exploration and exploitation, after conducting seismic surveys off China's coast. Among them, 16 were US concerns engaged in joint petroleum development in Chinese seas.[71] The first joint concern is between the China National Offshore Oil Corporation and the US companies Arco China Inc. and Santa Fe Minerals.[72] Under the contract signed in September 1982, foreign companies will provide most of the equipment. The South China Sea Oil Company, a branch of the China National Offshore Oil Corporation, will provide foreign companies with offices, living quarters, stockyards, oil supply, transport, geophysical prospecting ships, and some product equipment. The recent contract signing by Occidental and Exxon Natomas for offshore oil development in the South China Sea is another step taken by the US heavy machinery industry.[73]

In December 1983, the Phillips Petroleum Company of Bartlesville, Oklahoma, and the Shell Oil Company of Houston, Texas, signed a contract with China to explore for oil in an area of 1,094 square miles in the Pearl River mouth basin.[74] This brought to ten the number of US companies that have signed contracts for offshore oil exploration since September 1982.

On March 17, 1983, an agreement for building advanced, semi-submersible drilling rigs in China was signed between the China Offshore Platform Engineering Corporation and the Baker Marine Corporation of the United States.[75] According to the terms of the pact, Baker will invest $50 million in the rig and the Chinese corporation another $50 million.[76] The rigs to be produced will be used to contract for offshore drilling operations inside and outside China's territorial waters.

Another positive step in joint offshore development is the establishment of a joint venture, the China-Brown and Root Marine Engineering and Construction Company LTD.[77] This joint concern, which is owned by the China Offshore Platform Engineering Corporation and the US Brown and Root Company, will offer services including the design and supervision of marine engineering projects and the purchase and installation of equipment for such projects.[78]

All in all, by the end of 1983, despite the fact that bilateral trade had declined slightly, economic exchanges between the two countries had become extensive. Cooperation is being carried out in agricultural, industrial, and other sectors that are important to national economic development.

PERSPECTIVES ON THE BILATERAL RELATIONSHIP

Although the bilateral economic exchanges between China and the United States are quite extensive, greater achievements may be made in the future, taking into consideration relevant elements of the political, legal, and economic systems of both countries. In order to develop its economy, China has adopted and is stabilizing a policy that encourages international cooperation. Domestically, with the introduction of a tax and responsibility system, Chinese enterprises enjoy more discretion in production and management. They are allowed and able to conduct transactions with foreign concerns at their own initiative.

In the United States, it seems that the government has attached importance to its relationship with China. Efforts are being made by the United States toward the improvement of bilateral relations. Many US companies have participated in China's economic development program. Having gained experience in their transactions with the Chinese, they are confident that, although Chinese laws and the legal system need improvement, developing business with China is in the interests of the United States.

In addition, China and the United States are economically complementary. China is richly endowed with natural resources such as petroleum, coal, water, tungsten, vanadium, tung oil, etc. These resources offer areas for bilateral cooperation. In addition, the abovementioned rare metals, fuels, and raw materials are also important for further US economic growth.

Although China was thought to be an oil-poor country in the 1950s, extensive onshore and offshore oil fields have been discovered.

China's offshore oil offers a new area for international cooperation. Lying in the continental shelves of South China, these fields include the Bohai basin, an area of 80,000 square kilometers, the South China Sea basin, an area of 150,000 square kilometers, the East China Sea basin, an area covering 460,000 square kilometers, and two other promising basins including one in the North Gulf of the South Sea and one in the Yingge Sea.[79]

Almost all the above-mentioned areas are under survey or exploration by both Chinese and foreign enterprises. By the end of 1983, more than 40 foreign companies had joined China in searching for oil in the Chinese sector of the South China Sea since 1979. Geophysical surveys have been carried out, some 87,000 kilometers of seismic survey lines have been shot, a number of oil-and gas-bearing structures have been discovered, and several high-yielding oil and gas wells have been sunk.[80]

Large concession areas have been authorized by the Chinese government to enable foreign companies to conduct their activities. So far, 27 corporations from nine countries have signed 18 cooperative contracts with China after competitive bidding.[81] The Atlantic Richfield Company of the United States, after Total of France, was the second to sign a contract with China. It completed two exploratory wells in the first six months of 1983, one of which was expected to yield 1.2 million cubic meters of gas per day.[82]

In addition to rich oil resources, China has enormous reserves of coal. It is estimated that the country's coal reserve amounts to about 600 billion tons.[83] The largest and richest coal deposits are concentrated in the Shanxi, Hebei, Henan, Shandong, Anhui, Inter-Mongolia, Heilongjiang, and Guizhou provinces and autonomous regions. Coal resources in Shanxi provide a great potential for international cooperation. Eight large coalfields covering an area of 57,000 square kilometers exist. These deposits are very shallow and stable, both desirable characteristics for open mining.

China's oil and coal resources coupled with its modernization plan and open-trade policy provide a tremendous opportunity for international cooperation. The goal of the Chinese government is to quadruple industrial and agricultural output by the year 2000.[84] This modernization program itself requires foreign cooperation. The Chinese government therefore attaches great importance to economic and technological exchanges with foreign countries. Such foreign economic exchanges are to be expanded "in accordance with the principles of equality and mutual benefit" in order to create more markets for Chinese exports and to bring in advanced technology "suited to China's national conditions."[85]

Under the Sixth Five-Year Plan (1981-85) adopted at the Fifth Session of the Fifth National People's Congress on December 10, 1982,[86] a total of 230 billion yuan will be invested in capital construction. Top priority is given to energy and transportation, which will receive approximately 33.6 percent of the total investment. Other priority sectors include agriculture, textiles, other light industry, building materials, metallurgy, and chemicals. In addition, funds totaling 130 billion yuan are earmarked for upgrading existing enterprises.[87]

During the 1981-85 period, 890 large- and medium-sized construction projects are to be undertaken. Four hundred projects will be completed before the end of 1985, and the rest will be carried over into the next five-year plan period.[88] Among these projects will be 28 large coal mines, each with an annual capacity of over one million tons; 15 hydroelectric stations, each with an installed capacity of 400 megawatts or more; one nuclear power plant with an installed capacity of 300 megawatts; and 132 deep-water berths to be built in 15 harbors. In addition, there will be new railways (2,000 kilometers) and doubletracking and electrification of the existing railways (1,700 and 2,500 kilometers, respectively), as well as a number of new industrial installations.[89]

To carry out these and other development projects will require an enormous amount of capital and equipment. Importation of advanced technology and key pieces of equipment is crucial to achieve the technology transformation of existing enterprises, which is an important element in the current Five-Year Plan. Thus, the Chinese government has drawn up a plan for importing 3,000 items of advanced technology during 1983-85.[90]

The United States can play a significant part in helping China meet its modernization objectives by providing a wide range of goods and services that include, inter alia, agricultural products, advanced technology, and farm inputs, machinery, and equipment. In the development of its energy sector, especially offshore oil resources, China may utilize large amounts of US capital, technology, and equipment. Further, significant sales opportunities for the United States exist in other sectors to be expanded under the Five-Year Plan, such as cement, timber, chemicals, steel, paper making, and sugar refining. Thus, the United States has the opportunity to participate in numerous sales of analytical and scientific instruments, computers and peripherals, packaging equipment, energy conservation systems, etc.

As the competition facing the United States increases and as the trade dispute among the Western countries grows, the Chinese market will increasingly become more valuable to the United States.[91]

Despite the favorable political and economic environment, greater achievements may not be made before problems, political, legal, and economic, are solved. One underlying obstacle inhibiting faster development is the issue of Taiwan, although its actual effect is difficult to measure. At a few points, the US policy toward Taiwan, especially its arms sales, has caused serious problems in the bilateral relationship. Although the Taiwan issue is interesting and important, it will not be discussed in detail in this study. Other factors affecting the bilateral economic relationship include economic, legal, and technical issues.

The trade deficit is a major issue in the bilateral economic exchanges. Over the last ten years, China's trade deficit with the United States has amounted to about $10 billion,[92] although China has earned a surplus in its overall international trade. The Chinese attribute this unfavorable trade to US restrictions unilaterally imposed on textile imports from China.[93]

Because of basic differences in the two societies, trade problems may not be resolved very easily. For instance, in order to achieve a balanced trade, China tries to promote its exports to the United States. This effort immediately draws concern from industrial sectors such as apparel, textiles, bicycles, industrial fasteners, dinnerware, radios, and canned mushrooms. They fear that China may flood the US market with enormous quantities of low-price commodities that may in turn destroy a number of labor-intensive US industries. In order to reduce Chinese exports to the United States, US companies have filed a number of antidumping lawsuits.

These lawsuits have caused embarrassment for both countries. While the Chinese side claims that the antidumping lawsuits discriminate against Chinese products in the US market, the United States does not trust the pricing system in China.[94]

Another issue is the transfer of technology. In order to carry out its economic program, China needs to import technology and equipment from foreign countries. Although the United States has the world's most advanced technology and products to sell to China to feed its modernization plan, somewhat restrictive constraints are imposed by the export control laws. Despite the fact that China is being better treated than the Soviet Union and other Eastern European countries, US export controls have prohibited some potential large transactions. With the possible reduction in China's grain imports from the United States, this issue will become more obvious in bilateral trade.

The United States' financial unwillingness to subsidize US companies investing in China is another issue. It has put the country in a somewhat uncompetitive position compared with other Western countries.[95]

On the other hand, the bilateral exchange depends, to a large extent, on the continuity of current Chinese policy. It is unlikely that China will change its development policy, because it faces great pressure internally as well as externally. Thus, it must continue to increase its foreign economic relations in order to realize its modernization program. Although there may be shifts in development strategy, the general policy will remain unchanged. The remaining question on the Chinese side may be how to clarify and implement its laws.

To sum up, the Sino-American economic relationship has been established in a short time period. Although bilateral economic exchanges have become quite extensive, greater achievements could have been made had it not been for obstacles hindering full development. These obstacles include a mutual misunderstanding of each other's political and legal systems and their internal operation. The lack of some legal arrangements, such as for economic cooperation and the prevention of double taxation, contributed to the obstacles. Although China enjoys the MFN treatment in US markets, more favorable treatment would be available if China were a General Agreement on Trade and Tariffs (GATT) member country. The underlying obstacle is lack of mutual trust, which derives from the different social, historical, economic, legal, and cultural backgrounds of the two countries. Future bilateral economic exchanges depend on the mutual understanding of each other's legal and political systems and the establishment of procedures for accommodation. While the hard political issues may be unresolved for some time, the economic relations can be strengthened through bilateral efforts. The economic results of the bilateral relationship may in turn lead to mutual understanding and trust and more extensive cooperation between the two countries, which are in the interest not only of the countries concerned but also of the international community as a whole.

NOTES

1. See Joint Communique on the Establishment of Diplomatic Relations Between the United States of America and the People's Republic of China, January 1, 1979. Department of State Bulletin 79, No. 2022 (January 1979), p. 25.

2. The Taiwan issue was not resolved when the normal diplomatic relationship was established.

3. Richard H. Solomon, "The China Factor in America's Foreign Relations: Perceptions and Policy Choices," in *The China Factor* ed. by R. H. Solomon (Englewood Cliffs, Prentice-Hall, 1981), p. 2.

4. Ibid.

5. See William Clarke and Martta Avery, "The Sino-American Commercial Relationship," China, A Reassessment of the Economy, 94th Congress, 1st Sess., Joint Economic Committee, Washington, DC, July 1975, p. 512.

6. *China Business Review*, January-February 1978, p. 39.

7. See *China Business Review*, September-October 1976, p. 11.

8. See *China Business Review*, January-February 1982, p. 69.

9. Although the US market is still limited for China, Chinese goods became much more competitive after most-favored-nation status was granted reciprocally in 1980.

10. *China Business Review*, September-October 1978, p. 28.

11. Ibid.

12. Ibid.

13. Agricultural Trade Act of 1978, Public Law 95-501, 92 Stat. 1685.

14. Ibid., Section 202.

15. Ibid.

16. Ibid., Section 201.

17. *China Business Review*, November-December 1978, p. 36.

18. Ibid.

19. See US Department of Commerce, "Agreement Between the Government of the United States of America and the Government of the People's Republic of China Concerning the Settlement of Claims," in *US-China Commercial Relations: A Compilation of Basic Documents*, 1982.

20. Ibid., Article II.

21. Ibid. The two sides thereafter exchanged notes on September 28, 1979, extending the date to January 31, 1980.

22. Ibid., Article III.

23. The Chinese government requested that assets of China to be unblocked not be transferred or withdrawn without its consent. The notification was made in July 1979.

24. US Department of Commerce, "Agreement on Trade Relations."

25. See the Trade Act of 1974, Public Law 93-617, 88 Stat. 2056.

26. Ibid. The waiver can be extended for a 12-month period by the president.

27. For instance, US tariffs on textile imports from China were reduced by about 50 percent after MFN status was effected. See *International Trade News*, January 17, 1980.

28. Ibid.

29. Ibid.

30. After the MFN treatment became effective, bilateral trade increased to \$3.749 billion in 1980. This is compared with the total trade of \$171.3 million in 1977. See *China Business Review*, January-February 1982, p. 69.

31. See US Department of Commerce, "Agreement on Trade Relations," Article III.

32. Ibid., Article V.

33. Ibid., Article VI.

34. See "Message from the President of the United States," 97th Congress, 2nd Sess., House Document No. 97-190, June 2, 1982, p. 3.

35. Ibid., p. 1.

36. See US Department of Commerce, "Investment Incentive Agreement," in *US-China Commercial Relations.*

37. Ibid., Article III.

38. Ibid.

39. Over the last few years, the Chinese minister of foreign economic relations and trade and the US secretary of commerce have served as cochairpersons of the committee.

40. Zhang Wenjin, "The Recent Development of Sino-US Relations," *New York Times*, May 11, 1984, p. D9. Mr. Zhang is currently Chinese ambassador to the United States.

41. Christopher H. Phillips, "Progress in US-China Economic Trade" *New York Times*, May 11, 1984, p. D9.

42. Lionel H. Olmer, "Agreement for Peaceful Nuclear Cooperation," *New York Times*, May 16, 1984, p. A24.

43. "Sino-US Relations: Promises and Challenges," *New York Times,* October 3, 1983, p. D7.

44. See *China Business Review,* January-February 1982, p. 69.

45. Ibid.

46. "Sino-US Relations."

47. See "US-China Trade Down 5.5%," *New York Times*, February 3, 1983.

48. See *China Business Review*, January-February 1982, p. 69.

49. See "Soft-Pedalling a Massive Surplus," *Far Eastern Economic Review*, October 1, 1982, p. 48.

50. See "US-China Trade down 5.5%."

51. US House Subcommittee on Trade, "Report on Trade Mission to Far East," WMCP: 97-27 (Washington, DC, Government Printing Office, 1981), p. 52.

52. See "China's Trade Surplus Reaches a Record High," *New York Times*, January 30, 1983, p. A12.

53. Agreement Between the United States of America and the People's Republic of China in Treaties and Other International Acts. Series 9930 (Washington, DC, Government Printing Office,).

54. Article I. Grain Trade Agreement.

55. See *Asian Wall Street Journal*, December 21, 1981, p. 6.

56. *Asian Wall Street Journal*, January 24, 1983, p. 14.

57. Ibid.

58. *China Daily News*, November 5, 1983, p. 1.

59. See *Asian Wall Street Journal*, January 24, 1983.

60. See "US, China Firms Plan Swap of Marketing Rights," *Asian Wall Street Journal*, October 12, 1981, p. 22.

61. Ibid.

62. See *China Business Review*, January-February 1982, pp. 56-64.

63. Ibid.

64. See "US Firms Get a Chance to Help China Launch Major Hydroelectric Program," *Asian Wall Street Journal*, September 27, 1982.

65. *New York Times*, October 3, 1983, p. D8.

66. *People's Daily*, March 9, 1983.

67. See "Occidental in Pact with China on Coal," *New York Times*, March 9, 1983, p. D4.

68. The final agreement was signed by both parties on April 29, 1984. See *New York Times*, April 30, 1984, p. D1.

69. See "China Coal Projects Awarded to Fluor Company, *Hong Kong Standard*, May 3, 1982.

70. Ibid.

71. See "What the Chinese Want Now," *New York Times*, January 30, 1983.

72. See *Xinhua News Agency News Bulletin*, No. 12413, January 9, 1983, p. 9.

73. *New York Times*, October 3, 1983, p. D8.

74. *Asian Wall Street Journal*, December 5, 1983, p. 4.

75. See [Federal Broadcast Information Service on China (FBIS)] FBIS-CHI-83-054, March 18, 1983, p. B2.

76. Ibid.

77. See FBIS-CHI-83-014, January 20, 1983, p. B4.

78. Ibid.

79. *China Trade News*, April 15, 1982, p. 1.

80. Based on the results of primary surveys, China's offshore oil potential will be about equal to its onshore reserves. These surveys brought about the discovery of seven oil- and gas-bearing basins, including the Bohai Sea, the southern Yellow Sea, the East China Sea, the Taiwan shoals, the Pearl River mouth basin, the Yingge Sea, and the Beibu Gulf. These basins cover about one million square kilometers. See *Beijing Review*, December 19, 1983, p. 5.

81. *Beijing Review*, February 27, 1984, p. 11.

82. *Beijing Review*, December 19, 1983, p. 5.

83. *China Daily News*, October 6, 1982, p. 2.

84. The combined value of industry and agriculture output is to be raised to 2.8 trillion yuan from some 710 billion (to $1.4 trillion from $366 billion) by the end of this century. See "Peking Hopes, by 2000, to Quadruple Its Output," *New York Times*, September 3, 1982.

85. Ibid.

86. For excerpts of the text see the "Five-Year Plan," *Beijing Review*, May 23, 1983.

87. See the "Five-Year Plan," *Beijing Review*, May 23, 1983.

88. Ibid.

89. Ibid.

90. *Business America*, February 21, 1983, p. 38.

91. The United States could not reach an agreement with European countries at the last General Agreement on Trades and Tariffs meeting, France was even unwilling to attend the meeting because of the superiority of the United States and Japan in international trade in future industries. See *People's Daily*, December 11, 1982. At the same time, the United States could not resolve its trade disputes with European Economic Community countries in agricultural products. See *People's Daily*, December 14, 1982.

92. See *People's Daily*, February 5, 1983.

93. Ibid.

94. The Americans suspect that "trying to establish a margin of dumping duties or countervailing duties to offset subsidies in China is an Alice-in-Wonderland-type exercise." See Report on Trade Mission to Far East by Subcommittee on Trade of the Committee on Ways and Means of the House of Representives, 97th Congress, 1st Sess., WMCP: 97-27 (1981), p. 56.

95. For a detailed discussion of financial issues, see Chapter 4.

Chapter 2 China's Political and Legal Systems Pertaining to Foreign Economic Relations

> The People's Republic of China is a socialist state under the people's democratic dictatorship led by the working class and based on the alliance of workers and peasants.
>
> — **The Constitution**

China's legal system was formally established in 1949, although it can be traced back to the late 1930s. Long before the establishment of the government, a number of laws and decrees were issued by the then Central Government in liberated areas. Right after the liberation, China began to build its legal system. In 1949, the Common Program, which served as the basic legal document, was promulgated by the government. Then the first Constitution was adopted by the National People's Congress in 1954.

Unfortunately, the establishment and improvement of the Chinese legal system have suffered a great deal in its 30-year history. Despite the success scored by the state, many mistakes and setbacks have been experienced since the mid-1950s. The initiation and continuation of the "cultural revolution" constituted a grievous mistake.[1] In the period of cultural revolution, all laws were suspended, de facto, as well as instrumentalities that were charged with the enforcement of laws.

After the cultural revolution, the Chinese government began to pursue a more liberal and open-minded policy in its economic relations with foreign countries. Almost all Chinese laws concerning foreign economic relations were passed after 1978, which led to a dramatic increase in economic exchange between China and foreign countries. The most important of these laws was the newly adopted Constitution. It defines the function and power of each organ of the state as well as the rights and obligations of Chinese nationals and foreigners in China.

In a sense the Chinese politicolegal system is comparatively new. Like quite a few other countries, its system is not well known by people from foreign countries. Despite the fact that some studies have been carried out, many of them can hardly demonstrate the real operation of the politicolegal system. This is due to the short history of the Chinese government and the dramatic legal reform that makes China unique. Moreover, the cultural gap between Chinese and foreigners makes it almost impossible for the latter to fully appreciate the operation of the Chinese system.

As a practical matter, it is always important for those interested in doing business with a foreign country to understand that country's political and legal systems. It is therefore necessary for US citizens who are interested in doing business with China to understand the Chinese systems, process of decision making, and pertinent laws. Full understanding of the Chinese political and legal systems by Americans will help the latter to build up faith in carrying out economic activities in China and to plan their business better.

Owing to the newness of the structure of the Chinese government and the legal reforms, this chapter explores the subject briefly. Since the operation of the institutions is not familiar to foreigners, and since some important laws have just come into effect, this chapter cannot present a detailed analysis of their application.

THE STATE POWER

China is a unitary state. Its people's democratic dictatorship is called a "dictatorship of the proletariat."[2] The state power, which belongs to the people, is vested with the National People's Congress (the Congress). The local people's congresses at different levels exercise similar legislative powers within their own districts.[3] The reason for this unified exercise of state power is that "under the socialist system, there is a community of fundamental interests of the whole people. Therefore, the people's congresses can and must exercise state power in a unified way."[4] Since the National People's Congress exercises state power, other organs – administrative, judicial, and military –

are inferior and responsible to the Congress. The Congress is "the highest organ of state power,"[5] whereas its Standing Committee is its permanent executive body.[6] The legislative power of the state is exercised by the National People's Congress and its Standing Committee concurrently. The Congress is the superior body and is empowered to repudiate decisions adopted by the latter.[7] Article 62 of the Constitution authorizes the Congress to exercise the function of amending the Constitution: adopting laws; supervising the enforcement of the Constitution and laws: electing the president, the vice-president, the chairperson of the Central Military Commission, the president of the Supreme People's Court, and the procurator-general of the Supreme People's Procuratorate. The Congress is charged with deciding, upon nomination by the president, on the "choice of the Premier of the State Council, and upon recommendation by the Premier, on choice of the Vice-Premiers, State Councillors, Ministers, Auditor-General, and the Secretary-General of the State Council."[8] The membership of the Central Military Commission is decided by the National People's Congress upon recommendation of the chairperson of the commission.[9] Likewise, the Congress has the power to recall or remove from office the above-mentioned officials.[10]

In addition to its power of declaring war and peace, another important power of the Congress is "to approve the establishment of provinces, autonomous regions, and municipalities directly under the Central Government," and "to decide on the establishment of special administrative regions and the systems to be instituted there."[11]

The National People's Congress

Members of the National People's Congress serve for a term of five years.[12] The Congress meets in session once a year.[13] The Standing Committee may convene a session any time it deems necessary.[14] A session may also be convened upon the initiative of "more than one-fifth of the deputies" to the Congress.[15]

According to the Law of Organization of the National People's Congress (hereinafter referred to as the "Law of Organization"),[16] when the Congress is in session, all deputies are divided into different deputations according to the region from which they come.[17] Each deputation elects a chairperson and a vice-chairperson. Most work of the Congress is done in the deputations rather than in the Congress as a whole when it is in session. They decide the agenda before a session starts, and examine bills and drafts submitted to them. Once they finish their own review, the chairperson, vice-chairperson, or a third person may plead at the Presidium meeting or plenary session of the Congress.[18]

At each session, the Presidium is elected at a preparatory meeting convened by the Standing Committee.[19] The members of the Presidium preside over the Congress on a rotating basis. Within the Presidium, a number of elected standing chairpersons are responsible for its work.[20]

The Presidium, the Standing Committee of the Congress, the special committees, the State Council, the Central Military Commission, the Supreme People's Court, and the Supreme People's Procuratorate have the right to submit a bill to the Congress. Then the Presidium decides whether the bill should be examined by the deputations, or whether it should first be examined by a special committee and then by the deputations.[21]

One deputation, or 30 or more of the deputies, may submit a bill to the Presidium. The Presidium may put the bill on the agenda of the plenary session. It may also first assign it to a special committee to see whether it is proper to include it in the agenda and then, upon a report by the committee, decide whether it should be put on the agenda or not. Every bill must be adopted by the plenary session of the Congress before becoming law.[22]

Three deputations, or 10 percent of the deputies of the Congress, may propose the election, or removal from office, of those officials who are to be elected by the Congress under the Constitution.[23]

Deputies do not receive any salary from the Congress, although necessary allowances and other facilities are provided for business purposes. They are immune from arrest and trial, except when the arrest or trial is conducted with the permission of the Presidium.[24] Statements made or votes cast by deputies are immune from judicial review.

The Standing Committee

Since the Congress as a whole meets once a year for just a few days, its day-to-day functions are in fact carried out by the Standing Committee. Members of the Standing Committee are elected for a term of five years, as are the members of the Congress.[25]

The Standing Committee is empowered to exercise all the functions of the National People's Congress under law. These functions include: (1) interpretation of the Constitution and laws; (2) ratification of treaties with foreign countries; (3) annulment of laws and regulations by the State Council that are not in conformity with the Constitution or laws; (4) annulment of laws and regulations by local governments that are not in conformity with the Constitution; (5) appointment to and removal from office of government officials; (6) decisions of peace and war; and so on.[26]

In short, the Standing Committee is authorized to function as the essential legislative body of the State. Owing to the fact that it has the power to appoint and remove from office government officials, it also exercises, as the Congress does, administrative functions. Because of the importance of the work of the Standing Committee, its members are not allowed to "hold any post in any of the Administrative, judicial, or procuratorial organs of the State."[27]

The head of the Standing Committee is its chairperson. With the assistance of the vice-chairpersons and the secretary-general, the chairperson "presides over the work of the Standing Committee."[28] These members of the Standing Committee form its leading body, which handles its important day-to-day work.[29] Within the Standing Committee, there are a Credentials Committee and a General Office that is under the direction of the secretary-general. Other working committees may be established by the Standing Committee whenever it deems necessary.

In fact, the Standing Committee exercises considerably greater power than ever before. The expansion of the functions and powers of the committee is part of the plan to strengthen the system of the Congress. Peng Zhen, in his report, explained that, "As China is a big and populous country, the number of deputies to the National People's Congress should not be too small; but too large a number will make its work cumbersome. The Standing Committee is the permanent body of the National People's Congress, and all those on the Committee can be described as executive deputies to the Congress. Being few in number, they can meet frequently and carry a heavy load of legislation and day-to-day work."[30] Since its members are prohibited from taking on any other responsibilities, the Standing Committee can devote its full time to its own work.[31]

The chairperson and vice-chairpersons of the Standing Committee are not allowed to serve more than two consecutive terms.[32]

Special Committees

In order to strengthen the function of the National People's Congress, several special committees have been established within the Congress. At present, these include the Nationalities Committee, the Law Committee, the Finance and Economic Committee, the Education, Science, Culture, and Public Health Committee, the Foreign Affairs Committee, and the Overseas Chinese Committee. Other committees may be established by the Congress when it deems necessary.[33] The special committees are charged with the examination, discussion, and drawing up of relevant bills and resolutions.[34] Their work is carried out under the direction and leadership of the Standing Committee, when the Congress is not in session. Otherwise, they are responsible to the Congress.

A special committee comprises a director, several deputy directors, and members, who are all deputies of the Congress. They are nominated by the Presidium and elected by the plenary session of the Congress. The work of a special committee is carried out under the direction of the director assisted by deputy directors.

When a special committee thinks it necessary, it may suggest that experts be appointed as counsels of the committee. Counsels are appointed and removed from office by the Standing Committee.[35] They have no right to vote in the committee, but may nevertheless make comments at the committee meetings and give advice to the committee.[36]

The nature of the work of a special committee depends on its functions. For instance, the Law Committee is charged with examining bills submitted to the National People's Congress and to its Standing Committee or comments made by other committees regarding a bill.[37]

The Election of Deputies

Deputies of the National People's Congress are not directly elected by their constituents. Instead, they are elected from the deputies of congresses at the provincial level and from the army. The total number of national deputies is 3,500. The Standing Committee is empowered to decide the number of deputies of the National People's Congress that each provincial level congress may elect. A deputy from the countryside, however, represents one-eighth the number of constituents represented by a deputy from an urban area.[38]

Under the Election Law, all Chinese nationals who have reached the age of 18 are entitled to vote, except those who are deprived of the right by law or judicial decision. Voters directly elect deputies in their own election areas, which are divided in accordance with working units or residence.[39] Before voting, every voter is supposed to register.[40] A voter list is announced, and electors' certificates are distributed 30 days before the election.[41] An individual may make complaints regarding elections to the Election Committee established for the election area. The committee must make a decision in three days. If the individual is not satisfied, he or she may petition for judicial review, which is final.[42]

Candidates may be nominated by the units in which they work, by the election areas in which they reside, or by any parties or organizations, either jointly or separately. All voters are entitled to nominate candidates, if their initiative is supported by three other voters.[43]

On election day, voters should go to the election area to vote. When voters are not able to write, they may ask someone whom they trust to write down the names of the candidates they favor; it may also be requested in writing that someone else vote instead. The assignment is not valid, however, unless it is approved by the Election Committee in advance.

While deputies at grass-root-level congresses are directly elected by voters, members of congresses above county level are elected by the deputies of congress at the lower level.

Deputies at all levels may be recalled by the constituents. Everyone who is entitled to vote has the right to file a petition to recall a deputy with the congress of which he or she is a member.[44] If the deputy accused has been elected directly by constituents, a majority vote of the constituents is required in order to effect a recall. In case the deputy is elected by a lower-level congress, a majority vote of the congress members is required before the deputy is removed.[45]

OTHER STATE ORGANS AND THE PARTY

The President

The National People's Congress is the highest state organ. It elects the president and the vice-president of the country.[46] The president of China, however, is different from those of other countries. In 1954, Chinese President Liu Shaoqi in his "Report on the Draft of the Constitution of the People's Republic of China" stated, "In accordance with the circumstances of our country and based on the experience of building state organs since the establishment of the People's Republic of China, the function of the head of the state is jointly exercised by the National People's Congress and the President of the People's Republic of China. The head of our country is a collective one. At the same time, neither the Standing Committee nor the President . . . has the superior right over that of the Congress."[47]

The special feature of the presidency of China is that the presidential function is exercised concurrently by the president and the Standing Committee of the Congress. The president has no power or right to make decisions, while empowered to promulgate decisions made by the Congress and/or its Standing Committee. Although the presidency is an honorable position, the president has no administrative responsibility, except the power to nominate the premier of the State Council.[48] The president may, however, receive foreign diplomatic representatives "on behalf of the People's Republic of China."[49]

Basically, the president is charged with, pursuant to decisions of the Congress and its Standing Committee, promulgating statutes; appointing and removing from office the premier, vice-premier, state councillors, ministers, auditor-general, and secretary-general of the State Council; conferring state medals and titles of honor; issuing orders of special pardons; proclaiming martial law and states of war; and issuing mobilization orders.[50]

Other functions the president may exercise include the appointment and recall of plenipotentiary representatives abroad, and the ratification and abrogation of treaties and important agreements concluded with foreign states.[51]

Being elected by the Congress, both the president and the vice-president, who is the assistant of the president, may be recalled or removed from office by the Congress.[52]

The term of office of the president and vice-president is five years, as is that of the Congress. These officers are not allowed to serve more than two consecutive terms.[53] Nationals who have the voting right and have reached the age of 45 are eligible for election as president or vice-president.[54]

The State Council

The State Council is the central government of China. It is the executive body of the highest organ of state power, the Congress, and is the highest organ of state administration. The function of the State Council is to carry out the provisions of the Constitution and the statutes and resolutions adopted by the Congress and its Standing

Committee. The council is responsible to the Congress and its Standing Committee, and is supervised by them as well.

The functions and powers of the State Council are considerable. The most important ones include the powers: (1) to adopt administrative measures, to enact administrative rules and regulations, and to issue decisions and orders in accordance with the Constitution and statutes; (2) to submit proposals to the Congress or its Standing Committee; (3) to lay down the tasks and responsibilities of the ministries and commissions of the State Council; (4) to exercise unified leadership over the work of local organs of state administration at different levels throughout the country; (5) to draw up and implement plans for national economic and social development and the state budget; (6) to direct and administer work concerning civil affairs, public security, judicial administration, supervision, and other related matters; (7) to conduct foreign affairs and conclude treaties and agreements with foreign countries; (8) to direct and administer the building of national defense; and (9) to alter or annul inappropriate orders, directives, and regulations issued by the ministries or commissions.[55] Thus, virtually every aspect of the administration of the country is directed and administered by the State Council.

The State Council is composed of the premier, vice-premiers, state councillors, ministers of ministries and commissions, the auditor-general, and the secretary-general.[56] The premier has overall responsibility for the State Council, whereas the ministers have overall responsibility for their own respective departments.[57] Vice-premiers and state councillors assist the premier.

Two kinds of meetings may be held in the State Council, namely, the plenary meeting and the executive meeting. A plenary meeting includes all members of the State Council, whereas an executive meeting is attended by the premier, vice-premiers, state councillors, and the secretary-general.[58] The premier convenes and presides over both types of meetings. Although the premier is exclusively responsible for the State Council, important matters must be handled at either the plenary or the executive meetings.

There are, at the present time, a premier, four vice-premiers, and several state councillors. Every ministry may have a minister and two to four vice-ministers. A commission may have a minister, two to four vice-ministers, and five to ten other members.[59]

In order to strengthen supervision over finances and financial and accounting activities,[60] an auditing body has been established in the State Council that exercises its power though auditing the revenue and expenditure of all departments under the State Council, of the local governments at different levels, of the state financial and monetary organization, and of enterprises and undertakings. Under the direction of the premier, the auditing body exercises its supervision independently, free from interference of any kind.[61]

The day-to-day work of the State Council is carried out under the direction of the secratary-general. The secretary-general heads a general office in the State Council.[62]

The term of office of the State Council is the same as that of the congressional deputies. The premier, vice-premiers, and state councillors may serve no more than two consecutive terms.

The Chinese Communist Party

Article 5 of the Constitution provides that "all political parties and public organizations . . . are subject to the Constitution and laws." "The term of 'political parties'," said Han Yutong, a well-known jurist, "includes the Communist Party . . . . The party is not an organization outside the people; the Party members are no different from other individuals. As a result, neither the Party nor its members may have any privileges to disregard the Constitution or the law. On the contrary, they both should set up examples to be abided by the Constitution and laws, as well as with regard to the policy against privileges."[63]

The Constitution of the Communist Party of China stipulates that "the Party must conduct its activities within the limits permitted by the Constitution and the laws of the state."[64] Hu Yaobang, the secretary-general of the Chinese Communist Party, again emphasized this principle in his report to the Twelfth National Congress of the Party. He said, "It is impermissible for any Party organization or member, from the Central Committee down to the grass roots, to act in contravention of the Constitution and laws. The Party is part of the people. It leads them in making the Constitution and laws which, once adopted by the supreme organ of state power, must be strictly observed by the whole Party."[65]

To say the Party and its members must conduct their activities within the limit of law does not mean that the leadership of the Party in the country has been abolished. The Party still plays the leading role in the country. But its leadership is "mainly of political character."[66] The "Party's leadership is not realized through the arrangement of making the Party the supreme organ of the state. It is accomplished by the adoption of correct line, principles, and policies, as well as by the exemplary role of the Party members."[67]

Since the Constitution and laws reflect the Party's policy, which represents the people's interest, those laws have binding force over every aspect of life in the country.

The Communist Party system in China is very comprehensive. The Party is an integral body organized under its program and constitution. There are Party organizations at all levels coincident with the organization of governments at all levels. The highest leading body of the Party is the National Congress and the Central Committee elected by it. The leading bodies of local Party organizations are the Party congresses at different levels and their committees. The grass-roots organizations of the Party are Party branches at villages, schools, offices, city, neighborhoods, and so on.

Higher Party organizations are supposed to supervise lower organizations' work. Lower organizations report on their work to, and request instructions from, higher Party organizations. At the same time, they are encouraged to handle their own work independently.

Delegates to Party congresses are decided by elections, which are held by secret ballot.

As a basic principle of democratic centralism, individual Party members are subordinate to the Party organization; the minority is subordinate to the majority; the lower Party organizations are subordinate the higher Party organizations; and all the constituent organizations and members of the Party are subordinate to the National Congress and the Central Committee of the Party.[68] Decisions of Party organizations are made by majority rule.

In order to become a Party member, one must accept the Party's program and the Constitution and agree to carry out Party decisions. A new member, once admitted, should take an oath to the Party. Admission is normally made by a grass-roots branch upon receiving an application with two members' recommendations. Certain behavior is required from an applicant before he or she is admitted. Dues are collected from all members of the Party.

Although there is no provision in the law that requires high government posts to be reserved for Party members, most high-ranking government positions are held by members. It appears that recently more and more non-Party members have been elected to leading positions in universities and factories. A small number of non-Party members have even occupied important posts in the government.

THE SPECIAL ECONOMIC ZONES

Over the last few years, China has pursued decentralization and opening to the outside world's economic policy. In order to attract foreign investment and gain experience from cooperation with foreign partners, some special economic zones have been established in coastal areas of China. They were created to give foreign investors more incentives and are expected to set examples of foreign cooperation for the entire country.

A special economic zone is administered by the Chinese government. As in the rest of China, it has economic enterprises owned by the state, collectives, or private individuals. The majority of enterprises, however, are funded or run jointly by Chinese and foreign interests, or funded entirely by the latter. They may be established for processing or assembling for foreign customers, or to operate on a compensation trade basis.

China's special economic zones are special in terms of economic development and production management. Enterprises in the zones, by and large, organize and manage production in accordance with the market force themselves. At the same time, they are under the general administration of the local government of zones, which is under the leadership of the provincial government and then the central government. Enterprises in the special economic zones carry out their activities under the state plan. The state plan controls such things as urban planning, land use, the distribution of industries, and bank loans. But it plays only a guiding role.[69]

Presently, four special economic zones in China have been set up: Shenzhen, Zhuhai, Shantou, and Xiamen. The city of Shenzhen in Guangdong province is being transformed into one of the largest special economic zones in the world. The total area of the Shenzhen zone covers 327.5 square kilometers (one-sixth of the city). Ninety-eight square kilometers of land will be used for constructing projects, an area two-thirds of the size of Shanghai proper, China's largest industrial city.[70] The zone is to be divided into five sections. The westernmost end is the Shekou industrial area, which has been placed under the administration of the China Commercial Shipping Corporation of the Ministry of Communications.[71]

Since the establishment of the Shenzhen special economic zone, this city has developed very fast. Industrial output value increased by 101 percent in 1983 from 1979 before the special zones were created; agricultural output value increased 25 percent, financial revenue 600 percent, and local income in foreign exchange 140 percent. The proportion of industry in the zone has expanded rapidly. By the end of 1983, 164 new industrial enterprises had been set up in the city, of which 55 were built and put into operation in 1983. The special zone now has industrial enterprises in electronics, textiles, clothing, food, furniture, printing, building materials, and machinery.[72]

The Zhuhai special economic zone is located opposite Aomen (Macao). It has an area of 6.8 square kilometers, 45 percent of which is devoted to industry, 15 percent to residences, 5 percent to scientific research departments, and the remainder to parks, schools, medical and health facilities, and roads.[73]

According to a master plan prepared by the Zhuhai local government, the Zhuhai special economic zone should attract $2.1 billion in investment by the year 2000.[74] The master plan indicates that Zhuhai will become an increasingly industrialized city, envisioning that industrial output will grow to $1.1 billion by 2000, compared with $70 million in 1983. By 2000, industrial output is expected to account for about 90 percent of overall production.[75]

Zhuhai officials say foreign companies have already invested $100 million in the zone. Since its establishment, Zhuhai has signed 42 joint-venture contracts with foreign companies. Pledged foreign investment in the projects totals $1.3 billion. Of the 42 joint ventures, 16 are in industrial projects, 9 in transportation, 7 in tourism, 5 in property development, and 5 in commerce and trade. About half of the 42 projects have begun operations.[76]

The Shantou special zone is the one whose construction started later than the other two mentioned above. This special zone comprises two processing districts and four companies: (1) The Longhu processing district, which is located in the southwest section of Longhu village on the outskirts of Shantou city, encompasses about 1.6 square kilometers. (2) The port area, with a total area of 1.7 square kilometers, is located in the south of Longhu village and east of the fishery port. (3) The integrated agricultural development company has a total area of ten square kilometers covering the outskirts of Shantou and part of Chenghai county. Vegetable, flower, tree, pig, fish, shrimp, chicken, duck, and goose exporting bases are being built in the area. (4) A tourism company, the Special Economic Zone Development Company, and the service company are located in the economic zone.[77]

The Xiamen special economic zone is in Fujian province on China's southeast coast. The establishment of the zone was approved in October 1980. Xiamen, an island city, covers an area of 1,466 square kilometers, of which Xiamen proper takes up 123 square kilometers. Huli, which is part of the special zone, occupies an area of 2.5 square kilometers.[78] The construction of the zone is concentrated in Huli, which is an industrial district processing goods for export in the Xiamen zone.

In July 1979, the State Council, recognizing Hainan Dao's unique geographical, climatological, and economic circumstances, granted the island larger authority over investment policy. Most recently, Chinese government officials indicated that the building of Hainan Dao (Hainan Island) should follow the example of special economic zones in Guangdong province.[79] Hainan Dao is the second largest island of China, next to Taiwan. It has an area of 322 square kilometers, which is 32 times that of Hong Kong. The population of the island is 5.6 million, or 173 people per square kilometer.[80] The climate there is mild but humid. It has rich resources and seems to be an impressive area for foreign investment.

Although Hainan Island is not yet a special economic zone, it provides foreign investors with more or less the same preferential treatment as other special economic zones do. In addition, officials in Hainan have greater authority in handling foreign loans and investments. For instance, they have the authority to negotiate and approve foreign loans up to $3 million (compared with the prefectures of Zhanjiang, Foshan, and so on, which can approve foreign loans up to $1.5 million), and to retain up to 70 percent of its foreign currency earnings.[81]

In order to coordinate its large-scale investment program, the Hainan International Trust and Investment Corporation (HITIC) was established in March 1980. It has a registered capital of RMB 50 million yuan. The HITIC serves to absorb foreign investment, sponsor all types of investment projects, handle credit and trust business, and engage in consulting work.[82] In fact, it functions as the Chinese partner in Hainan.

In these special economic zones, foreign firms can invest their money in building factories and running enterprises and other undertakings. Many types of businesses permitted in the zones are completely foreign owned, managed, and operated. At the same time, foreign investors may participate in joint ventures with their Chinese counterparts. They are provided with the necessary conditions and accorded preferential treatment by the local government. While the Chinese government protects their assets, due profits, and other legitimate rights and interests (not further defined in the statute), the foreign investors are subject to the laws and decrees of the country.

The first set of Regulations on Special Economic Zones in Guangdong Province (hereinafter referred to as the Regulations) was adopted by the Standing Committee of the Fifth National People's Congress on August 26, 1980.[83]

Under the Regulations, an administrative body, which is called the Guangdong Provincial Administration of Special Economic Zones (hereinafter referred to as the Administration), was established at the provincial level of Guangdong "to exercise unified management of the special zones on behalf of the Guangdong Provincial People's Government."[84]

In order to start a business in the special zones, an investor should apply to the Administration and secure from it licenses of registry and use of land.[85] Since products of the special zones are mainly for exportation, and since preferential treatment is provided thereof, when the products are to be sold in the domestic market, the producer "must have the approval of the . . . Administration . . . and pay customs duties."[86]

A key characteristic of the special economic zones is special incentives to foreign investors. The preferential corporate tax is one of them. The said tax rate for enterprises with foreign investment is 30 percent in the rest of China, but only 15 percent in the special economic zone. Article 14 of the Regulations provides:

> The rate of income tax levied on the enterprise in the special zones is to be 15 percent. Special preferential treatment will be given to enterprises established within two years of the promulgation of these regulations, enterprises with an investment of US $5 million or more, and enterprises involving higher technologies or having a longer cycle of capital turnover.

When investors reinvest profit for five years or more, they may "apply for exemption of income tax on profits from such reinvestment."[87]

Although investors may rent a piece of land in the special zones, "the land in the special zones remains the property of . . . China."[88] Article 2 of the Provisional Rules on Land Management in the Shenzhen Special Economic Zone further provides that the land in the special zone is under the unified management of the government of Shenzhen City, and that the city government may requisition it when it deems necessary for construction or in accordance with laws and decrees.[89]

In order to make enterprises in special zones accessible to the Chinese labor market, labor service companies run by local governments have been set up in each of the special zones. The Regulations provide:

> Chinese staff members and workers to be employed by enterprises in the special zones are to be recommended by local labor service companies or recruited by the investors with consent of the . . . Administration . . . . Enterprises can test them before employment and sign labor contracts with them.[90]

Normally, an employment contract will include: (1) the rights to employ and fire, and resign, of the employer and employee, respectively; (2) the responsibility or duty of the employee; (3) salary and bonus as well as work hours; (4) labor insurance, welfare, and labor protection; and (5) work discipline. Individuals who have not reached the age of 16, however, are not to be employed under the law.[91]

Over the last few years, numerous contracts between Chinese and foreign enterprises have been signed concerning projects in the special economic zones. A number of joint ventures, coproduction ventures, and wholly foreign-owned enterprises have been set up in the special zones. By the end of January 1983, agreements on 1,589 projects in the Shenzhen special zone had been reached.[92] The total investment under contract amounts to RMB 3.1 billion yuan, or about 10.3 billion Hong Kong dollars.[93] The first contracts tended to involve either the processing of imported materials or components or compensation trade. At the initial stage, projects did not involve a great amount of money. Since 1980, however, agreements have been entered into on a number of big projects, 35 of which required the investment of 10 million Hong Kong dollars. Seven others involved investments exceeding 100 million Hong Kong dollars.[94] Now, about 80 percent of the contracts are for joint or cooperative ventures.[95]

The same thing has happened in other special economic zones as well. For instance, between 1979 and 1980, Xiamen concluded 103 contracts with foreign enterprises.[96] In order to induce foreign capital to transform Xiamen's existing industries and increase exports, 25 factories have been selected as the key units for developing economic cooperation with foreign countries.

Today, all the special zones are becoming prosperous. Interviewed by the correspondent of *People's Daily*, Liu Tianfu, the governor of Guangdong province, said that "over the last three years, about 14,000 contracts were signed by the province with foreign enterprises, involving more then $2.6 billion."[97] Obviously, the majority of the contracts involve projects in the special zones. Referring to the changes brought about in Guangdong, Governor Liu said, "The special economic zones have taken a lead in the development. The total output of the special zones has more than doubled in the last three years. Shenzhen and Zhuhai were desolate and out-of-the-way border areas. Today, both of them have begun to take the shape of cities."[98]

LAWS RELATED TO FOREIGN INVESTMENT

The Joint-Venture Law

In order to expand international economic cooperation and technological exchange, China adopted its joint-venture law on July 1, 1979,[99] and the Regulations for the Implementation of the Law of the People's Republic of China on Joint Ventures Using Chinese and Foreign Investment (hereinafter referred to as the "Regulations on Joint Ventures") were promulgated by the State Council on September 20, 1983.[100] The adoption of the Joint-Venture Law marked the beginning of a new era in the history of China's economic relations with other countries. China's previous experience in the operation of joint ventures was with the Soviet Union, Poland, and Tanzania.[101] In adopting the Joint-Venture Law, China cleared the way for participation in joint ventures on Chinese soil by nationals and by commercial entities of all foreign countries.

China's Joint-Venture Law, which comprises fifteen articles, establishes a legal basis and general framework for the operation of joint ventures in China. Article 2 of the statute states that "all the activities of a joint venture shall be governed by the laws, decrees, and pertinent rules and regulations of the People's Republic of China."[102]

The scope of the Joint-Venture Law is broad and open ended. The law does not confine investment to capital construction; rather it permits investment in all areas, including agriculture and light industry.

The fundamental issue of joint ventures is control or ownership thereof. Unlike some other countries that have prescribed upper limits to the permissible proportion of foreign investment in a joint venture, China established instead a general rule for the permissible lower limit of the percentage of foreign investment. The second paragagh of Article 4 of the statute provides that in the registered capital of a joint venture, the proportion of the investment contributed by foreign participants shall in general not be less than 25 percent.[103]

Although the typical ratio of equity ownership will find the Chinese partner with 51 percent of the equity and the foreign partner with 49 percent,[104] China allows foreign partners to have more than 50 percent shares in some cases. Li Xiannian, then Chinese vice-premier, once stated, "China does not confine herself to the established international practice of 51 percent and 49 percent. . . . The proportion of investment of foreign companies can be higher than 50 percent."[105] In some instances, a Chinese partner may hold 45 percent interest,[106] whereas in other instances, China even allows foreign investors to have a 75 percent share.[107]

Joint ventures with 50-to-50 percent ownership are also permissible in China. A venture may be participated in by more than one Chinese party. For instance, Volkswagenwerk AG of West Germany signed a preliminary agreement with China to produce its Santana model in Shanghai, China. This venture is to be owned 50 percent by Volkswagenwerk, 35 percent by Shanghai Tractor & Automobile Corporation, and 15 percent by Bank of China's Shanghai branch.[108]

A joint venture in China takes the form of a limited liability company, the control of which is in proportion to the capital invested in the joint venture. Since no ceiling is established for the maximum percentage of equity ownership allowed for foreigners, theoretically a venture could be owned entirely by non-Chinese. The Joint-Venture Law, which generally fixes the lower limit of foreign participation at 25 percent, on the other hand, seems to be an attempt to ensure that foreign participants' contribution to the venture is sufficiently substantial to motivate them to make a meaningful commitment to its success.

The parties may make their respective contributions in a variety of forms. Cash, capital goods, site value, and industrial property rights are all listed as possible contributions to equity.[109] Very often one may find that Chinese partners prefer to make contributions in kind rather than in cash, whereas foreign partners are encouraged to provide cash and technology.[110] The Chinese contributions may include labor, raw materials, rights to plant sites, factories, and component parts.

As the valuation of intangible contributions can be an extremely complex matter, Article 5 provides that "the various contributions referred to in the present article shall be specified in the contracts concerning the joint venture or in its articles of association, and the value of each contribution (excluding that of the site) shall be ascertained by the parties to the venture through joint assessment." Ren Jianxin, one of the Chinese officials involved, has said that the valuation of the rental fee would be made by the local people's government, taking into consideration such factors as the purpose of the joint venture and the fees charged to neighboring ones.[111] Mr. Ren also stated that the actual fee reached in such instances would not exceed current land rates in neighboring countries.[112] A Japanese firm stated that its store rent was comparable with rents in New York and Hong Kong.[113] In the ES Pacific hotel venture case, China secured 51 percent equity for the contribution of the site.[114] The hotel agreement further provides that the joint venture will pay 3 percent of its annual revenues for the use of the site.[115]

The determination of the percentage of ownership is crucial under Chinese law, for it involves the appointment of a board of directors and the sharing of profits, risks, and losses. Article 4 of the Joint-Venture Law states that "the profits, risks, and losses of a joint venture shall be shared by the parties to the venture in proportion to their contributions to the registered capital." The actual distribution of net profits is subject to certain deductions from gross profit.[116] Taxes, reserve funds, bonus and welfare funds for workers and staff members, and expansion funds of the joint venture are deducted according to pertinent regulations and the articles of association.[117]

Another issue within the context of ownership and profit sharing concerns the transferability of shares by the parties to the venture. Under Chinese law, a party must secure the consent of the other party or parties in order to transfer its share. To be specific, Article 5 of the Joint-Venture Law provides that the transfer of one party's share in the registered capital shall be effected only with the consent of the other parties to the venture. Thus, it seems that China has adopted the general rule and practice with regard to the transfer of shares in a closed corporation.

Management of a joint venture is just as important as the ownership thereof. The Chinese law on joint ventures adopts the system of a board of directors vested with the supreme power in the management of the company. Article 6 of the Joint-Venture Law specifies that a joint venture shall have a board of directors with a composition stipulated in the contracts and the articles of association. The number of directors appointed by each party is proportionate to the shares held by the party. Once the board is established, the directors can be removed only by the appointing party.[118] The board has a chairperson who is a Chinese national appointed by the Chinese side. Foreign participants to the venture appoint one or two vice-chairpersons.[119] The chairperson is in charge of calling and presiding over the meetings of the board of directors. Nevertheless, chairpersons cannot make significant decisions independently.

The board is empowered by the statute to direct all fundamental matters concerning the venture.[120] The list of such issues includes expansion projects, production and business programs, the budget, the distribution of profits, plans concerning manpower and pay scales, the termination of business, and the hiring or appointment of the president, vice-president(s), chief engineer, treasurer, and auditors as well as the determination of their functions, powers, and remuneration.[121]

The board of directors is the highest authority of a joint venture in deciding all major issues concerning it.[122] These major issues include, inter alia, its expansion plans, production and business programs, budget, distribution of profits, and appointment or hiring of the president, chief accountant, and other important posts.[123] In addition, the board of directors is also empowered to hire and dismiss workers and establish wage scales according to actual jobs.[124]

Decisions of the board, however, are to be reached by the members through "consultation . . . on the principle of equality and mutual benefit."[125] This provision ensures the participation of foreign members on major problems. It also demonstrates that China expects a joint venture to be conducted as a partnership in the sense that the parties will attempt to reach a consensus on all board decisions. Should negotiations fail, however, problems may be resolved by a majority or two-thirds vote as provided by the articles of association. In an interview, Rong Yiren stated, "Primarily, the board of directors of the joint venture will manage the business of the enterprise through consultation and cooperation. By consultation on vital problems, the interests of both parties – the majority and the minority – will be looked after. . . . Generally speaking, the board of directors should reach unanimous decisions through consultation. It can also be stipulated in the joint-venture agreement or articles of incorporation that in case of failure to reach a unanimous decision on some important issue, other measures will be adopted."[126] Although "important decisions should be made by consensus rather than by voting, and this law [the Joint-Venture Law] spells out a variety of matters that constitute important decisions, the Ministry of Foreign Economic Relations and Trade has stated that only decisions that revise the articles of association, terminate a joint venture, or increase, transfer, or mortgage its capital, or call for its merger with another organization, will require unanimity; all other decisions may be taken by a two-thirds vote or a simple majority."[127]

A joint venture's president and vice-presidents are the key personnel among the executives responsible for the daily routine work. They are to be chosen from the various parties to the joint venture.[128] Although foreign partners cannot be chairpersons of the board of directors, "they can be president or vice-presidents."[129] It is reported that in some recent ventures, the Chinese have agreed to having a foreigner as president for an initial period such as five years. Some other contracts provide for rotation and a continuing balance between Chinese and foreign managers.[130]

The Joint-Venture Law also provides that procedures concerning the employment and discharge of workers and staff members are to be stipulated in the articles or by contract.[131] This is an issue of importance to foreign investors who want to maintain a level of control over daily plant operations. As China is a socialist country, there is virtually no free labor market in the country. Prospective workers and staff members are initially recommended for employment by the departments in charge of joint ventures or labor authorities and are accepted by the joint ventures after passing qualifying examinations, with priority given to those with high marks.[132] The remuneration of the president, vice-presidents, chief engineers, chief accountant, and auditors are determined by the board of directors.[133] The board's power with regard to these matters is in accordance with its power to hire the personnel in question.

One general policy matter over which the board does not have complete discretion is the purchase of certain types of items. The Joint-Venture Law stipulates that in the purchase of raw and semi-processed materials, fuels, and auxiliary equipment, joint ventures must give first priority to China's resources. It also provides that such materials may be acquired on the world market with the venture's own foreign exchange funds in exceptional circumstances.[134]

Since China's economy is state planned, plans for Chinese enterprises are formulated by a central authority. In order to integrate joint ventures with this planned system, the Regulations on Joint Ventures require them to file their plans with the Chinese authorities.[135] Nevertheless, the Chinese authorities concerned are prohibited from issuing directives on production and operating plans to joint ventures.[136]

When a joint-venture contract is negotiated, both parties are often concerned about the proportion of products to be sold in China and abroad. A joint venture must export a certain amount of its products to earn some foreign exchange to balance its foreign exchange payments, and to constantly improve the quality of its products and management through the competition on the international market. However, the Regulations on Joint Ventures do not mechanically demand that all joint ventures market the major part of their products abroad or balance their foreign exchange receipts and payments. Items produced through joint ventures that China urgently needs or imports for its modernization drive can be sold chiefly on the Chinese market.[137] Under these circumstances, any shortage of foreign exchange of a joint venture will be offset by the superior department in charge of the Chinese participant or the department that originally gave approval to the venture through the adjustment of its retained quota of foreign exchange.[138] Prices of both Chinese raw materials and finished products sold domestically will be aligned with prices paid and charged by state-owned enterprises.[139]

Since the adoption of the statute, quite a few joint ventures have been set up in China. In the four years since the adoption of the Joint-Venture Law in 1979, 105 joint ventures were established.[140] A total of $13 billion in foreign funds was absorbed, of which $5,000 was direct foreign investment.[141] At the initial stage, the common feature of those ventures is small size; the average investment per venture is about $3.48 million.[142] They are basically engaged in service and consumer productions such as hotels, food processing, home electricity, etc.[143] Having gained experience in running smaller projects, China now is able to cooperate with foreign countries in large joint projects. Since 1983, joint ventures have been established for the renovation of existing enterprises and for the production of sophisticated equipment. The average amount of investment per project is about $18.88 million.[144] This trend seems to represent current Chinese policy on joint ventures. Addressing the matter, Feng Tienshun, an adviser of the Foreign Investment Bureau of the Ministry of Foreign Economic Relations and Trade, said, "In the last two years, we ran a few small joint ventures. But the effect isn't apparent. They haven't played much of a role in our economic development, so we don't want to continue with them."[145] He indicated that China will not "use joint ventures for unimportant items."[146]

Taxation

The Chinese tax system is entirely new. Not long ago, Chinese enterprises, both state owned and collective owned, were paying profits rather than tax to the Treasury. Starting at the end of 1982, a tax system has been introduced to the economy. Under the new system, enterprises are required to pay tax in proportion to their profits to the government. This tax institution, which provides for incentives for enterprises, is an extension of income tax laws on joint ventures and foreign companies adopted since 1980.

According to China's Joint-Venture Tax Law (as amended),[147] joint ventures registered in China are subject to taxation on their worldwide income, based on the income derived from "production, business, and other sources."[148] Income from other sources refers to dividends, bonuses, interest, and income derived from leasing or trademark, copyright, and so forth.[149]

The basic tax rate of joint ventures is 30 percent, with a local surtax of 10 percent.[150] This brings the total tax rate to 33 percent. In special circumstances, this surtax can be eliminated or reduced by the government of the province, municipality, or autonomous region in which the joint venture is located. A tax rate of 10 percent is levied on a foreign participant remitting its share of the profits out of China.[151] By doing this, China has followed the practice of many countries of levying a tax on the payment of dividends to foreign shareholders.

Since joint ventures in petroleum, natural gas, and other resources may derive high profits, the Joint-Venture Tax Law makes it clear that matters involving these resources will be governed by a separate tax law.[152]

A number of tax incentives are provided for in the Joint-Venture Tax Law. It allows a newly established joint venture that is scheduled to operate for a period of ten years or more to apply for a full exemption from its tax during its first two profit-making years and a 50 percent reduction in its third, fourth, and fifth profit-making years.[153] The first profit-making year is defined as the year in which a joint venture begins to make a profit after taking into account any loss carryovers. In case there are losses in the initial stages of running the operation, the first profit-making year is the one in which a balance remains after deducting from the profit of that year the losses that have been carried from the previous losing year. However, the period allowed for offsetting a year's losses by profits gained in the subsequent years cannot be longer than five years.[154]

Since 80 percent of China is rural, the Joint-Venture Tax Law further provides that joint ventures in "low-profit" operations such as farming or forestry or ventures located in remote, undeveloped, outlying areas may apply for a 15 to 30 percent reduction in income tax for an additional ten-year period. The reduction is subject to the approval of the Ministry of Finance.[155]

Aware of the problem of double taxation, the Joint-Venture Tax Law provides for a credit against Chinese tax for foreign taxes.[156] Nevertheless, the amount allowed for tax credit cannot exceed the amount of income from foreign countries according to Chinese income tax law and at Chinese tax rates.[157]

On December 13, 1981, the Income Tax Law of the People's Republic of China concerning Foreign Enterprises (hereinafter referred to as "Foreign Enterprise Tax Law") was adopted.[158] This statute covers two categories of taxpayers. The first consists of "foreign companies, enterprises, and other economic organizations which have establishments in the People's Republic of China engaged in independent business operations, cooperative production, or joint business operations with Chinese enterprises."[159]

Under the Foreign Enterprise Tax Law, income tax on foreign enterprises is assessed at progressive rates for the parts in excess of a specific amount of taxable income.[160] While the annual income below 250,000 RMB is taxed at 20 percent, the highest tax rate is 40 percent of the part exceeding 1 million RMB.[161]

In addition to the progressive taxes, a 10 percent local tax will be assessed on taxable income, making the total range from 30 to 50 percent. This method of imposing local tax differs from that used in the Joint-Venture Tax Law, under which the local tax is calculated at 10 percent of the basic tax paid.[162]

A foreign enterprise that has a small scope of production and a low profit level may be granted reductions or exemptions from the local surtax by provincial-level governments.[163] Enterprises engaging in low-profit operations such as farming, forestry, and animal husbandry for ten years or more may receive a tax exemption for their first profit-making year and a 50 percent tax reduction for their second and third profit-making years.[164]

The second category of taxpayers covered by the statute consists of foreign companies, enterprises, and other economic organizations that do not set up establishments in China but that have "China-source" income such as interests, royalties, dividends, and rents. The tax rate for this sort of income is 20 percent without local surtax.[165] In any event, although tax holidays and incentives are provided by the statute, wholly foreign-owned enterprises are not provided with as favorable treatments as are joint ventures.

Foreign Exchange Control

One of the most important concerns for foreign investors is foreign exchange control. China has so far adopted the Provisional Regulations for Exchange Control of the People's Republic of China (hereinafter referred to as the "Provisional Regulations").[166] Under this statute, enterprises with overseas Chinese or foreign capital and joint ventures with Chinese and foreign investment that have their income in foreign exchange must deposit all their foreign exchange with the Bank of China and pay out of their accounts all expenditures in foreign exchange.[167]

Coincident with Article 10 of the Joint-Venture Law, which grants a right of repatriation for foreign participants, Article 24 of the Provisional Regulations provides that enterprises with overseas Chinese capital, enterprises with foreign capital, and foreign partners in Chinese and foreign joint ventures may apply to the bank of China to remit abroad their net profits after tax, as well as other legitimate earnings. Foreign enterprises and partners "should apply to the General Administration of Exchange Control or its branch offices for transferring foreign exchange capital abroad by debiting the foreign exchange deposit accounts of the enterprise concerned."[168]

China is a young country although with a long history. Despite its efforts, China's legal systems are still imperfect, to some extent insufficient to cope with current issues. Its laws are new not only to foreigners but also to the Chinese themselves. Especially, the actual application of the laws almost remains unknown, for there is no publication of court decisions or authoritative interpretation of laws. In addition, owing in part to the lack of experience of the Chinese government, at least partly, laws adopted tend to be simplified, which is likely to cause confusion in their application. In order to solve these problems, legal education of the society as a whole is necessary. New laws, especially more concrete laws, should be adopted to meet current situations.

NOTES

1. See Peng Zhen, "Report on the Draft of the Revised Constitution of the People's Republic of China," November 26, 1982, at the fifth session of the Fifth National People's Congress of the People's Republic of China, 25(50) *Beijing Review* 11 (1982).

2. The nature of state power is defined as the people's democratic dictatorship in the Common Program of 1949, in the Constitution of 1954, and in the documents of the Eighth National Congress of the Chinese Communist Party held in 1956. See Peng, "the Report," p. 12.

3. See "The Constitution of the People's Republic of China," adopted on December 4, 1982, by the Fifth National People's Congress of the People's Republic of China at its fifth session, Article 2, 25(52) *Beijing Review*, 12 (1982).

4. See Zheng, "the Report," p. 20.

5. Ibid., Article 57.

6. Ibid.

7. Ibid., Article 62.

8. Ibid.

9. Ibid.

10. Ibid., Article 63.

11. Ibid.

12. Ibid., Article 60.

13. Ibid., Article 61.

14. Ibid.

15. Ibid.

16. "The Law of Organization of the National People's Congress of the People's Republic of China," *People's Daily*, December 15, 1982. The law is in Chinese only.

17. "Law of Organization of the Congress," Article 4.

18. Ibid.

19. Ibid., Article 5. The secretary of the Congress is also elected at the preparatory meeting. The preparatory meeting of the first session of a Congress is convened by the Standing Committee of the previous Congress.

20. Ibid., Article 6.

21. Ibid., Article 9.

22. Ibid., Articles 9 and 10.

23. Ibid., Article 15.

24. Ibid., Article 44. When the Congress is not in session, permission of the Standing Committee must be secured before a deputy is arrested or tried.

25. "The Constitution," Articles 65 and 66.

26. Ibid., Article 67.

27. Ibid., Article 65.

28. Ibid., Article 68.

29. See "the Constitution," Article 68, and "Law of Organization of the Congress," Article 25.

30. See Peng, "the Report," pp. 18-19.

31. Ibid., p. 18. Peng Zhen also reported that the "organization of the Standing Committee has been strengthened, too."

32. See "the Constitution," Article 66.

33. Ibid., Article 70.

34. Ibid.

35. See "Law of Organization of the Congress," Article 36.

36. Ibid.

37. Ibid., Article 37. The purpose of the establishment of the Law Committee was to strengthen the legal system in China and to avoid possible conflicts between different laws. See Xi Zhongxun, "Report on the Draft of the Law of Organization of the National People's Congress," *People's Daily*, December 15, 1982.

38. See "The Election Law of the National and Local People's Congresses, Articles 13 and 14 (Chinese version only), *People's Daily*, December 16, 1982. This law does not apply to elections in the army.

39. Ibid., Article 22. The number of candidates is required by law to be larger than the number of deputies to be elected. Generally speaking, however, candidates do not contest each other in the election. Instead, their resumés are circulated, sometimes along with their policy statements.

40. In practice, the administration in each election area prepares a voter list instead of asking voters to register themselves.

41. "Election Law," Article 24.

42. Ibid., Article 25.

43. Ibid., Article 26.

44. The deputy who is accused may make a response to the petition. Since the law came into force, some cases of recall involving deputies at the district level have been reported.

45. When the Congress is not in session, the Standing Committee of the Congress may make a decision by vote. In such a situation, a majority vote in favor is required.

46. "The Constitution," Article 79.

47. The translation is supplied by this author. For the original Chinese version, see *The People's Handbook of 1954*; and Xiao Weiyun, "Restoration and Development of Our System of Presidency," *People's Daily*, December 28, 1982.

48. See "the Constitution," Article 62.

49. Ibid., Article 81. Other state organs may also act on behalf of the country in certain circumstances. For instance, the Standing Committee may conduct business in the state's behalf. The State Council, acting as the Central Government, may carry out activities on behalf of the state. For more discussion, see Weiyun, "Restoration and Development."

50. See "the Constitution," Article 80.

51. Ibid., Article 81.

52. Ibid., Article 63. The vice-president is the immediate successor of the presidency in case of vacancy. If there are vacancies of both the president and vice-president, the chairperson of the Standing Committee of the Congress may

temporarily act as the president until a new one is elected. See "the Constitution," Article 84.

53. Ibid., Article 79.

54. Ibid.

55. Ibid., Article 89.

56. See "The Law of Organization of the State Council of the People's Republic of China," Article 2 (Chinese version only), *People's Daily*, December 15, 1982; and "the Constitution," Article 86.

57. "The Constitution," Article 86.

58. "Law of Organization of the State Council," Article 4.

59. Ibid., Article 9.

60. See Peng, "the Report," p. 18.

61. See "the Constitution," Article 91.

62. "Law of Organization of the State Council," Article 7.

63. See *People's Daily*, November 29, 1982.

64. See "Constitution of the Communist Party of China," adopted by the Twelfth National Congress of the Communist Party of China on September 6, 1982, 25(38) *Beijing Review* 10 (1982).

65. See 25(37) *Beijing Review* 27 (1982).

66. See Zhou Gucheng, "Combination of the Party Policy and the People's Will," *People's Daily*, November 30, 1982. Mr. Zhou is a famous historian and a member of the Committee for Revision of the Constitution of China.

67. Ibid.

68. See "Constitution of the Communist Party," in general.

69. For detailed discussions, see *Beijing Review*, January 23, 1984, p. 31.

70. See 24(50) *Beijing Review* 17-18 (1981).

71. Ibid.

72. *Beijing Review*, January 23, 1984, p. 28.

73. 24(50) *Beijing Review* 19 (1981).

74. *Asian Wall Street Journal*, April 2, 1984, p. 12.

75. Ibid.

76. Ibid.

77. 24(50) *Beijing Review* 20 (1981).

78. Ibid.

79. Premier Zhao Ziyang, on his way back from Africa, visited the island with State Councillor Fuang Yi. They discussed with local officials the future development of Hainan Dao and expressed the idea that more liberal measures should be taken in order to attract foreign investment. See *China Daily News*, February 17, 1983.

80. See *China Daily News*, February 19, 1983.

81. See "Hainan," *China Business Review*, January-February 1983, p. 44

82. Ibid.

83. The Chinese version can be found in *People's Daily*, August 27, 1980. These regulations can be regarded as sample provisions, for regulations related to the Xiamen special economic zone are similar to it.

84. Ibid., Article 3.

85. Ibid., Article 7. In order to attract foreign investment, land rent is lower, and equipment and raw materials used by such enterprises are exempt from import duties.

86. Ibid., Article 9.

87. Ibid., Article 16.

88. Ibid., Article 12.

89. These regulations were adopted by the Standing Committee of the Fifth Guangdong Provincial Congress on November 17, 1981.

90. See "The Regulations on Special Zones in Guangdong Province," Article 19.

91. See the Provisional Rules on Labor and Wage Management in the Guangdong Special Economic Zones, Article 5. These rules were adopted by the Standing Committee of the Fifth Guangdong Provincial Congress on November 17, 1981.

92. "1,589 foreign investment projects have been signed with Shenzhen," *People's Daily*, March 3, 1983.

93. Ibid.

94. Ibid., p. 19.

95. *China Reconstructs*, July 1983, p. 14.

96. *People's Daily*, March 3, 1983.

97. See *People's Daily*, December 8, 1982.

98. Ibid.

99. The Law of the People's Republic of China on Joint Ventures Using Chinese and Foreign Investment, adopted on July 1, 1979, at the second session of the Fifth National People's Congress; promulgated on July 8, 1979.

100. For an English version, see *Beijing Review*, October 10, 1983.

101. Yao Zhuang, "The Positive Role of the Joint Venture Using Chinese and Foreign Investment," *Renmin Ribao*, July 24, 1979. The successfulness of these ventures, however, requires independent research.

102. Ibid., Article 2.

103. Ibid., Article 4.

104. There were at least three early joint ventures in which Chinese partners secured a 51 percent share while foreign partners secured 49 percent. These included: (1) a hotel venture between the China International Travel Service and ES Pacific; (2) a hotel venture between the China International Travel Service and Zhong Mei; and (3) a food service venture between the Civil Aviation Administration of China and China Air Catering of Hong Kong. See "What New Ventures, Increased Power for Chao Mean for Companies," *China Business Review*, April 30, 1980, p. 57.

105. 27 *Beijing Review* 4 (1979).

106. For instance, the International United Shipping and Investment Joint Venture. See "Signs of Flexibility from China," *Far Eastern Economic Review*, April 4, 1980, p. 136.

107. For instance, the Sanyo Refrigerator Manufacturing Venture. See "Lessons for Companies in Japanese Route to Joint Ventures in China," *Business China*, September 12, 1979, p. 127

108. See *Asian Wall Street Journal*, December 13, 1982.

109. Law on Joint Ventures, Article 5.

110. It was reported that "In one [joint venture] under negotiation, where the foreign investor wishes its contribution to consist of technology and a small amount of cash, the foreigner also wants to be paid by the venture for part of the technology in the form of a royalty under a license. The Chinese side has

said that, in these circumstances, 85 percent of the capital contribution of the foreigners should be in cash or the equivalent, and only 15 percent of the capital can constitute technology." See Jerome A. Cohen, "Equity Joint Ventures," *China Business Review*, November-December 1982, p. 24.

111. Ren Jianxin, "Selling Technology to China." A speech delivered at the National Council for US-China Trade, Washington, DC, 1979. Copies may be obtained from the National Council, Suite 350, 1050 17th St., NW, Washington, DC, U.S.A.

112. Ibid. In one instance, the Chinese reportedly based the value of land rental upon comparable European prices. See "Chinese Joint Venture Provides Guidelines for Future Equity Deals," *Business Asia*, March 28, 1980. p. 99.

113. See "Foreign Consumer Goods, for Man-in-the Street: Watches Lead the Way," *Business China*, May 28, 1980, p. 74.

114. See "What New Ventures, Increased Power for Chao Mean for Companies," *Business China*, April 30, 1980, p. 59.

115. Ibid.

116. Law on Joint Ventures, Article 7.

117. Ibid.

118. Ibid., Article 6.

119. Ibid.

120 Ibid.

121. Ibid.

122. Regulations on Joint Ventures, Article 33.

123. See 29 *Beijing Review* 30 (1979).

124. The statement was made by Wei Yuming, vice-minister of economic relations and foreign trade. *Beijing Review*, October 24, 1983, p. 9.

125. Law on Joint Ventures, Article 6.

126. See "An Exclusive Interview with Rong Yiren," *China Business Review*, September-October 1979, p. 6.

127. Cohen, "Equity Joint Ventures," p. 23.

128. Law on Joint Ventures, Article 6.

129. See "Rong Yiren on Joint Venture," 29 *Beijing Review* 27 (1979).

130. See Cohen, "Equity Joint Ventures," p. 25.

131. Law on Joint Ventures, Article 6. It seems that, in practice, employees of a joint venture usually sign a contract with the venture. For instance, every staff member of the above-mentioned food service venture between the Civil Aviation Administration of China and China Air Catering of Hong Kong has signed a contract with the venture. The joint venture has the right to fire its employees according to their behavior. In addition to this right, the venture enjoys the discretion of giving bonuses to and imposing punishment on its employees within the provision of the contracts.

132. Shen Shiaoming, "China's New Law on Joint Ventures Using Chinese and Foreign Investment," 34 *Southwestern Law Journal* 1880. Despite the unfamiliarity of both Chinese and foreigners with this kind of labor market, no problem has ever been reported.

133. Law on Joint Ventures, Article 6.

134. Ibid., Article 9.

135. Regulations on Joint Ventures, Article 56.

136. Ibid., Article 56.
137. Ibid., Article 64.
138. Ibid.
139. Ibid., Article 66.
140. *Beijing Review*, October 24, 1983, p. 9.
141. Ibid.
142. *China Daily News*, October 31, 1983, p. 3.
143. Ibid.
144. Ibid.
145. "China Policy Changes in '82 Slowed Foreign Investment," *Asian Wall Street Journal*, March 14, 1983, p. 10.
146. Ibid. It was reported that a Chinese-US oil joint venture was established in China on March 16, 1983. The venture, which has a capital of $20 million and is owned 50 percent by both the Chinese and US sides, is the largest joint venture set up so far. See *China Daily News*, March 18, 1983.
147. The Income Tax Law of the People's Republic of China Concerning Joint Ventures with Chinese and Foreign Investment, adopted on September 10, 1980, at the third session of the Fifth National Congress. For an English version, see 19 *International Legal Materials* 1451 (1980).
148. Ibid., Article 1.
149. Ren Jianxin, "China's Foreign Economic and Trade Law–Work Is Progressing." A speech given in the United States in January 1981.
150. Income Tax Law of Joint Ventures, Article 3.
151. Ibid., Article 4.
152. Ibid, Article 3.
153. Ibid., Article 5.
154. Ren, "China's Foreign Economic and Trade Law."
155. Income Tax Law of Joint Ventures, Article 5.
156. Ibid., Article 16. Most features of the law seem analogous enough to corporate taxation. For example, the Chinese "cost of sales" is analogous to the concept of "cost of goods sold" used in US accounting practice.
157. See Ren, "China's Foreign Economic and Trade Law."
158. This law was adopted in the fourth session of the Fifth National People's Congress. It came into effect on January 1, 1982.
159. See Foreign Enterprise Tax Law, Article 1.
160. Ibid., Article 3.
161. Ibid.
162. Ibid., Article 4.
163. Ibid.
164. Ibid., Article 5.
165. Ibid., Article 11.
166. For the Chinese version of the statute, see *Renmin Ribao*, December 19, 1980.
167. See Provisional Regulations, Article 22. Apparently, these foreign exchange regulations do not present any difficulty to foreign enterprises.
168. Ibid., Article 24.

Chapter 3 Political and Legal Systems of the United States Pertaining to Foreign Relations

If you go to an American town, as a journalist or perhaps a lawyer sent by a client considering moving his plant there, your first question will be, "Who's the Mayor?" Your second question will be "Who's the boss?"

– **W. Michael Reisman**

The United States is a heterogeneous society. Its federal democracy represents the diverse, sometimes conflicting, interests of its constituents. Ever since the Declaration of Independence of July 4, 1776, the national government has been receiving input from diversified interests. Although the formal framework of the government remains unchanged since 1789, its operation has undergone substantial changes. For instance, the division of power designed by the Founding Fathers between Congress, the president, and the courts has virtually lost its original form. This is due to many factors, such as the delegation of power by Congress to the president, the interpretation of the Constitution and law by the courts, the growth of the political parties' role, the growth of interest groups (business, labor, and so forth), and the changed structure of international trade and international politics.

This chapter briefly explores the basic structure of the government under the Constitution, the parties' role in US politics, the part played by interest groups and the financial system in decision-making processes, and the internal operation of the legislative and executive branches. Like the previous chapter, it must be radically abbreviated. A comprehensive picture would require volumes. Owing to the complex nature of the society, only crucial fundamental issues directly pertinent to international trade will be discussed. Obviously, this chapter is for the benefit of Chinese readers; the previous chapter is for US readers.

As the potential Chinese readers are more familiar with US administrative decision making and judicial review, these aspects of the government will not be emphasized. Nonetheless, owing to the importance of the administrative process and its direct and, to some extent, crucial effect on foreign economic relations, a brief introduction will be conducted along with the discussion of federal bureaucracy.

STRUCTURE OF THE US DEMOCRACY

The Constitution of the United States basically divides the central or federal government into three branches: Congress, the president, and the judiciary. In terms of the document of 1789, Congress is given legislative power, the president is charged with the responsibility of carrying out and enforcing the laws, and the courts apply laws in particular cases.

The Constitution assigns to Congress the powers "to . . . provide for the common defense and general welfare of the United States . . . to regulate commerce with foreign nations . . . to define and punish piracies and felonies committed on the high seas, and offenses against the law of nations; to declare war . . . and to make rules concerning captures on land and water; to raise and support armies . . . to provide and maintain a navy . . . to make all laws which shall be necessary and proper for carrying into execution the foregoing powers. . . ."[1] In theory, Congress has power over virtually everything, for it is the law-making body in the United States. "Whatever difficulties Congress may have in exercising this power are owing to reluctance on the part of its members . . . or to organizational difficulties within Congress, or to difficulties arising from local pressures on members."[2]

One of the potent weapons Congress has is commerce power. Commerce, as defined by Chief Justice Marshall,[3] is not merely trade, "it is intercourse."[4] With this broad judicial interpretation, Congress has been able to regulate every aspect of interstate commerce, intrastate commerce (which has an impact on the former), and international commerce. Under the commerce clause, Congress has found the authority to regulate "every species of commerical intercourse between the United States and foreign nations."[5] It is through this power that Congress imposes tariffs and export and import controls, grants the MFN status to foreign countries, and imposes embargoes on those foreign countries that the United States deems unfriendly. Congress now can do almost everything with the help of this power unless vetoed by the president.[6]

As far as foreign economic relations are concerned, the commerce power is by no means the limit of Congress. Under the applicable enumerated powers in the Constitution, it can regulate activities by US citizens and entities abroad. Taxation of the income of a US citizen living abroad or a US corporation doing business abroad is one of the techniques used by Congress to regulate foreign relations.

Treaty power is still an important power that Congress possesses in relation to foreign affairs. The simple language in Article II, Section 2, Clause 2, declares that the president "shall have the power, by and with the advice and consent of the Senate, to make treaties, provided two-thirds of the Senators present concur. . . ." Despite the fact that the president has more often than not bypassed this clause under the guise of executive agreements, this power is still very important. It prevented the United States from becoming a member of the League of Nations and made it possible for the United States to join the United Nations. The Senate, under this clause, has refrained from giving consent to the Genocide Convention for many years. Since the Senate does not formally advise on treaties during the negotiating process, in order to secure their consent, today some senators are included in the negotiations and are appointed to delegations by the president.[7]

Another important power of Congress is the appropriation of funds.[8] With this power, Congress may be able to induce the executive to handle a matter in the manner of congressional choice. It may even stop the executive from carrying out certain actions.

The Constitution vests the administration of the law in the executive.[9] In addition to the power of making treaties subject to the advice and consent of the Senate, as mentioned earlier, the president shall have the power to "appoint Ambassadors, other Public Ministers and Consuls." The president is also empowered to receive "Ambassadors and Public Ministers." These provide the president with most direct power in relation to foreign affairs. Another power concerning foreign relations is the enforcement of treaties by the president. Under the Constitution, laws adopted by Congress and treaties concluded by the United States are the supreme laws of the land. The president is required to "take care that laws be faithfully executed. . . ." The president, however, has more powers than those listed in the Constitution. This is the result of the delegation of power by Congress.[10] In recent years, presidents have greatly increased their authority in international relations.

With the powers granted both by the Constitution and by congressional custom, the president is charged with negotiating treaties and conducting other activities related to foreign affairs, authorized to negotiate and conclude agreements on particular subjects. The president has used this delegation of power to make many executive agreements that are in the nature of treaties. Without the consent of the Senate, the approval of Congress, or the support of a treaty, presidents from Washington to Nixon have made many thousands of agreements, of different degrees of formality and importance, on matters running the gamut of US foreign relations.[11]

After the judgment in *Goldwater* v. *Carter*,[12] the president seems to have secured the power to terminate an international treaty without consulting the Senate or the Congress as a whole.

In addition to the responsibility for administering laws, the president shares responsibility for the adoption of laws, having the power to veto a bill adopted by Congress, though the veto itself may be overridden.

The Constitution also designates the president as "Commander in Chief of the Army and Navy of the United States."[13] Presidents have interpreted their authority in this realm broadly and dynamically, and their position as commander in chief of the armed forces has become one of their most influential powers in the foreign policy field. Throughout its history, the United States has been involved in numerous armed conflicts and undeclared wars largely under presidential authority. The competence of the executive, however, since the passage of the War Powers Resolution,[14] is controversial.

The federal courts in the United States are authorized to exercise jurisdiction of suits by foreign ambassadors or cases to which foreign consuls are party and of suits between two states under Article III of the Constitution. Their principal participation in foreign affairs is to interpret the Constitution, laws, and international treaties when a case is brought before them. In history, there have been occasions on which the courts were asked to decide cases involving foreign affairs. In almost all those cases, the courts followed the pattern of foreign policies adopted by the president and Congress.[15]

CONGRESS AND THE COMMITTEE SYSTEM

The Congress of the United States is a bicameral body, consisting of a House of Representatives and a Senate. One hundred senators constitute the Senate, with two from each of the states. The size of the House is determined by an act of Congress, with the membership allocated to the states in proportion to the size of the population of each state. At present, the number of the membership of the House is 435, determined by an act of Congress in 1911. A study conducted by the *Congressional Quarterly* shows that the members of Congress are mainly from the following groups of citizens – lawyers, businesspersons, public servants, professional educators, and farmers. It is estimated that in the ninety-sixth Congress, the number of lawyers declined for the first time in history to "just over 50 percent of the membership."[16]

The term of a Congress is two years with at least two sessions. In January of each odd-numbered year, Congress holds its first session. The second session is convened in January of each even-numbered year.[17] The president is entitled to call special sessions of Congress under Article II, Section 3, of the Constitution.

The terms of all members of the House, which is two years, expire simultaneously: hence, a new organization starts at the opening of each new Congress.

A senator's term is six years. One-third of the senators are elected every two years on a staggered basis. As a result, the Senate is a more continuous body than the House.

The leading member of the House is the Speaker, whereas the Senate is presided over by the vice-president of the United States. The two national parties of the House put forth their candidates for Speaker. The candidate of the majority party is elected. The Speaker is the most important member in the House. His or her importance is seen as strengthened by "reason of the authority vested in him under the House rules and his acknowledged leadership position in the party."[18] The Speaker is vested with the authority, among other things, to recognize members who wish to obtain the floor, to interpret and apply the rules of procedure, to decide questions of order, to schedule legislation on the floor, to appoint members of select and conference committees, and to refer bills and other matters to committees. Taking into account the importance of procedural matters in legislation, this kind of power and authority has incredible value.

The Speaker also serves as a spokesperson for his or her party and the House. In case the president's office becomes vacant, the Speaker is after the vice-president in the line of succession.

Although authorized by the Constitution to preside over the Senate,[19] the vice-president does not enjoy much prestige nor have as much power as the Speaker of the House of Representatives does. Unlike the Speaker, the vice-president is not a member of the body over which he or she presides.[20] The important factor that makes vice-presidents powerless is that they may not be the leader of the dominant party either in the Congress or in the Senate. The Senate does, however, elect a president pro tempore, who has the right to preside whenever the vice-president is absent. The president pro tempore is chosen by a straight party vote of the majority party. This official, however, is not as powerful as the Speaker in the House. The person who is really powerful in the Senate is the majority leader.

Article I, Section 5, of the Constitution authorizes each house of Congress to "determine the rules of its Proceedings." Because of the fact that senators' terms are staggered, the Senate is viewed as a continuous body. Its rules are normally upheld by the majority of remaining members and carry through succeeding Congresses without changes. One of the best-known rules, Rule XXII, the filibuster rule, however, underwent a major change in 1974. Under the previous Rule XXII, senators had the freedom of unlimited debate. Using this rule, a senator, sometimes working in cooperation with other senators, could make a lengthy speech in order to defeat a bill. The strategy is that when the Senate is tied up with business, the sponsors of the bill in debate may surrender. Senator Strom Thurmond made a continuous speech for 24 hours and 18 minutes in opposition to a pending civil rights bill in 1957 under this rule.[21]

As a minority could use this rule to block a majority's opinion, the rule was viewed as undemocratic. Under pressure from its liberal members the Senate amended it. The amendment provides that unlimited debate by a senator is permitted, unless a majority of three-fifths of the senators sign a motion, known as a "cloture motion," to close off the debate. If the motion is signed, the presiding officer, in two days time, must present it to the Senate for a yea-and-nay vote without debate. If the motion is decided affirmatively by three-fifths of the entire membership of the Senate, the pending measure becomes the unfinished business of the Senate and must be disposed of before anything else can be taken up.

The amendment of Rule XXII, however, does not help very much, for it is often bypassed. One of the techniques invented by James B. Allen to evade this rule proved successful. In 1976, Allen managed to win compromises by continuing to filibuster after cloture with "such parliamentary maneuvers" as demanding quorum calls and roll-call votes on dozens of amendments. The time consumed in calling the role did not count against Allen's one-hour limit. A few months later, Senators Howard M. Metzenbaum and James Abourezk renewed the record of filibuster to tie up debate for nine more days by using Allen's technique, in order to block a vote on a natural gas-pricing bill.[22] Although filibusters may delay the adoption of bills, it seems that they are unable to effectively prevent the adoption of laws.

Despite the discontinuity of the House of Representatives, the majority of the rules have survived every Congress. One of the rules dating from 1841 is that a member of the House is not allowed to occupy more than one hour in debate on any question.[23] The members of the House can bring a debate to a close by a motion of previous question. If the majority of the members present vote in favor of the motion, the debate will be cut off.

In addition to rules from previous sessions, the Rules Committee of the House of Representatives is authorized to report any special rules or regulations at any time and have them considered immediately. If the rules are adopted by a majority vote of the House, they become binding. A study shows that more than one-half of the cases considered in the House at each session are governed by special rules initiated by the Rules Committee.[24] Unanimous consent is another technique adopted by the House (as well as the Senate).

The committee system is a part of the formal organization of Congress. Most of its work is done at committee level. The committees have been established in accordance with the nature of the work Congress has. Generally speaking, there are four kinds of committees: select, joint, conference, and standing. Select committees are ad hoc bodies created for a specific purpose and for a specific length of time. When their work is accomplished, they are terminated. They may be transferred into a standing committee when the nature of the work requires.

Joint committees are composed of members of both Houses. The function of this sort of committee is to coordinate the routine work of both houses of Congress.

Conference committees are used by Congress to eliminate differences between the two houses when adopting a bill. They are composed of members from both houses, too. These committees are to adopt a version of a bill by either house or a compromise of the two, or rewrite a bill by themselves. When a bill is adopted by a conference committee, the committee must report to both houses of Congress. In most cases, each "will accept a conference committee report routinely."[25]

Standing committees are the most important. They are permanent miniature legislative bodies in Congress. Most of these committees are divided into subcommittees. Members of Congress serve on one or more committees and subcommittees.[26] The memberships of those committees are apportioned between the parties roughly in accord with their relative strength in Congress. Because of the expertise and special interests of the members of the committees, opinions of standing committees are easily accepted by each house on the floor. In fact, to some extent, the committees rather than the entire Congress function as the legislature. Once a bill survives the standing committee in charge of it or is recommended by the committee, it has a good chance of being adopted by Congress.

One of the standing committees in the House is worth special mention: the Rules Committee. The function of the Rules Committee, which is characterized as a body between the standing committees and the House floor,[27] is as follows: (1) to propose making or changing the rules for the creation of committees, and to direct them to make investigations; and (2) to report resolutions relating to the hour of daily meeting and the days on which the House shall sit, and orders relating to the use of the galleries during the electoral count. Generally, the responsibility of the House Rules Committee is to schedule the flow of business of legislation. The importance of the committee rests on the fact that a bill may be adopted or killed by means of procedure or special rules issued by the committee. The power of this committee is incredible. Walter Kravitz commented, "In short, the Committee on Rules is to a large degree the governing committee of the House. To it the House has largely delegated the power to regulate procedure vested in the House itself by the Constitution. Furthermore, by virtue of its influence in determining the order and the content of floor business, the Committee may also function as a 'steering' committee, steering the House in whatever direction the exigencies of the hour appear to demand."[28] Although the powers of the Rules Committee have been somewhat curtailed, it remains a dominant power in the House.

Another important actor in the committee system is the committee chairperson. Chairpersons have the power to arrange meetings for their committee and to decide on the agenda of business. They are also authorized to select a professional staff to do research for the committee and to appoint members for subcommittees. Since legislators may have policy preferences about a certain matter, the selection of researchers and especially subcommittee members is of some importance for the adoption or defeat of a bill. In addition to these powers, a chairperson is also empowered to decide whether a public hearing for a bill is necessary or not. When a conference is necessary, chairpersons are the natural representative of their committees. Owing to the importance of committee chairpersons, the posts are also decided roughly in accordance with party strength in each house of Congress. All committee chairpersons are members of the majority party.

A bill that will become law if passed by Congress with the approval of the president may have its genesis with a lobby group, an agency of the White House, perhaps with the recommendation of the president, or a private individual. The first draft or a recommendation of a bill needs a sponsor in Congress in order to get onto the route of the legislative process. The Constitution requires that all bills for raising revenue originate in the House of Representatives, whereas bills concerning other matters may be introduced by either a senator or a representative. Sponsorship demonstrates some commitment to the bill by the sponsor. The selection of sponsors may decide to a large extent the fate of a bill. When a bill is introduced, it will be assigned to a committee by the Speaker of the House. At the committee level, the bill will be examined preliminarily to decide whether it should be studied and considered by the full committee or by a subcommittee. The chairperson of the committee will decide whether a special subcommittee should be established or not. Whether the bill is considered by a full committee or by a standing or special subcommittee, it usually is the subject of hearings. The chairperson determines whether to hold hearings and invite witnesses to testify about its virtues and shortcomings, and makes recommendations to the committee. These hearings may be public or closed. Usually, interested government agencies are permitted to comment before nongovernment sources are heard.[29] After considering the bill, the subcommittee reports its recommendation to the full committee. If it decides negatively, the bill will be killed within the subcommittee.

Although the subcommittee's decision to table, endorse, or reshape a bill is often accepted by the full committee, the committee may kill a bill simply by not reporting it out for a floor debate. A committee can hold a bill as long as it likes. Although a discharge petition signed by a quorum of 218 members of the House will force the committee to report the bill out, this procedure is a difficult requirement to meet. Even if the committee decides to report out a bill, it may greatly alter the character of the bill by approving major changes at "markup" sessions. When a bill is reported out of the committee, it will be put on the calendar.

Committee chairpersons, sometimes with the cooperation of subcommittee chairpersons, can decide whether a public hearing should be held or not. How such hearings will be conducted is also at their discretion.

A bill that has survived the committee is reported to the House, and, as mentioned earlier, placed upon the appropriate calendar (a list of business pending). Unless the bill reported is in the nature of private, noncontroversial, or privileged measures, the chairperson of the reporting committee must request a hearing before the Rules Committee. When the request is granted, the chairperson, along with interested members of the committee, will probably appear before the Rules Committee and plead for the granting of a special rule or resolution calling for the bill's consideration forthwith by the House.

The Rules Committee then will decide whether a special rule should be granted or denied, with considerable consequences for the fate of the bill. In case the Rules Committee decides to grant a special rule, the terms of debate, time allowed for floor consideration, and mode of floor amendment will be set out in the resolution. By virtue of this power, the committee can delay or kill a bill by procedures or issuing special rules.

Except some bills that may be considered at the informal meetings of the House, which are called the "Committee of the Whole," all bills passing the Rules Committee are required to be debated on the floor and voted on by the representatives.

When a bill passes the House, it is sent to the Senate, where it is referred to an appropriate committee for consideration. Then, more or less the same procedure will be followed as in the House. Sometimes, the two chambers may be only in general agreement with regard to a bill; they may not agree on every provision or on all the versions of the bill. Should such a case occur, a conference committee will be created to resolve the differences. When a compromise or agreement is reached in the conference committee, the committee reports to each house for final approval.

After both chambers adopt the bill, it is first signed by the Speaker of the House and then by the presiding officer of the Senate. Lastly, the bill is carried to the president of the United States.

The president of the United States has three options regarding the bill: (1) approve and sign it, in which case the bill will become law; (2) do nothing, in which case the bill becomes law in ten days without the signature of the president, unless Congress has adjourned in the meantime (then the bill is dead); or (3) veto the bill. In the event that the president vetoes a bill, two-thirds of the members of each house are required to vote for it in order to override the veto and make the bill into law.

In addition to these formal rules and procedures, congresspersons have to observe unwritten but generally and traditionally recognized norms in Congress.[30] It suffices to mention some of the norms, such as loyalty to the institution, seniority and apprenticeship, specialization, and accommodation.[31]

Also, upon voting a bill, members of Congress have to take into consideration the opinions of their constituents. Even though not many voters know what is going on in Congress, there are always a few in almost every district who are well informed of a few issues of vital importance to them. Usually, these constituents possess resources important to the congressperson, for example, potential campaign contributions, favorable coverage in a newspaper, endorsement by an important local union, and so on. These constituents certainly have direct influence on the members of Congress elected from their districts. As a result, although Congress members have their own preferences and freedom in lawmaking, they may feel "under constant pressure from constituents."[32]

THE FEDERAL BUREAUCRACY AND THE ADMINISTRATIVE PROCESS

The president is the administrative head of the executive branch of the government. As such, presidents must faithfully administer the laws,[33] whether these laws have been adopted by their party or by the opposite party. To carry out their executive responsibility, the executive government has been established with numerous agencies, both temporary and permanent, and 13 executive departments.[34] Presidents constantly set up central review and coordination units. These help formulate new policies and eliminate interagency differences in the government. At the same time, they provide interest groups with access to policy making.

The basis for executive power is found in the opening of Article II, Section 1, of the Constitution: "The executive power shall be vested in a president of the United States." In addition to the powers set forth in the Constitution, the statutes adopted by Congress have conferred upon the president specific authority and responsibility covering a wide range of matters. The president has the power, by and with the advice and consent of the Senate, to appoint officers. The Constitution also gives presidents the power to "require the opinion, in writing, of the principal officer in each of the executive departments, upon any subject relating to the duties of their respective offices." Hence, a cabinet was considered by the drafters as necessary for the function of the government, and provisions were made for its establishment. Starting from the administration of George Washington, there has been a cabinet in the government. The difference between each administration is in the size of its cabinet and bureaucracy. The growth of the cabinet and bureaucracy is a feature common to all administrations. The total number of people serving in the government at the time of Washington was 780, whereas the present number is around 2.5 million. (This figure does not include the over 2 million people serving in the armed forces.)[35]

Because of the huge size of the bureaucracy and the formation of interest groups, the president can hardly hear public opinions. Commenting on his experience, former President Carter said, "One thing about being President or governor or a member of Congress is that the voices you hear in a state capital or in Washington are the strident voices, the narrowly focused voices, and the selfish voices."[36] Former President Ford agreed that "there [was] a growing gap, a yawning chasm . . . between the public and policy makers."[37] Because of the president's lack of direct contact with the public and loose control over the executive units, and because of the fact that these administrative agencies were established by acts of Congress, both appointed officials and professionals "tend to become involved in the decision-making activities."[38]

To manage the government today, the president has a team comprising the executive office of the president, the 13 cabinet secretaries and their assistants, the vice-president, task forces, special commissions, and personal friends.

The executive office of the president was first created by President Roosevelt in 1939. Under the authority of the Reorganization Act of 1939, various agencies were transferred to the executive office by the President's Reorganization Plans I and II of 1939.[39] Subsequently, the composition of the office has been changed by each president to correspond to the goals of the administration. The main divisions now include the White House Office, Office of Management and Budget, Council of Economic Advisers, National Security Council, Office of Policy Development, Office of Science and Technology Policy, etc.

The White House Office is the most important division of the executive office of the president. It is the most immediate assistant and advisor to the president. Unlike cabinet secretaries, the staff of the executive offices are not chosen in accord with special regional or political patterns, but for their ability to aid and assist presidents in such matters as they may direct.

Having intimate contact with the president, the highest-ranking assistants and advisors usually become very influential. They in fact occupy "top-ranking policy-making" positions.[40] Every administration has its handful of powerful staff members. They play a major or even decisive role in shaping government policy.

In addition to the policy-making function of the leading members, the White House Office facilitates and maintains communication with Congress, the individual members of Congress, the heads of executive agencies, the press and other information media, and the general public for the president. As such, the White House Office has become indispensable to the president.

The creation and maintenance of the office have changed the structure and modes of operation of the executive branch of the government. Communication between the president and the cabinet departments now must go through the pipeline of the White House Office.

The cabinet is composed of 13 departments. A department is a major unit of administrative activity. The head of the department is usually called the "secretary," except the head of the Department of Justice, who is called the "attorney general." For the administration of departmental affairs, the secretary has an undersecretary and several assistant secretaries. All the secretaries, undersecretaries, and assistant secretaries are appointed by the president with the advice and consent of the Senate. These appointments, however, are usually made by the president with consideration of the need for harmony within the party, geographical balance, the wishes of interest groups, and so on. As a result, the appointees may not have a strong relationship with the president; they may not be as loyal as the president's assistants are to the president. Generally speaking they perform a less important role in decision making than top officials in the White House Office do, although some of the secretaries, such as the secretaries of defense, state, and treasury as well as the attorney general, may be strong forces in the cabinet.

The cabinet secretaries may also be weak because of their relationship with their own departments and the bureaucrats in those departments. Appointed by the president, secretaries are viewed as outsiders by the bureaucrats of the department to which they are appointed. They expect them only to work in the department for a couple of years or even just a few months. They do not consider them as persons who know the organization, the policies, and the goals of the department. So, new appointees find themselves in a framework of established relationships. They face a bureaucratic structure with great resistance to change. In fact, most of the organization is staffed by those who have been working there for many years and who are called "middle-management" career people, some of whom cannot be fired by the president under law.[41] They are familiar with the ways things can or they think should be done. These middle-management career people constitute about four-fifths of the office and bureau chiefs.[42] If the secretary pushes too hard to have something done, he or she may meet with resistance from these bureaucrats because the president cannot fire them. Nevertheless, if secretaries identify themselves with their department, they and the department may risk losing support, or even the cutting off of funds by the White House.

Owing to these institutional elements and customs, the bureaucracy or the administrative agencies can be quite powerful. As one of Kennedy's White House aides, frustrated at the bureaucracy, once put it, "Everyone believes in democracy until he gets to the White House and then you begin to believe in dictatorship, because it's so hard to get things done. Every time you turn around, people just resist you, and even resist their own job."[43]

The power base of these bureaucrats is multiple. Every department or agency has been established under a specific act of Congress. It treats itself to some extent as an independent body. In addition to this statutory relationship, a department may have a direct "bureau-legislative" relationship with either a standing committee or subcommittee of Congress.[44] At the same time, a departmental constituent may base its autonomy on support from other constituents or a top official in the executive branch.

As a practical matter, these administrative agencies are very important to economic activities within the country and its economic relations with foreign countries. They function as legislative as well as judicial bodies. Most of the statutes adopted by Congress, as in other countries, are very general. In order to implement a law, supplemental rules and enforcing regulations are usually adopted at the administrative level. For instance, Congress adopted the Export Administration Act and left the Commerce Department to write enforcement regulations. The Treasury Department and the Internal Revenue Service exercise law-making power in implementing the tax laws, as another case in point.

Even though laws adopted by Congress may be concrete, their application in fact is still subject to administrative interpretation. A good example is the countervailing duty statute. Congress did not make it clear whether the statute should be equally applicable to nonmarket economy countries. When a countervailing duty petition against import from a nonmarket economy country was filed with the Commerce Department in 1983, the department had to decide whether the statute should be applicable to imports from such countries.

The administrative agencies may exercise judiciary functions in conjunction with the enforcement of laws. An obvious case is the International Trade Commission's (ITC) investigative function in antidumping lawsuits.

Basically, the decision-making function of the administrative agencies is the result of the delegation of power by Congress for "the need for effective government."[45] Although administrative agencies enjoy significant discretion of law making, they are not free from political accountability. Congress can influence these agencies through the appropriation of funds, for administrative agencies are dependent on public funding to support their operation. Also, judicial review provides interested parties with opportunities for relief.

Second, presidents may use their veto power to block the enactment of laws affecting agencies to control them. They may also influence agencies by exercising their power to appoint and remove federal officers.[46] Despite the considerable effect of this power, the president may, however, run highly political risks, when replacing a high-ranking official who is backed up by influential constituents. In practice, the president usually employs less drastic measures, such as the modification of the organizational structure of the agency in question, in order to effectuate his influence over decision making of the administrative agency.

Third, administrative agencies' actions are subject to judicial review.[47] Judicial review influences administrative actions through providing relief for the individual person who is harmed by a particular agency decision. In recent years, with the development of technology and economic activities in dealing with diversified agency decisions, the courts generally lack reliable empirical information and expertise in deciding complex cases. Nonetheless, judicial review has become more stringent than it was a couple of decades ago.

In addition to these legal checks, administrative agencies constantly receive pressure from outside sources, including lobbyists, trade associations, lawyers working for big corporations, and even personal friends. These groups of people usually have their inputs into regulations by supplying information, publicizing shortcomings of a regulatory action by executive agencies, or submitting comments at formal hearings.[48] A US scholar summarized: "The federal bureaucracy is permeated by networks of government-private interest group alliances. In most cases, the private groups which are represented are particular businesses and/or industries, with government bureaus and agencies acting as their supporters and protectors against other government bodies, other interests, and the general public."[49] This kind of close relationship between governmental agencies and the interest groups, in fact, represents two-way support. On the one hand, private interest groups get support from government agencies. On the other, the private interest groups can put pressure upon the executive branch as a whole, or upon the legislative branch, Congress, to adopt or reject a bill that may have a direct or indirect effect on these governmental agencies. Since many government officials are from major industrial and financial corporations, investment houses, and corporate law firms, their relations with these interest groups are naturally very close and the basis of their support can be very solid.[50]

In making rules or regulations, administrative agencies are required by the Administrative Procedure Act to solicit opinions from interested parties.[51] When a statute requires rules to be made on the record, the administrative agency concerned must conduct trial-type hearings and provide interested parties the opportunity to testify and cross-examine adverse witnesses before adopting a rule.[52]

If the statute in question does not direct the administrative agency to adopt rules on the record, the agency must follow notice-and-comment procedures provided for by Section 553 of the Administrative Procedure Act. First, it must notify the public by publishing the matter in the *Federal Register*, a daily official publication by the US government. The notice should include the substance of the proposed rule or a description of the subjects and issues involved. It should also contain the legal basis of the proposed rule. The second step is for the interested parties to submit their comments on the proposed rule to the administrative agency.[53] Finally, the agency, after considering the comments from interested parties, must issue with the final rules a concise general statement of their basis and purpose.

If an interested person is not happy with the agency rules, an action can be brought to enjoin their enforcement or to challenge their validity. The reviewing court decides whether the rules were made within the agency's jurisdiction.[54] It also decides if the agency, by adopting the rules, is violating constitutional rights, and whether procedural requirements have been met. The court is also supposed to determine whether the agency's factual analysis was reasonable.[55]

In any event, the federal bureaucracy has become a very important part of the government. The regulatory function played by administrative agencies is indispensable for implementing governmental policies and laws.

POLITICAL PARTIES AND ELECTION CAMPAIGNS

The political party system in the United States is essentially a two-party system. Both parties, the Democratic and the Republican, aim at winning elections. They serve primarily as linkage institutions – linking the government to the general public and linking different constituencies in the government. Parties are supposed to recruit and nominate candidates for government posts. In order to do so, they must bring political issues, including economic issues, to the attention of the public and educate the public about them. In Congress as well as in state legislatures, the political parties may be viewed as instruments to organize support for or forces against a piece of legislation at a given time. Although the emergence of interest groups has diminished the importance of the parties' role in political life, they still represent diverse interests of the democracy.

Owing to the goals set out by them,[56] the organization of the parties in the United States is very loose. Membership in either party does not create any obligation. Neither party has a definite, card-carrying, dues-paying membership. It is not necessary for persons to do anything except declare themselves members of one party or the other. Some states require voters to indicate their membership in a party at election time, whereas others do not require even this measure of affiliation. Although the membership is without formal commitment, members may feel some moral obligation and become loyal to the party they are attached to.

Coincident with the objective of winning votes and thereby running public offices, the parties have committees that correspond to the various levels of government: local, state, and national. These committees are treated as the executives of each convention. A convention is a more numerous group than a committee and meets less frequently.

The highest organizational level of each party is the national convention, which meets every four years. Its function is to nominate the party's presidential candidate. The national committee operates continuously between the party conventions, as do committees at other levels. It is composed of four people from each state.[57] The day-to-day work of the national committee is handled by the national chairperson and his or her staff members in the headquarters in Washington, DC. The essential function of this committee is to assist in the direction of, and to raise funds for, the presidential election campaign.

In addition to the national committee, each major party has established a Senatorial Campaign Committee and a Congressional Campaign Committee. They are composed of members of the Senate and the House of Representatives, respectively, to aid members in election or reelection to office.

State and local committees also serve such functions as assisting members of the party to run for public office.

To run successfully for a public office or the presidency, a two-fold process is required: party nomination and election. In order to be elected, an election campaign has become indispensable. This requires both manpower and finances. Although election campaigns need millions of hours of labor, each major party seems to be able to secure this without having to pay substantial salaries. Most of the citizens participating in the political activities receive very little or no cash in return. The incentive for this voluntary work may be manifold. Volunteers at lower levels work for a certain candidate whose policy is in their favor. At a higher level, however, campaign workers, such as consultants, may work for future political and economic reward from the office elected.

Publicity is the way to win public support or votes. Candidates need to make as many personal appearances to the public as possible. Appearances on television and radio and in the press as well as direct mails have proved to be essential campaign methods. But all these activities cost a lot of money. In 1972, Richard Nixon spent a record of $61 million in the general election.[58] The cost of all the campaigns around the country in the 1982 House election totaled $1 billion, it is estimated. When managers of the campaign commented that it was the most expensive campaign in history, Jody Powell, an ex-White House aide, agreed that "but then, they all are nowadays."[59] It seems that a good deal of money went to buy television and radio spots. Mailing is also expensive. Robert Price, the former deputy mayor of New York and a veteran campaign manager, concluded that, for a congressional campaign, "One district-wide mailing will cost at least $20,000. Two brochures . . . cost another $20,000."[60]

The expenditures are very important for winning votes. After the House election campaign in 1982, officials of both the Democratic and Republican parties agreed that fund-raising advantages played a critical role in preserving Republican seats, "especially those of incumbents, in close races." Charles T. Manatt, chairperson of the Democratic national committee, said that "the money advantage alone gave them [Republicans] 10 or 12 seats." He said that the money advantage prevented a "solid defeat" from turning into a landslide. Nancy Sirnot, executive director of the National Republican Congressional Committee, agreed with Manatt's estimation. She said that it "sounds plausible to me" and added that Republican money "preserved many seats that might have gone down otherwise."[61]

The importance of fund raising cannot be easily exaggerated, but who are the contributors? Traditionally, candidates can get a good amount from national committees, county committees, and other party groups. The rest of the necessary money must be raised through solicitation. It seems that the bulk of the election expenditure is from friends, or friends of friends, or labor or business. "The biggest givers are likely to be firms with government contracts, or with hopes of getting one."[62] After the reforms of election campaign regulations in 1974 and 1976, direct financial contribution by these companies became unlawful.

The contributions can be made in various ways. They may be made directly to party committees. The contributors may buy a page advertisement in a party pamphlet for $15,000. They may buy a $1,000 President's Club ticket. Or they may pay $100 or more for a "campaign" or testimonial dinner. They may also contribute by attending $1 coffee receptions.

Owing to the loose organizational nature of the parties and the reliance upon campaign financing by candidates and its importance to them, the parties' role has eroded in Congress and in the executive and other federal, state, and local offices. Individual senators or representatives have to compete with candidates from their own party in elections. They must represent the interest of a certain group or groups in order to raise funds for election or reelection. Hence, a legislator "may be less concerned about sanctions his party leadership could bring to bear on him than the possible sanctions likely to be invoked by the interest groups whose support he has had or seeks."[63] An example of the party erosion in Congress is the cooperation of southern Democrats with the Reagan administration in passing the president's economic proposals in 1981. Switches from one party to another by congresspersons further indicate the weak party leadership in the legislature.[64]

Because of the indispensable nature of election campaign funds, they are regulated by law. In 1907, a law was passed to forbid corporations chartered under federal law, such as national banks, from making any contributions to any political campaigns and to forbid all corporations to make contributions to national campaigns.[65] In 1925, Congress adopted the Corrupt Practices Act, placing limits on the amount of money that could be spent by candidates for election to the Senate or the House. Revising the act, Congress fixed the amounts to a maximum of $25,000 for a Senate candidate and $5,000 for a House candidate.[66] In 1971, the Federal Election Campaign Fund Act was adopted by Congress.[67] This act requires candidates to file reports on campaign contributions for federal offices.

A major reform of election campaign regulations took place in 1974, in the political aftermath of Watergate. The Federal Election Campaign Act Amendment of 1974 was adopted.[68] This act was further amended by the Federal Election Campaign Act Amendment of 1976.[69] These amendments make it unlawful for any national bank, any corporation organized by law of Congress, or any government contractor to make contributions to election campaigns with the purpose of influencing the nomination for election or reelection for federal office. They set a limit of $1,000 on contributions by individuals for any election for a federal office. A person is prohibited from making contributions aggregating to more than $25,000 in any calendar year. Corporations and labor unions are not allowed to make contributions for political purposes.

Under these amendments, political comiittees may be created for the purpose of campaign finance. A political committee is "any committee, club, association, or other group of persons which receives contributions or makes expenditures during a calendar year in an aggregate amount exceeding $1,000." A committee is required to have a chairperson and treasurer. The treasurer is required by law to keep an exact account of "(1) all contributions made to or for such committee; (2) the identity of every person making a contribution in excess of $50, and the date and amount thereof . . .; (3) all expenditures made by or on behalf of such committee; and (4) the identity of every person to whom any expenditure is made." A political committee may give up to $5,000 toward a candidate in a federal election. In a presidential campaign, a committee may make a $5,000 contribution to each candidate in a general election.

A Federal Election Commission was established under these reforms. It was designed to serve as a bipartisan watchdog.

Another important provision of the amendments is to establish a Federal Election Campaign Fund. Under this provision, all individuals paying income taxes may designate on the tax form, at no cost to themselves, that $1 be paid to a fund maintained by the US Treasury. Candidates running for the presidency may accept financial support from those funds under the condition that they are then no longer qualified to receive contributions from individuals or political committees in the general election campaign. In addition to this, a candidate must also have received "contributions which in the aggregate exceed $5,000 in contributions from residents of each of at least 20 states, and . . . contributions certified with respect to any person . . . do not exceed $250." In the 1980 presidential election campaign, both Carter and Reagan chose to accept financing from this public funding for the general election, accepting financing from individuals and political action committees (PACS) only in the primaries.[70]

Although people have not yet come to an agreement as to the effect of the reform, the limitation on spending for campaign advertising and the disclosure provisions are of significance, despite the modest scope of the amendments.

PRESSURE GROUPS AND LOBBYING

A pressure group in general is an association of individuals with a common interest. It imposes pressure upon the government to influence its decision making. Pressure groups send people who are known as lobbyists to Washington as their resident representatives to conduct lobbying. In reality, pressure groups, lobbyists, and lobbying are really more or less the same thing with different headings. Also, in addition to professional lobbyists, lawyers and trade associations are two other very influential lobbies in governmental decision making. (For the purpose of this section, the term "lobbyists" shall include both fulltime lobbyists and others, such as lawyers.) It is estimated that 80 percent of the largest US companies either employ law firms or have set up their own offices for lobbying purposes in Washington, DC.[71]

It is said that lobbying is just as old as legislation, and that pressure groups are as old as politics. As early as when the Adamses went to attend the First Continental Congress in Philadelphia, they encountered "the same kind of pressure tactics that the congressman is subject to daily in Washington today." Even before they reached Philadelphia, they were met by a group of lobbyists.[72]

Lobbyists influence the legislative process through providing information, organizing political support and opposition, and the use of money. This is reflected in the Regulation of Lobbying Act of 1946. This law, through the requirement of registration, defines a lobbyist as an "individual, partnership, committee, association, corporation, and any other organization or group of persons" who "by himself, or through any agent or employee or other persons in any manner whatsoever, directly or indirectly, solicits, collects, or receives money . . . to be used principally to aid, or the principal purpose of which person is to aid in . . . passage or defeat of any legislation by Congress of the United States."[73] Lobbyists are employees of interests groups, such as oil, highway, dairy industries, and so forth. One of the major jobs of lobbyists is to develop friendly relations with people in the legislative and executive branches, from leading members down to the staff of a committee or an office. As such, former legislators are the best candidates to be lobbyists. They not only have personal contacts with incumbents but also have insight into how the game is played. In the 20 years after the second world war, 23 senators and 80 representatives became lobbyists or consultants in Washington, DC, when they left Congress.[74]

In order to carry out their functions effectively, lobbyists adopt different techniques. Campaign contributions have long been an effective means of influencing the decision-making process. The lobbyists or interest groups spend hundreds of millions of dollars on election campaigns. In 1980, 25 candidates for seats in the House raised in excess of $200,000 apiece. Most of the money had an origin in interest groups.[75] These are all indirect influences.

Lobbyists also serve as sources of legislative research for decision makers. They may submit a formal report or comment. They may provide information simply by talking to congresspersons, very often their staffs, and letting them know the possible effects of a legislative action. In this regard, lawyers are considerably persuasive, because they know the laws and have detailed information from their clients. "At the executive and regulatory agencies, some Washington lawyers ply the halls daily for their clients in off-the-record meetings with officials."[76] "First they would try to convince us how fair it was for them to have a special exemption to some general tax provision added to the bill in committee. If that didn't work, they would urge that their company was being ruined by some unfair provision. Finally, they would start telling you how much business they were doing in your state,"[77] commented an aide to the Senate Finance Committee.

Lobbyists may even draft legislation themselves for the legislators. John Thomas Taylor of Legion lobby once boasted informally that he "personally had written between 1,500 and 2,000 bills" in his first ten years as head of the lobby.[78]

The lobbyists' direct influence is important and effective. It nevertheless needs the cooperation of legislators. Sometimes lobbyists have to use direct methods in conjunction with indirect techniques in order to effect their influence. In addition, lobbyists have to be very attentive and careful, for even the slightest negligence could cost millions of dollars to their companies. In 1952, Rod Markley, Ford Motor Company's Washington managing director, found, after a brief telephone call, that the House Banking and Currency Committee, persuaded by Ford's competitor, had introduced a three-word change in the amendment to the Defense Production Act passed from the Senate, which in turn passed the floor of the House. This three-word amendment, if it had passed, would have deprived Ford of an income benefit of $35 million. Well aware of the disadvantage of the bill, Markley lost no time in pointing out the insidious nature of the amendment to its sponsors just before the House-Senate conference, and, at the same time, started mounting opposition from Ford's auto dealers. Fortunately for Ford, three days later, the amendment was deleted in the wee hours of the morning in a conference that lasted until 5 A.M.[79]

Lobbyists do not confine their activities to Congress. They also develop strong ties with the executive branch. The "iron triangle," as they call it, which includes interest groups, congressional subcommittees, and their relevant federal agencies, is the end product of the game. In fact, lobbyists very often go to the executive first.[80] They have their voices heard at formal hearings conducted by administrative agencies and through informal and private meetings. Sometimes, the administrative agencies may ask lobbyists, for example, lawyers, to research a certain issue or even to draft regulations. In 1968, the Commerce Department asked an advisory committee of some 15 private lawyers and accountants to draft regulations for direct foreign investment.[81] A good relationship with the executive is just as important as with Congress. "Very often, the symbiotic relationship becomes so pronounced that the private interest group comes to make its own policies and regulations, with the federal agency serving to legitimate its actions."[82]

The same thing happens in Congress, too. Even some congresspersons do not deny their representation of certain interests. Senator Boies Penrose once explained to some businesspersons that "I believe in a division of labor. You send us to Congress; we pass laws under . . . which you make money . . . and out of your profits you further contribute to our campaign funds to send us back again to pass more laws to enable you to make more money."[83]

Penrose's candor is no longer heard from decision makers. With the evolution of the human community, congresspersons feel they should appear more responsive to their constituents' interests. The techniques used by lobbyists are also in the process of development. In addition to campaign contributions and other lawful donations, lawmakers receive money through giving speeches. The amount of the payment, which is called an "honorarium," may not exceed $2,000 per speech under the law. In 1981, 25 senators received more than $25,000 from honorariums. Senator Jake Garn received $48,000 in honorariums in 1981. Senator Richard G. Lugar received $8,500 from five Minneapolis speaking appearances within 30 hours. Referring to the nature of the honorariums, Senator William Proxmire said, "If you are Chairman of the Banking Committee, you don't have to speak at all. All you have to do is show up. You can read the phone book, and they'll be happy to pay your honoraria."[84]

To say that lobbyists are active in Washington, DC, does not mean that they are carrying out unlawful activities. Lobbying is protected by the First Amendment, which guarantees the freedom of speech by individuals.[85] In 1946, Congress adopted the Regulations of Lobbying Act.[86] The act requires lobbyists to register with the Senate and the House of Representatives and to file quarterly financial statements disclosing their expenses. The persons who are required by this law to register are those who try to influence Congress by "direct communication."[87] This law is in fact without much force, for a good many lobbyists do not usually report their expenses fully.[88]

The traditional influence of pressure groups in US politics through election campaign funds has not undergone a substantial change despite the reform effort in the 1970s. Before the reform, campaigns were funded almost solely by individual contributions. Although there were PACs, they were little known by the public. With the restrictions on individual contributions, pressure groups have established PACs under all kinds of names. Today, "PACs are the growth industry in Washington, DC." In 1974, there were 589 PACS; today, the number is more than 3,000.[89] Interest groups use PACs to make campaign contributions instead of individual ones. In the 1979-80 election cycle, business PACs alone gave about $35 million to congressional and presidential campaigns. It is estimated that by the 1984 elections, PACs will contribute over $100 million to congressional candidates alone.[90]

Interest groups through PACs enjoy the same latitude in influencing the decision-making process as they did before, because of the loopholes in the 1974 amendments.[91] PACs have proved to be effective in the new circumstances. For instance, on May 26, 1982, the House voted 286-133 to kill a bill that would have forced used car dealers to tell consumers of any known major defects in the cars they sell. Between January 1979 and April 1982, the used-car-dealers PAC, NADA, gave a total of $742,371 to those voting to kill the bill. Of those who voted against the bill, 82 percent received campaign contributions from NADA, while 31 percent of those who voted for it received money from NADA.[92] It may be too early to tell the exact power and function of PACs in US politics. Terry Dolan, head of the National Conservative PAC, however, told Salt Lake City's KU-TV in 1980 that "we could elect Mickey Mouse to the House or Senate."[93] Nevertheless, this is not to say that PACs or the interest groups can obtain whatever they want at any given time, "but all groups engaged in the process can achieve some of their goals."[94]

THE MONETARY AND FINANCIAL SYSTEM

US monetary and financial institutions may play an important part in the decision-making process, too. In addition to having their own interest group, they influence government actions through their special relationship with the government and through business operations.

The major financial institution is the Federal Reserve System.[95] The system was established on December 23, 1913, when President Woodrow Wilson signed the Federal Reserve Act.[96] Although the system functions as the central bank of the United States, it is different from central banks of other countries. First, it is not a single bank. Instead, it consists of 12 Federal Reserve banks located in 12 districts. These Federal Reserve banks are in turn owned by the Federal Reserve member banks.

Under the Federal Reserve Act, all national banks are members of the system.[97] In addition, state-chartered banks may also be admitted into the system. As of June 30, 1979, there were 5,404 commercial banks that were members of the system. Of the total number, 4,493 were national banks, whereas the remaining 1,011 were state chartered.[98] These member banks had 79 percent of the total assets of insured commercial banks.[99]

Member banks are required to become stockholders of the Federal Reserve banks. Ownership of this sort, however, carries only limited rights, such as electing some directors of the members' Federal Reserve banks and receiving a dividend of 6 percent on its stock holdings.

The system operates in a comparatively independent pattern. It is empowered to carry out its business in accordance with its best judgment, but is subject to such guiding principles and restrictions as Congress may prescribe. In other words, the system must endeavor to attain the general economic goals of the government, while any means for achieving the ends may be employed by the system at will.

The system is run by the board of governors, previously known as the "Federal Reserve Board," the Federal Open-Market Committee, and the Federal Advisory Council.

The board of governors is composed of seven members. Appointed by the president with the advice and consent of the Senate, members of the board serve for 14 years.[100] The terms are staggered so that only one term expires every two years.[101] In addition, the president is empowered to designate one member as the chairperson and one as the vice-chairperson of the board; each serves for four years.

The primary purpose of the board of governors is to give instructions and advice for the operation of the 12 Federal Reserve banks. Its functions can be categorized into two classes, namely, supervision and regulation of the operating units of the domestic payments and credit mechanism, and the formulation of national policy as delegated to the board by Congress.

The board is empowered to examine the Federal Reserve banks, to adjust the district boundaries, and to suspend and remove bank officers. It may also require the Federal Reserve banks to establish branches or keep accounts in foreign countries.

Another field of supervision is the board's power in relation to member banks. First, it is empowered to receive state banks into the Federal Reserve System. Second, it may remove from office directors and officers of the member banks. It may permit directors, officers, or employees of one member bank to act in a similar capacity in another. Also, the Federal Reserve System has a strong influence on loan funds and interest rates.

The system's direct contact with the government is through the chairperson of the board of governors. The chairperson keeps close contact with both the executive branch and Congress, meeting frequently with three officials who are in charge of shaping and implementing the federal government's financial policy: the secretary of the Treasury, the chairperson of the president's Council of Economic Advisers, and the director of the president's Office of Management and Budget. Together with these three officials, the chairperson participates in informal discussions with the president regarding national financial policies.

As far as the legislative body is concerned, the chairperson of the Federal Reserve System has a liaison relationship with the committees dealing with, or interested in, banking and monetary affairs. More often than not, chairpersons speak before relevant committees of every Congress about the board's views and judgments with respect to legislation concerning financial matters under consideration in Congress. At the same time, Congress may ask the board of governors to study various subjects.

Another leading body within the Federal Reserve System is the Federal Open-Market Committee. Made up of the seven members of the board of governors and five elected representatives of the Federal Reserve banks, the committee has full control over all open-market operations of the Federal Reserve banks. No Federal Reserve bank may engage in, or refuse to engage in, open-market operations except in accordance with the directives and regulations adopted by the committee.[102]

The Federal Advisory Council, which was established by the Federal Reserve Act, serves as a formal channel of communication between the banking and financial community and the board of governors. The council is composed of 12 members selected by the

Federal Reserve banks of their respective districts. It has the power to discuss general business operations with the board and to make recommendations regarding matters within the board's jurisdiction.[103] Thus, the council's power of recommendation ranges from the general objectives of the Federal Reserve System to the specific operation of the Federal Reserve banks and member banks.

Owing to its statutory status and huge assets (including its member banks), the Federal Reserve System plays an influential role in the national financial decision making. For instance, although the Treasury Department has responsibilities with regard to the functioning of the credit market and monetary mechanisms, it seeks the advice of the officials of the system before a final decision is made in these areas.

Unlike central banks in other countries, which are subordinate to the Treasury, the Federal Reserve System is a coordinate, not a subordinate, cog in the administrative machinery. Its financial decisions may, at the same time, have binding force on the Treasury. A joint resolution of the two houses of Congress provides that the "primary power and responsibility for regulating the supply, availability, and cost of credit in general shall be vested in the duly constituted authorities of the Federal Reserve System, and that Treasury actions relative to money, credit, and transactions in the Federal debt shall be made consistent with the policies of the Federal Reserve."[104]

The relationship between the Federal Reserve System and the Treasury is a two-way street. The Treasury's administration of US monetary reserves and conduct of various other financial activities are equally important to the operation of the Federal Reserve System. Conversely, the system's operations in the domestic and international financial markets profoundly affect conditions in the credit market. This in turn affects the decision and law making of the federal government.

In fact, the decisions and policies of the Federal Reserve System may have far-reaching effects at both national and international levels. The rise and fall of interest rates in the last three years is an example. With the system's growth targets for money supply far below the growth of the gross national product (GNP), the immediate result of the gap between money growth and GNP growth was an increase in interest rates. High interest rates led to the appreciation of the dollar in relation to other currencies. The average value of the dollar in terms of currencies of the ten major industrial countries rose 30 percent from August 1980 to August 1981.[105] At the same time, the high interest rate slowed down domestic investment and significantly increased the burden of servicing debt obligations by a few countries. Both are of much concern to the government and may have a direct impact on US economic policy at home and abroad.[106]

In conclusion, as a heterogeneous, quintessential capitalist country, the United States has the most complicated political and legal systems. The internal operation and decision making of the US government receive inputs from many sources. Also, laws of the United States are much more comprehensive and complicated than those of any other countries. As a result, it is difficult for foreign countries, especially those with different political and legal systems, such as China, to comprehend US law making and application. It is also difficult to have these countries' views represented, for they usually do not have lobbies in Washington, DC.

The complex law-making procedures coupled with the effects of interest groups and political parties make it difficult to change current laws, although some are apparently insufficient and unsuitable for present circumstances.[107] It seems that more efforts should be made by the US government to amend its laws to balance the interests among domestic industries, different social groups, and foreign interests.

NOTES

1. See the Constitution of the United States, Article I, Section 8. Legislative powers are also conferred on Congress in other articles. For instance, the power to admit new states and to govern federal territory and other property is derived from Article IV, Section 3, whereas the power to propose constitutional amendments is conferred by Article V.

2. Bob Eckhardt and Charles L. Black, Jr. *The Tides of Power* (New Haven, Yale University Press, 1976), pp. 14-25.

3. John Marshall, secretary of state in the administration of John Adams, was nominated as chief justice of the Supreme Court in January 1801 and took his oath of office on February 4, 1801. The court presided over by Marshall decided quite a few cases having a significant effect on US constitutional law. Marshall is probably the most famous US judge.

4. Gibbons v. Ogden, 9 Wheat 1, 189 (US 1824).

5. Ibid., p. 193. See also Felix Frankfurter, *The Commerce Power Under Marshall, Taney and Waite* (Chicago, Quadrangle Book, 1964-first published 1937), pp. 31-32, 61-62.

6. For a detailed discussion, see Eckhardt and Black, *Tides of Power*, pp. 12-38; and Louis Henkin, *Foreign Affairs and the Constitution* (New York, Foundation Press, 1972), pp. 69-71.

7. See Henkin, *Foreign Affairs*, pp. 131-132.

8. See the Constitution of the United States, Article I, Section 8.

9. Constitution of the United States, Article II.

10. In his *Foreign Affairs and the Constitution*, Professor Henkin commented that the president had secured more power "by accretion, some will say by usurpation, never effectively recaptured." See Henkin, *Foreign Affairs*, p. 38.

11. Ibid., p. 177.

12. 481 F. Supp. 949 (DDC 1979), rev'd 617 F. 2d 697 (DC Cir. 1979), vacated and remanded with directions to dismiss 444 US 996, 100 S. Ct. 533, 62 L. Ed. 2d 428.

13. See the Constitution of the United States, Article II, Section 2.

14. Under this statute, the president's power of commander in chief is limited to some extent. It requires the president to: (1) consult with Congress before taking a military action and after the introduction of armed forces; and (2) report to Congress the necessity of using force, the legal basis for taking the action, and the estimated scope and duration of the hostilities or involvement. It also gives Congress the power to stop military action by joint resolutions or bills. See USC Title 5, Section 1541-48.

15. For recent examples, see Banco Nacional de Cuba v. Sabbatino, 376 US 398, 84 S. Ct. 923, 11 L. Ed. 2nd 804 (1963); First Nat'l City Bank v. Banco Nacional de Cuba, 406 US 759, 92 S. Ct. 1808, 32 L. Ed. 2nd 466 (1972); Alfred Dunhill of London Inc. v. Republic of Cuba, 425 US 682, 96 S. Ct. 1854, 48 L. Ed. 2nd 301 (1976); Sokoloff v. National City Bank, 239 NY 158 (1924); Bank of China v. Wells Fargo Bank and United Trust Co., 104 F. Supp. 59 (ND Cal. 1952), aff'd 209 F. 2nd 467 (9th Cir. 1953); Goldwater v. Carter, 444 US 996 (1979).

16. *Inside Congress*, Congressional Quarterly, 2nd ed. (Washington, DC, Congressional Quarterly, 1979), p. 96.

17. The Constitution of the United States, Article I, Section 4, requires the Congress to assemble at least once a year. Section 2 of the Twentieth Amendment provides that the opening meeting of the Congress "shall begin at noon on the 3rd day of January."

18. Albert B. Saye, John F. Allums, and Merritt Pound, *Principles of American Government*, 8th ed. (Englewood Cliffs, Prentice-Hall, 1978), p. 293.

19. Article I, Section 3, of the Constitution provides, "The vice president of the United States shall be the president of the Senate but shall have no vote, unless they be equally divided."

20. The vice-president is not entitled to cast a vote, except when it is necessary to break a tie.

21. Saye et al., *Principles of American Government*, p. 296.

22. *Inside Congress*, Congressional Quarterly, 2nd ed. (Washington, DC, Congressional Quarterly, 1979), p. 13.

23. Saye et al., *Principles of American Government*, p. 295.

24. Ibid.

25. Max J. Skidmore and Marshall Carter Wanke, *American Government: A Brief Introduction*, 2nd ed. (New York, St. Martin's Press, 1977) p. 100.

26. The 1977 revision of the Senate committee system generally limits each senator to membership on two major committees and one minor committee and three subcommittees and two subcommittees of the minor committee.

27. Ted Siff and Allan Weil, *Ruling Congress* (Washington, DC, Congressman Publisher 1975) p. 119.

28. Walter Kravitz, "A Short History of the Development of the House Committee on Rules," Library of Congress, Legislative Reference Service, February 17, 1969.

29. David C. Saffell, *The Politics of American National Government*, 3rd ed. (Boston, Little, Brown, 1978), p. 267.

30. As a tradition, senators rather than the president select the federal judges in their state serving at district court.

31. For a detailed discussion concerning the identification and determination of the norms, the way that the norms become unwritten rules of Congress, and the possible consequences of violating the norms, see Saffell, *Politics of American National Government*, Chapter 7.

32. Theodore J. Lowi and Randall B. Ripley, *Legislative Politics USA*, 3rd ed. p. 162.

33. See the Constitution of the United States, Article II, Section 3.

34. The constitutions of the departments and agencies are described in detail in *The United States Government Manual 1981-82* (Washington, DC, 1982.).

35. Edward S. Greenberg, *The American Political System* (Cambridge, Winthrop Publishers, 1977), pp. 342-343.

36. See "Ford and Carter Tell of Difficult Communication in Government," *New York Times*, February 11, 1982, p. A14. President Carter attributed this to the consequence of forming interest groups. He said that "quite often, public officials only hear the voices of organized groups . . . and those groups speak much more narrowly and stridently than the people they represent, the doctors or the lawyers or the peanut farmers."

37. Ibid.

38. See Greenberg, *American Political System*, Chapter 11,; Saffell, *Politics of American National Government*, Chapter 9; and Grant McConnell, *The Modern Presidency* (New York, St. Martin's Press, 1976), Chapter 4.

39. The establishment of divisions and the functions of these divisions were set out in Executive Order 8248 of September 8, 1939.

40. Greenberg, *American Political System*, p. 352; and Saffell, *Politics of American National Government*, p. 310.

41. See Civil Service laws, USC Title 5, Section 3301, and Executive Order No. 10577, as amended 41831.

42. Saye et al., *Principles of American Government*, p. 277.

43. Thomas E. Cronin, "Everyone Believes in Democracy Until He Gets to the White House: An Examination of White House-Departmental Relations," in *Perspectives on the Presidency*, edited by Aaron Wildavsky (Boston, Little, Brown, 1975), p. 363.

44. For more detailed discussion, see Richard F. Fenno, Jr., "The President's Cabinet," in Wildavsky (ed.), *Perspectives on the Presidency*.

45. Ernest Gellhorn and Barry B. Boyer, *Administrative Law and Process*, 2nd ed. (St Paul, West Publishing Co., 1981), p. 13.

46. There are currently 2.8 million federal employees, of which 3,000 are appointed and may be removed by the president. The rest of the people within the category of competitive service cannot be fired without cause by the president

under Civil Service laws. This information was secured through a telephone interview with Mr. Richard Hurt, public service specialist, Office of Personel Management of the US government.

47. Ever since the Supreme Court's decision in Marbury v. Madison, 5 US (1 Cranch) 137 (1803), the court has asserted the power to review the constitutionality of administrative decisions.

48. The lobbying techniques and their effect on decision making will be discussed in the following sections.

49. Greenberg, *American Political System*, p. 346.

50. Richard Barnet concluded that "between 1940 and 1967 . . . all the first and second level posts . . . were held by fewer than four hundred individuals who rotate through a variety of key posts. The temporary civilian managers who come to Washington to run America's wars . . . were so like one another . . . that, apart from a few Washington lawyers, Texans, and Mavericks, it was possible to locate the offices of all of them within fifteen blocks in New York, Boston, and Detroit." See Richard Barnet, *The Roots of War* (Baltimore, Penguin Books, 1972), pp. 48-49.

51. USC Title 5, Section 551-701 et. seq.

52. Administrative Procedure Act, Sections 556 and 557.

53. For example, in March 1984, the Commerce Department requested comments from semiconductor and computer manufacturers on its proposed regulations that would prevent the sale or resale of high-tech products to countries other than those in the North Atlantic Treaty Organization, Japan, Australia, or New Zealand. "US Sets Trade Curb for Digital," *New York Times*, March 19, 1984, p. D5.

54. Administrative Procedure Act, Section 706.

55. See Gellhorn and Boyer, *Administrative Law*, p. 269.

56. Unlike dominant political parties in some other countries, parties in the United States are more concerned about winning elections than adopting policies. They treat the adoption of policy as an instrument to win elections rather than a separate goal of the parties.

57. According to the revised system of the Democratic party, each state committee consists of one man, one woman, the state chairperson of the party, and the highest-ranking officer of the opposite sex of each state's Democratic party. The Republican party's national committee is composed of a man, a woman, and a Republican governor or the majority leader of the party from each state.

58. Herbert E. Alexander, *Financing the 1972 Election* (Lexington, DC Heath, 1976).

59. Flora Lewis, "TV, Money and Votes," *New York Times*, November 5, 1982, p. A27.

60. Andrew M. Scott and Earle Wallace, *Politics, USA – Cases on the American Democratic Process*, 3rd. ed. (1969), p. 241.

61. Adam Clymer, "Campaign Funds Called a Key to Outcome of House Race," *New York Times*, November 5, 1982, p. A1.

62. See Scott and Wallace, *Politics, USA*, p. 214.

63. William J. Ronan, "The Power to Govern," in *The Power to Govern, Assessing Reform in the United States*, edited by Richard M. Pious (New York, Academy of Political Science, 1981), p. 253.

64. In mid-1983, Democratic Representative Phil Gramm of Texas resigned from Congress and announced that he would run for reelection as a Republican. Gramm is not the only case. Over the years, a number of congresspersons have switched parties, but not all of them chose resignation as a precondition. See *New York Times*, January 6, 1983, p. A25.

65. 60 Congress, 2nd Sess., Ch. 321, 35 Stat. 1092 (1909).

66. 69th Congress, 2nd Sess., Ch. 368, 43 Stat. 1070 (1925).

67. Public Law 92-178, 85 Stat. 563 (1971).

68. Public Law 93-443, 88 Stat. 1263 (1974).

69. Public Law 94-283, 90 Stat. 475 (1974).

70. Margaret Peterson, "Leaders of the PAC," *Public Citizen* (Fall, 1982), p. 21.

71. Mark J. Green, *The Other Government* (New York, Norton, 1978), p. 170.

72. Karl Schriftgiesser, *The Lobbyists* (Boston, Little, Brown, 1951), p. 4.

73. 79th Congress, 2nd Sess., 69 Stat. 839 (1946).

74. Skidmore, *American Government*, p. 152.

75. Ibid.

76. See Green, *The Other Government.*

77. Ibid.

78. Schriftgiesser, *The Lobbyists*, p. 50.

79. Richard Austin Smith, "The Company's Man in Washington," in Scott and Wallace (eds.), *Politics, USA*, p. 120.

80. A resident automobile executive once said, "You have to take your case to the administration first. We are interested in the Treasury for many reasons – all the way from international finance and export restrictions to corporate taxes. The taxes may start in the exercise section at the Treasury, which is quite a way from the Secretary's Office. . . . You have to get into these operations to be effective . . . . We . . . want to shape things before they emerge." see Smith, "The Company's Man," pp. 121-122.

81. Green, *The Other Government*.

82. Greenberg, *American Political System*, p. 347.

83. Mark J. Green, James M. Fallows, and David R. Zwick, *Who Runs Congress?* (New York, Bantam Books 1972), p. 8.

84. *New York Times*, January 10, 1983, p. A16.

85. Buckley v. Valeo is a case in point. See 424 US 1, and 96 S. Ct. 612 (1976).

86. 79th Congress, 2nd Sess., 69 Stat. 839 (1946).

87. This direct communication criterion was decided in US v. Harriss by the Supreme Court in 1954.

88. The Senate Government Operations Committee stated in 1976 that only 20 to 40 percent of lobbyists who should register do register and only 1 percent of money spent on lobbying in Washington is ever reported. Also see Saffell, *Politics of American National Government*, p. 109; and Skidmore, *American Government*, p. 155.

89. Peterson, "Leaders of the PAC," *Public Citizen* (Fall, 1982), p. 21.

90. Ibid.

91. For a detailed discussion about how interest groups evade the provisions of the 1974 amendments, see Rodney N. Smith, "Federal Election Law, Part II: What You Can Get Away With!" *Campaign and Elections* (1982), p. 10.

92. Peterson, "Leaders of the PAC," *Public Citizen* (Fall, 1982), p. 21.

93. Ibid.

94. Ibid. This statement reflects the theory of pluralism: Pluralism accepts that organized groups or interest groups have become politicized on a continuing or intermittent basis. They make their claims through or upon the institutions of government. On the other hand, both the forms and functions of government are a reflection of the activities and claims of such groups. However, pluralism further asserts that interests that are widely held in society may be reflected in government without their being organized in groups. In other words, although interest groups try to influence governmental decision making, governmental decisions may reflect interests of more than one group, for groups balance one another. For a detailed discussion, see David B. Truman, *The Governmental Process*, 2nd ed. (New York, Alfred A. Knopf, 1971).

95. The US economy is an important and interdependent part of the world economy. The economic and financial developments in the United States naturally have a significant effect on the world economy; in turn, they are affected by the latter as well. The US monetary and financial activities are likewise an important part of the world monetary and financial system. The Federal Reserve banks actively carry out international transactions and participate in international monetary and financial institutions. This section, however, does not examine the Federal Reserve System's activities in the international domain, which are beyond the scope of this chapter.

96. See Federal Reserve Act, Ch. 6, 38 Stat. 251.

97. See Federal Reserve Act, Section 2(3). The statute is available in Frederic Solomon, William H. Schlichting, and Jeffrey Cooper, *Banking Law, Vol. 4* (New York, Mathew Bender 1982).

98. Federal Financial Institutions Examination Council Annual Report 9 (1979).

99. Ibid.

100. Federal Reserve Act, Section 10(1), 12 USC Section 241.

101. Ibid., Section 10(2), 12 USC Section 242.

102. Ibid., Section 12 A(b), 12 USC Section 263(b).

103. Ibid., Section 12, 12 USC Section 262.

104. *Monetary, Credit, and Fiscal Policies: Report of the Subcommittee on Monetary, Credit, and Fiscal Policies of the Joint Committee on the Economic Report, Congress of the United States* (Washington, DC, Government Printing Office, 1950), p. 18.

105. Robert Solomon, "The Elephant in the Boat?: The United States and the World Economy," 60 *Foreign Affairs: America and the World* 575, (1981).

106. President Reagan complained about the banks' high interest rate at a breakfast meeting with reporters at the White House. See "Reagan Criticizes Banks Over Rate," *New York Times*, February 24, 1983.

107. Examples may be found in the export control and import administration laws, both of which will be discussed in the following chapters.

Chapter 4 Financial Issues of the Bilateral Exchange

The experience of various countries has told us that rational utilization of foreign capital and technology is an effective way to speed up economic development in one's own country.

– Ji Chongwei

Since the 1960s, the world economy has become more interdependent. Closer economic contacts, scientific and technical exchanges, and cooperation between nations have developed. The economic development of any country has become inseparable from its participation in the broad exchange of material, scientific, and cultural wealth with other countries in the world. History witnesses that almost all the developed countries have taken advantage of foreign capital in the course of their economic development.[1] For instance, in the United States, railroads in the 1800s were built with British capital, which had an enormous effect on US economic development. Many developing countries and regions where rapid economic growth has been achieved have also utilized a considerable amount of foreign capital.

China has a population of 1 billion people and an area of 9.6 million square kilometers. It is committed to building itself into a nation with modern industry, agriculture, national defense, and science and technology. This ambitious modernization plan requires tremendous amounts of capital and advanced technology. As a socialist and densely populated country, China will draw primarily upon its own funds in carrying out the economic program, while at the same time making use of foreign funds.

The United States is a country with a capital-intensive economy. It is capable of helping to meet Chinese financial needs. But to what extent, and under what conditions, will the two countries carry out financial cooperation?

CHINA'S UTILIZATION OF FOREIGN FUNDS

Evolution of Policy

In the formative years of the People's Republic of China, the Chinese leaders hewed to a policy of economic and technical cooperation exclusively with the Soviet Union and Eastern European countries. This policy continued to the early 1960s when friendly relations with the Soviet Union broke off. Having learned a lesson from this experience, a policy of strict self-reliance was adopted by the Chinese government. It drew upon its own funds and aimed to import only what was essential for the socialist construction plan. The imports were basically financed through export earnings. This strict self-reliance policy continued to the late 1970s, when the "Gang of Four" was thrown out of power.

The decade of the 1970s brought dramatic changes to China's stance toward international finance. These important changes include "the arrangement of a number of supplier credits, the establishment by the Bank of China of first, mutual deposit accounts and later, full correspondent relations with foreign banks, and the establishment of representative offices of foreign banks in China."[2]

Only since 1978 has China begun to borrow from developed countries to finance capital goods imports for development projects. It first agreed to a mutual-deposits scheme whereby the Bank of China and foreign banks would deposit funds with each other denominated in their respective national currencies. Since the foreign banks usually deposited more funds than the Bank of China did, the scheme in fact operated as a program of interbank loans. Later, China began to accept external commercial bank credit in the form of deposits with the Bank of China and supplier or buyer credits in the form of deferred payments.

A more open-minded policy was adopted at the end of 1978. In 1979 and 1980, following the conclusion of trade agreements with several developed market economy countries, China negotiated some credit arrangements.[3] Since 1979, China has accepted government loans from Japan, Belgium, and other countries, and has signed export credits agreements with more than ten countries, including Britain, France, Italy, and Canada.[4] Under an agreement with Japan, the Japanese Overseas Economic Cooperation Funds provided loans to finance six construction projects: two ports, three railways, and one power station. The amount of the loans, according to the agreement, was to be determined by the two parties in the light of the progress of the projects. The loan, effected for the year 1979-80, was 106,000 million yen (more than $400 million).[5] In addition to these agreements, the Bank of China and the China International Trust and Investment Corporation (CITIC) have reached a number of agreements with commercial banks in various countries to establish reciprocal accounts. The Bank of China alone has signed buyer credit agreements for a total of more than $12 billion with Britain, France, Italy, Canada, Sweden, Australia, West Germany, Belgium, Norway, and Argentina.[6]

The features of China's loans have changed gradually with the change of policy. Most of the loans China borrowed in 1979 and early 1980 were "general trade credits not linked to any specific projects,"[7] whereas most of the loans borrowed since 1980 have been project related.

The Bank of China is the borrower of most of the loans initially borrowed by China. For instance, in May 1979, the Bank of China signed a loan contract with 18 French banks to provide China with financing for 85 percent of the purchase price of French exports valued at $6.85 billion. These French franc-financed exports to China include automotive, chemical, and electronics equipment. The 15 percent of the purchase price not covered was to be financed by Chinese down payments.[8]

At the same time, the early foreign creditors were usually single lenders. Subsequently, China began to make use of syndicated loans. The first syndicated Eurodollar loan by foreign banks was signed in February 1980, with the arrangement of a $300 million facility by Union des Banques Arabes et Françaises.[9]

With the establishment of joint ventures and the autonomy acquired by Chinese domestic enterprises, loans for specific projects have become quite popular. For instance, in 1981, a $50.2 million syndicated loan was arranged by American Express to finance imports of Italian machinery by the Yan Shan Petrochemical General Corporation. This loan is, in fact, a cross between an export credit and a commercial loan.[10]

Making use of foreign funds has now been adopted as one of China's foreign economic policies.[11] Various forms of absorbing foreign loans have been employed by China. These include (1) export credits, including buyer's and seller's or deferred payment; (2) government loans, such as the loan offered by Ex-Im Banks, government export agencies, or governments themselves; (3) loans from international organizations, such as the International Monetary Fund (IMF), the World Bank, and the International Development Association (IDA);[12] and (4) commercial loans from private banks.

Certain principles have been adopted by the Chinese government in borrowing foreign funds. The basic principle is self-reliance with external assistance as a supplement. In his speech at Brussels, Wei Yuming, the then vice-minister of the Import-Export Commission and Foreign Investment Commission of China, stated, "We shall rely primarily upon our own accumulation funds for capital construction. The amount of foreign funds to be utilized must fall in line with our capacity to use it fully and our capability to repay."[13] The principle of equality and mutual benefit is the guideline in negotiating economic agreements. "Such agreements will only be signed if no political conditions of any kind are attached and no clauses encroaching or infringing on our rights and interests are included."[14] The economic results of investments and guarantees of repayment and equitable profits are also treated as principles in Chinese borrowing. Addressing the matter of the utilization of foreign funds, Bu Ming, the chairperson of the board of directors and president of the Bank of China, said, "The prime consideration is the economic effectiveness the loan will provide."[15]

Since the Chinese government considers economic return as the primary goal, it makes use of mainly low-interest or interest free loans from foreign governments or international monetary organizations.

China's Financial Institutions

China's financial system has undergone a major change in the last few years. Following the establishment of the Chinese government in 1949, the People's Bank of China took over all the financial organizations in the country. In the period of 1950-52, when the rampant long-standing inflation of the old government still threatened the national economy, the then Central People's Government unified finances and the management of cash. The People's Bank of China played a key role in the reform. In 1955, the bank issued the new currency RMB, whereby inflation was curbed.

For about 30 years after the establishment of the government, banks in China functioned as "cashiers" of the Ministry of Finance, for the latter was charged with appropriating funds for state-owned enterprises. It is estimated that by the end of 1978, 70 percent of the total sum of the fixed assets and working funds in state-owned enterprises had been appropriated by the Ministry of Finance.[16]

Since the system could neither allocate funds rationally nor make full use of them,[17] major organizational reforms took place in 1983. Under the present system, the People's Bank of China functions exclusively as the national central bank of the country. As the central bank, it engages mainly in the study and formulation of overall policies on national monetary affairs, strengthening the management of credit funds and maintaining the stability of currency, so as to change the overdecentralization of credit funds and stimulate the national economic development.[18] The bank is also charged with issuing currency, setting interest rates, devising a nationwide credit plan, setting accounts, supervising finance and foreign exchange, and other functions of central banks. In addition, it operates in the international monetary system on behalf of the Chinese government.

Other functions of the People's Bank of China include supervision and coordination. It coordinates and examines the operations of all monetary organizations, such as the Industrial and Commercial Bank of China, the Agricultural Bank of China, the Bank of China, and the People's Insurance Company of China, chiefly by economic means.[19] The specialized banks must carry out the decisions made by the People's Bank of China and its council, a policy-making organization subordinate to the bank.[20]

Among the specialized banks, the Industrial and Commercial Bank of China is a newly established one.[21] Its task is to take over the credit and deposit functions performed by the People's Bank. In accordance with monetary policies and credit plans approved by the latter, the former administers deposits for industrial and commercial enterprises and loans for their circulating funds and technical transformation, and handles the settlement of accounts and urban residents' personal savings deposits.[22]

The Bank of China is charged with handling foreign exchange through supervision over the State Administration for Foreign Exchange Control.[23] Its functions also include administering savings deposits, loans in relation to imports and exports, and so on.[24] In addition, it may be authorized or entrusted to negotiate credit matters on behalf of China.[25]

The Bank of China grew very fast. It had 190 domestic branch offices by the end of 1983. Its overseas offices number about 275, located in Hong Kong, Singapore, London, Luxembourg, Tokyo, and other international financial centers.[26]

The Bank of China plays an important part in China's economic system. In addition to the numerous credit contracts of several billion dollars it has signed up on behalf of China, it is the major supplier of foreign exchange for domestic enterprises. By the end of 1982, it had lent to domestic enterprises a foreign exchange of about $11.5 billion, which is more than three times the foreign investments in joint ventures, oil exploration and exploitation, and compensation trade.[27] It also provides export credits for Chinese enterprises. The first export credit was made in early 1982, when a Norwegian shipping concern, Edesvik, ordered four supply ships from China at a total cost of $30 million.[28] The transaction was financed jointly by China and Norway. About 80 percent of the equipment for the ships was imported from Norway. The Norwegian Export Finance Authorities, a government agency, provided export credits for the equipment. The Bank of China provided export credits for the remaining 20 percent, or about $6 million of the $30 million contract at annual interest rates between 8.5 and 8.75 percent.[29] Stanley Yuan, an official of China's Ministry of Machine Building, said that foreign buyers might be able to borrow up to 70 percent of a ship's value from the Bank of China at annual interest rates of less than 9 percent.[30]

Since 1981, the Bank of China has been actively participating in syndicated loans. In August 1981, it comanaged two syndicated loans to a Spanish highway corporation for $45 million.[31] Syndicated loans managed and comanaged by the bank in September 1982 totaled $140 million to two Brazilian corporations.[32] In the same month, it also participated in a $93 million syndication to a Venezuelan real estate corporation.[33] Two other bigger syndications participated in by the Bank of China were a $160 million syndication to help Venezuelan small businesspersons get subsidized credit and a $175 million syndication to Denmark's privately funded Ex-Im Bank.[34] In January 1983, the Bank of China participated in a $10 million syndicated loan for a joint project in China.[35] The syndicated credit, which was arranged by the London-based Nordic Bank, was to be used for financing the first stage of a hotel project in Shaanxi province. The Bank of China would provide $2.5 million of that loan and the remainder would be funded by Nordic Bank and several European banks.[36]

With development of its international financial activities, the Bank of China has begun arranging syndicated loans. In June 1983, the bank for the first time took the lead in making the arrangement for a $98.7 million syndicated loan to finance the construction of a hotel and office complex in Canton, China.[37] It approached the Chartered Bank, the Royal Bank of Canada, the Bank of Tokyo, the First National Bank of Chicago, and the Industrial Bank of Japan to join it.[38]

In order to facilitate the absorption of foreign funds and help foreign investors cooperate with interested regions, departments, or enterprises in China for short- and/or long-term joint ventures or other kinds of ventures as well as consultant services, the State Council set up the CITIC in 1980. The CITIC handles primarily long-term investments in China by overseas Chinese investors from Hong Kong and Macao, as well as those from other parts of the world. It also helps organize joint ventures with Chinese and foreign investments as well as other types of enterprises.

The role of the CITIC has been more and more felt. It has established relationships with a number of foreign banks doing international business. A subsidiary has been incorporated in Hong Kong, and a representative office has been set up in Paris. The most innovative and remarkable success it has achieved was its issuing of 10 million worth of yen bonds in 1981 in Tokyo. The Japanese yen-denominated debenture was underwritten by the Nomura Securities Company, the Daiwa Securities Company, and the Bank of Tokyo, with an annual interest of between 9.1 and 9.2 percent.[39]

Another function of the CITIC is investment in domestic industries. By the end of 1981, it had invested in a molybdenum mine in Hubei province and a phosphate mine in Yunan province with commercial credits.[40] Most recently, the CITIC signed up an economic cooperation agreement with the Fujian provincial government to import advanced technology and equipment and to renovate enterprises. Both parties agreed that they would try to organize joint ventures or coproduction concerns with foreign investors.[41]

In order to complete the transformation of financial institutions, the People's Construction Bank, which was created in 1954, was reestablished in 1979 to channel budget grants and loans to investment projects.[42]

The People's Construction Bank is responsible for conducting medium-and long-term loans for enterprises and allocating investments for the state. Under the leadership of the State Council and the Ministry of Finance, the bank, which has 2,500 branches throughout the country, operates, in fact, as an independent economic unit rather than an organ for allocating funds. Through its supervision and management over capital construction, it sees to it that the best possible economic results will be obtained from its loans. Explaining the bank's guidelines of operation, Wu Boshan, president of the bank, said, "The new method [the switch from the system of government allocations to bank loans] will be applied to investments in projects undertaken by enterprises practicing independent business accounting and having the ability to repay the loans, such as industry, commercial loans, and transport, land reclamation, animal husbandry, aquatic products, commerce, tourism, and cultural undertakings."[43] Under the bank's procedure, enterprises engaging in capital construction sign up contracts with the bank for loans. Annual interests are charged by the bank, and the loans are repaid according to the contracts. "The bank will," Mr. Wu further stated, "neither allocate funds nor extend loans for projects which do not conform to the state construction policy or which do not have the necessary condition for construction."[44]

To supplement the function of the Construction Bank, another specialized bank, the China Investment Bank, was established on December 23, 1981. The China Investment Bank has a capital of RMB 4 billion yuan ($2.3 billion), which is being used to make medium and small ($3 to $5 million) loans to capital construction projects, conduct feasibility studies using World Bank investment criteria, and invest in joint equity ventures with Chinese and foreign companies.[45] The charter of the bank stipulates that its business will include seeking long- and medium-term loans from international monetary institutions and other resources.[46]

Currently, the bank operates as an intermediate monetary institution in handling loans from the World Bank for small- and medium-sized projects.[47] The first loan agreement between the China Investment Bank and the World Bank was signed in December 1982.[48] According to the contract, the latter agreed to provide the former with $70 million. The money would in turn be lent to Chinese enterprises for renovation and transformation.[49]

Other banks, such as the Agricultural Bank, which chiefly handles credit for the agricultural departments and rural areas, may also be involved in foreign investments.[50]

China's Borrowing Practice

The lines of credit available to China are clearly substantial, as is the country's potential for external borrowing. The Chinese government, however, is very cautious and selective in using foreign loans. In December 1983, China announced that it owed a total of $3 billion of foreign debts at the end of September 1983.[51] Those loans were mainly from the IMF, the World Bank, and Japan, at highly favorable rates. One of the reasons for China's slowness in borrowing is that the level of interest rates in the international financial market is too high. Although China has usually enjoyed favorable terms from foreign sources, the London Inter-Bank Offered Rate interest rates have been at a level that seems exorbitant. "Interest rates on commercial loans are usually higher than we can afford," said Chen Muhua, the minister of Foreign Trade and Economic Relations. "For instance, many of our enterprises cannot afford an interest rate of 17 or 18 percent."[52]

Another factor affecting China's borrowing seems to be the specific purpose of the loans. Most of the loans are earmarked for limited, specific purposes. Since China's national economy had been undergoing a readjustment in the last few years, not much equipment has been imported. As a result, many of the credits remain unused.

In its practice, it appears that China has been more inclined to ask for soft loans from international organizations and government export agencies. The Chinese government has indicated that "whenever possible, loans with the most favorable terms (such as bilateral, long-term, low-interest loans and IDA-type credits) will be used first, the officially guaranteed medium- and long-term loans such as Ex-Im Bank credits, and then export credits."[53]

China tried successfully to secure cut-rate export credits subsidized by foreign governments. In commercial credit transactions, China sometimes demands that foreign partners cover any interest cost above the preferential rates governments give. For instance, in the $50.2 million loan to Yan Shan, the Chinese party agreed to pay 7.5 percent annual interest, which was the internationally agreed-upon rate for export credits when Yan Shan contracted to buy the machinery from Italy in 1980.[54] Italy's export credit agency was to pay participating banks the difference between the said interest rate China would pay and the market rate at that time.[55]

Despite the fact that China has made great efforts to provide a legal environment for investment in the country, some specific laws related to subjects such as bankruptcy, mortgage, and security interest do not yet exist. As a result, "the security options available to foreign lenders have generally been limited to guarantees, assignments of proceeds, and ad hoc arrangements, all of which are generally provided for in the loan documentation."[56] Although foreign loans are secured by private contracts, it seems that no problem has occurred in practice.

The generally adopted method of providing security is guarantee. In an export credit arrangement, both the foreign export agency and a Chinese agency may guarantee the transaction. The Bank of China has been very active as a guarantor in export credits and compensation trade transactions.[57] In a few other cases, loans were guaranteed by other agencies in China. For example, both the $8 million loan by the First National Bank of Chicago to Fujian[58] and the $26 million loan by First National Boston Ltd. to the China Ocean Shipping Company in 1980 were guaranteed by the Ministry of Communications.[59] In the above-mentioned Yan Shan transaction, the loan was guaranteed by the Beijing Economic Development Corporation.[60]

Another feature of China's borrowing practice is its reluctance to pay management and commitment fees. This practice, however, is not consistent. In the export credit arrangement with France in 1979, the Bank of China agreed, for the first time, to pay the management and commitment fees of the proceeds.[61]

THE US FINANCIAL FACILITIES

The US finance suppliers are the Ex-Im Bank of the United States and commercial banks. Operating under different rules and regulations, they form an interface of private commercial efforts and government policy, competing with financial institutions from other countries at the international level. In addition to the competition with foreign financial facilities, US financial institutions have to compete with Chinese domestic entities when their capital comes into the Chinese market.

The Ex-Im Bank

The Ex-Im Bank of the United States was established in 1934.[62] In 1945, Congress passed the Export-Import Bank Act of 1945,[63] whereby the bank received its statutory status. Established as an independent agency of the US government,[64] the purpose of the bank is "to aid in financing and to facilitate exports and imports and the exchange of commodities between the United States . . . and any foreign country or the agencies or nationals thereof."[65]

Managed by a five-member board of directors appointed by the president,[66] the bank provides for two kinds of assistance, namely, buyer credits or project financing and supplier credits. The buyer credit is direct lending. Pursuant to this program, the Ex-Im Bank participates in private contracts financing the export of US products. Although the bank may provide a direct loan from 30 to 45 percent of the contract value,[67] occasionally its loan participation may be increased to 75 percent of the contract price.[68] At the same time, foreign buyers are required to finance at least 15 percent of the contract price according to the bank's policy. The amount of direct loans the bank may offer depends mainly on foreign competition, the availability of private capital, and the bank's exposure in a certain country.

Applications for the bank's preliminary commitment may be made by foreign buyers, US exporters, or US commercial banks. The final application for a direct lending must be made by a foreign buyer, however.

The guiding principles of the bank were described by John L. Moore, Jr., president and chairperson of the Ex-Im Bank of the United States, as (1) to meet the terms of foreign competitors, and (2) to correct imperfections in the financial market.[69] To carry out this policy, the bank "must not compete with the private sector,"[70] when the latter is capable of financing a project. Since the bank is a government agency, the conformity of its activities with overall US foreign and economic policy is regarded as one of its basic operating principles.[71] Needless to say, like Ex-Im Bank credits from other countries, credits of the Ex-Im Bank of the United States are available only for the purchase of US products.

Another type of the Ex-Im Bank's program of supplier credit is indirect lending. The major functions of the bank in this program are those of insurers and guarantors. It may act as an coinsurer or reinsurer of policies of insurance issued by the Foreign Credit Insurance Association.[72] In addition, it may also act as a guarantor of loans provided by private banks to finance US exports. Other programs, such as discount loan and cooperative financing, are also carried out by the bank.

The availability of the US Ex-Im Bank facilities to China was brought into issue right after the establishment of diplomatic relations between the two countries.[73] The issue, however, became a procedural matter when then Vice-President Walter Mondale visited China in August 1979 and promised that $2 billion in Ex-Im Bank credits would be made available to China over five years.

The major procedural issue is the Trade Act of 1974. Under Section 402(b) of the act, nonmarket or Communist countries may not be eligible to participate in any Ex-Im Bank programs until and unless the president of the United States has submitted to Congress a report indicating that said country does not deny its citizens the right of emigration.[74] The president, however, may waive this prohibition, by executive order, if it is determined that such a waiver will substantially promote the objectives of the statute.[75]

Assured by the Chinese leaders' commitment that freedom of emigration would be enjoyed by Chinese nationals, President Carter waived the restrictions set out in the Trade Act of 1974.[76] Thus, the Ex-Im Bank has been allowed to issue China credits and loan guarantees ever since.[77]

The first US Ex-Im Bank preliminary approval for granting credits to China was made in late 1980, when a contract for purchasing US equipment was concluded.[78] Under the contract, a West German-built Baoshan steel project (in Shanghai) would purchase $80.5 million of US equipment, 75 percent of which would be financed by the Ex-Im Bank at an annual interest rate of 8.75 percent.[79]

In June 1983, the US Ex-Im Bank approved its first two loan guarantees under the 1982 Export Trading Company Act. The loan guarantees are to help domestic companies sell logs and machinery valued at more than $31 million to China.[80]

Commerical Banks

Unlike the Ex-Im Bank, commercial banks' activities are regulated by the National Bank Act.[81] At the same time, they are affected by Chinese domestic laws.

The main restriction of US statutes affecting commercial lending is the lending limit set out by the National Bank Act. The statute provides: "The total obligation to any national banking association of any person, copartnership, association, or corporation shall at no time exceed 10 percentum of the amount of the capital stock of such association actually paid in and unimpaired and 10 percentum of its unimpaired surplus funds."[82] Obligations such as overdrafts, standby letters of credit, leases on personal property, and loans are all subject to this lending limit. The federal regulations further define the term "unimpaired surplus" as: (1) 50 percent of reserve for possible loan losses; (2) subordinated notes and debentures; (3) surplus; (4) undivided profits; and (5) reserve for contingencies and other capital reserves.[83]

The statute, however, has made a few exceptions to this lending limit, some of which are significant. One of these is that a standby letter of credit may not be subject to the limit under the following circumstances: (1) Prior to its issuance, the customer pays the bank, or the issuing bank sets aside, sufficient funds to cover the bank's maximum obligation; and (2) the comptroller of the currency finds that a particular standby letter of credit will not expose the bank to the similar risk of loss as would a loan to the account party.[84] An affirmative determination of the comptroller may be made if the issuing bank participates in an OPIC program. For example, a commercial bank may issue a standby letter of credit in the form of an insurance policy, when it works in cooperation with the OPIC to protect other banks or investors from political or commercial risks of overseas projects.[85]

The impact of this statute on US commercial bank investments in China is that when the banks decide to invest, they have to be certain of the legal and economic status of the borrower. It seems that the crux of the issue is how to distinguish a government agency from an independent entity. Before the completion of economic reforms, and the status of different Chinese entities becomes more distinguishable, the issue may constitute a serious problem. It will be difficult to separate the two. The potential difficulty is that today quite a few enterprises have formed themselves into joint concerns. Whether these companies should be treated as separate entities or one company under the National Bank Act seems a question pending resolution. Besides, owing to the Chinese tax laws, which will be discussed later, US commercial banks may tend to lend funds to China's state banks rather than directly to Chinese enterprises. If that is the case, the 10 percent ceiling may be easily satisfied. At the same time, the National Bank Act may treat China's state banks as government instrumentalities or agencies. Since loans to foreign governments and their agencies and instrumentalities must be combined under the statute with regard to lending limit,[86] commercial banks may not be able to invest through Chinese state banks as much as they wish.[87]

Exceptions may be made to the combination of loans requirement if the borrower meets either the "means" or "purpose" test.[88] Under the means test, a borrower is required to show that it has resources or revenue of its own sufficient over time to service the loan obligation.[89] The purpose test may be satisfied if a borrower can show by written representation that the loan proceeds will be used in the conduct of the business.[90] These two tests will be applied when a loan is made. Only documentation is required in order to satisfy the tests. A lending bank should, under law, obtain the following documents: (1) a statement and supporting documentation describing the legal status and the degree of financial and operational autonomy of the borrowing entity; (2) financial statements for the borrowing entity for a minimum of three years prior to making the loan or for each year less than three that the borrowing entity has been in existence; (3) financial statements for each year the loan is outstanding; (4) the bank's assessment of the borrower's means of servicing the loan, including specific reasons justifying that assessment; and (5) a loan agreement or other written statement from the borrower that clearly describes the purpose of the loan.[91]

Commercial banks' activities are, as mentioned above, affected by China's laws as well. The most important statutes concerning foreign bank activities are the Foreign Enterprise Income Tax Law and the Detailed Rules and Regulations Implementating the Foreign Enterprise Income Tax Law (referred to in this chapter as "the Regulations").[92]

Under the Foreign Enterprise Income Tax Law, foreign banks are subject to a withholding tax equal to 20 percent on their interest derived from loans to Chinese enterprises.[93] Chinese borrowers are required by the statute to act as withholding agents, unless the following exceptions can be applied: (1) loans made to the Chinese government or China's state banks by international finance organizations; (2) loans given at a preferential interest rate by foreign banks to China's state banks; and (3) interest on deposits of foreign banks in China's state banks at a rate of interest lower than that prevailing in the international financial market.[94]

State banks are further defined by the Regulations to include the People's Bank of China, the Bank of China, the Agricultural Bank, the Construction Bank, the Investment Bank, and the CITIC.[95] International finance organizations include the IMF, the World Bank, the IDA, the International Fund for Agricultural Development, and other finance organizations of the United Nations.[96] As far as the second exception, the preferential interest rate, is concerned, the Regulations provide that it should be "at least 10 percent less than the general prevailing interest rate in the international financial market" in order to apply the exception.[97]

Foreign bankers have made efforts to avoid the withholding tax. They try to loan to China's state banks, and then the latter relend to the real Chinese borrowers.[98] Some have tried to recharacterize the loans as a lease or installment sale, with interest built into the lease price or installment.[99] Whatever tax shelter may be introduced, the Chinese withholding tax makes commercial lending to China difficult.

Competitiveness

The focus of financial competition in the newly established Chinese market is interest rate. A delegation from the Guangxi Zhuang autonomous region, which was seeking $4 billion in commercial loans in Hong Kong, indicated that the interest rates offered by the commercial banks, between 10 and 15 percent, were "too high."[100] "What we are looking for are interest rates between 7 and 9 percent," said a member of the delegation.[101]

The bulk of the loans borrowed by China is either Ex-Im Bank credits or government-guaranteed bank loans provided at an interest-subsidized rate substantially below market rates. It was estimated that more than half of the $30 billion in credits China had accepted by mid-1982 were in the form of foreign export credits.[102] The major supplier of government export credits is Japan, whereas Britain, Australia, Italy, France, Sweden, Canada, and the United States have all made efforts to finance projects in China. For example, the Japanese Ex-Im Bank offered a loan of about $1,500 million for energy resources in 1981.[103] Reports show that Japan extended $203 million in credit to China in 1979 and $228 million in 1980.[104] At the beginning of 1982, the Japanese government agreed to extend 60 billion yen ($244 million) to China for financing industrial projects and commodity purchases in Japan.[105]

The basic feature of the credits accepted by China is a low-interest or interestfree loan with long duration. The Japanese Overseas Economic Cooperation Funds' loan to China, which amounted to $400 million, set the interest rate at 3 percent, with repayment beginning from the eleventh year and being paid off in the thirtieth year.[106] The Japanese Ex-Im Bank's $1,500 million loan for constructing coal mines and oilfields has an interest rate of 6.25 percent. The credit will be repaid in installments in 15 years after each project has been put into operation.[107] Belgium's $31.5 million loan has the most favorable terms. It is interest free with a duration of 30 years.[108] Japan's loan extended in early 1982 is a preferential export credit. It carries an interest rate of 3 percent per year with a grace period of 10 years.[109]

One of the competitive techniques employed by foreign investors in China's finance market is the agency-bank arrangement. Under this arrangement, government agencies, such as the Ex-Im Bank, may make agreements with commercial banks. The government agency may agree to make up any interest differential between the fixed rates and the prevailing market rates, plus an agreed-upon margin. If the market rate goes above the agreed-upon rate, the agency will pay the difference to the commercial bank. Otherwise, the bank is required to refund the agency the margin above the agreed-upon interest rate. In 1973, Japan made an agency-bank arrangement sale of the Technip-Speichem petrochemical complex to China.[110]

In addition to the competition from other countries, US banks have to compete with Chinese financial institutions. China is now is a good position to finance some projects with its own foreign exchange reserves. By the end of September 1983, it had $14.07 billion in reserves.[111] As a result, Chinese banks as well as the CITIC are able to offer low-interest-rate loans to domestic enterprises. In 1983, the Bank of China alone provided 130 million yuan in local currency loans and $50 million in foreign exchange loans for more than 80 joint ventures of Chinese and foreign investment in China.[112]

Owing to the low interest rate of Chinese banks, Chinese concerns and joint ventures may be induced to switch their debt obligations from foreign to Chinese banks. In this regard, the Jinling Hotel case sheds some light. The 814-room luxury hotel has been jointly developed by China International Travel Service's Nanjing branch and Shing Kwan Pte Ltd. of Singapore, owned by S.P. Tao, chairperson of Singapore Lan Ltd. In 1980, the Nanjing branch obtained a $35.2 million 12-year loan from Wardley Ltd., a unit of the Hong Kong & Shanghai Banking Corporation. Before the completion of the project, which was scheduled for 1983, the China International Travel Service, Janjing branch, decided to prepay the loan in late 1982.[113] The reason for this prepayment was not given by the borrower. It was said, however, that the hotel project had been refinanced by the Bank of China with lower interest rates and a longer duration.[114]

The US financial facilities do not appear as competitive as those of other countries, despite the efforts made by the Ex-Im Bank of the United States and US commercial banks.

Among the US institutions, the Ex-Im Bank is in a better position to meet international competition. In addition to its direct loan and guarantee program, the bank may also make discount loans to banks that finance medium-term export sales on a fixed rate of interest. The discount loans provide subsidized interest rates. Under this program, if an eligible bank decides to borrow from the Ex-Im Bank (or sell the eligible export obligation to it), the bank will charge an interest rate of 1 percent below the commercial bank's yield on the export loan. This program is, however, subject to strict approval of the Ex-Im Bank. Unless the applicant bank certifies that it is not prepared to finance the export transaction, if the said subsidized interest rate can be obtained, the Ex-Im Bank will not agree to make the commitment.

The major difficulty with the US Ex-Im Bank seems to be its shortage of funds. Unlike its European and Japanese counterparts, the bank is funded solely through debt service payments on outstanding loans and borrowings from the Federal Financing Bank at prevailing market rates. In order to sustain its operation, the bank can neither offer export credits at very low interest rates nor extend large discount loans to domestic banks. As a result, the interest rates it offers are more often than not higher than those of other Ex-Im Banks in Japan or Europe. Since the bottom line of the competition is preferential and/or subsidized interest rates, the US Ex-Im Bank's competitiveness depends, to a large extent, on the availability of funds, which seems insufficient to the bank.[115] Also, the organization of the US Ex-Im Bank itself presents difficulties. It is organized to deal with the financial institutions of a developed country and does not fit into the current international financial situations. It seems that the bank needs to be reorganized to be able to deal with developing countries that have different financial institutions.

In addition to the Ex-Im Bank facilities, commercial banks may also secure assistance from other institutions, such as the Foreign Credit Insurance Association, the Private Export Funding Corporation,[116] and the OPIC. Owing to the limited subsidy program of government agencies and private organizations, US commercial banks' competitiveness depends largely on the situation in the international financial market and the competition from Europe and Japan.

The final legal issue that may hinder US banks in lending is that they are not allowed under the banking regulations to invest more than 10 percent of their capital in nonbanking business. As competition sharpens, more and more European and Japanese banks are trying to make direct investments in Chinese projects. This ceiling may constitute potential difficulty for US banks in their efforts to make direct investments in China.

IMPLICATIONS OF WORLD BANK MEMBERSHIP

China is one of the founding members of the IMF and the International Bank for Reconstruction and Development. But it was unable to exercise its representative power until 1980 when it resumed its seat in the organization. In March and April of 1980, the Chinese government negotiated separately with the two organizations for the restoration of China's representation in the IMF and the World Bank. Thanks to the efforts made by both parties, agreements were reached and China was reseated in the two organizations in mid-1980.

In order to match the size of the country, the IMF executive directors, upon request by China, decided to increase China's subscription to the IMF to about $1.57 billion or $1.2 billion special drawing rights.[117] Thus, the amount of China's subscription to the IMF exceeds that of all but the United States, the United Kingdom, West Germany, Japan, France, Saudi Arabia, and Italy.[118]

Ninety percent of the Chinese quota was subscribed in Chinese currency, some of which the IMF subsequently may be able to use in currency loans to other countries. The remaining 10 percent was paid in special drawing rights.[119]

China's subscription to the World Bank was also expanded. It was increased from 7,500 to 12,000 shares, the value of each share then being about $120,000. Member countries acquiring shares are not required to provide currencies to cover the entire amount of the subscription. Nonetheless, they are required to pay a small portion in capital, while the larger part is in the form of callable capital, that is, money the World Bank could ask its members to provide to pay off its borrowing in private capital markets.[120] Ninety percent of China's subscription was made in the form of callable Chinese currency. The other 10 percent, or $144 million, was paid in capital.

The increase of China's quota in the World Bank group is of great significance and importance. Since both organizations have a weighted voting system,[121] an increase of one member country's quota represents an expansion of the influence of the country over decision making in them.

The significance of China's membership in the IMF is at least threefold. First, having restored its representation, China now has the obligation to provide the fund, upon request, information of, inter alia, official holdings at home and abroad of gold and foreign exchange; total exports and imports of merchandise; international balance of payments, including trade in goods and services and capital transactions; and national income.[122] The information required is deemed crucial, by international creditors, in deciding the soundness of financing projects in a certain country. It has proved to be helpful in enhancing China's already fair standing with commercial lenders from foreign countries.

Second, Article 8 prohibits member countries from imposing "restrictions on the making of payments and transfers for current international transactions"[123] as well as from engaging in "discriminatory currency arrangements or multiple currency practices."[124] Hence, China and the United States have been put on the same footing not to restrict the payment of international transactions. This may make businesspersons, including bankers, feel more certain that their economic interests are protected when dealing with each other. Since China's foreign exchange statute was newly adopted and many foreign businesspersons are not familiar with it, the Chinese obligation under the IMF may serve as a further guarantee of their rights.

Third, being a member of the organization, China is eligible for IMF assistance. Under the Articles of Agreement, an IMF member may purchase a certain amount of foreign currency from the fund with an equivalent amount in its own currency paid to it. A member may request a purchase if it has a need based on its balance of payments, or its reserve position, or unfavorable developments in its reserves. When the exchange transaction is concluded, the purchasing member has the obligation to repurchase its own currency paid to the fund in the transaction. In addition, the fund may accelerate the repurchase if it deems appropriate.

The assistance may be obtained under a standby or similar arrangement. Under the standby arrangement, a member is assured by the IMF that it will be able to use the fund's resources up to a prescribed amount during a certain period. The general objective of the arrangement is to help member countries solve balance-of-payment problems. Normally, the standby arrangement is for one year. "If, however, a longer period is requested by a member and considered necessary by the fund to enable the member to implement its adjustment program successfully, the standby arrangement . . . may extend up to but not beyond three years."[125]

In early March 1981, the IMF approved a $550 million loan to China under a standby arrangement. Under the arrangement, China would draw down $450 million special drawing rights (equivalent to $550 million) over the following 12 months. The loan would help China meet its international payment obligations while it carried out economic adjustments. Before March 1981, China had drawn about $550 million against its reserves.

China "places much hope in the World Bank."[126] It takes some time, however, before a World Bank loan is made to a member country. "Usually, when a country is admitted into the bank, a number of procedural steps have to be taken before that country can go to the loan window."[127] Cautioned on the procedures followed by the World Bank, a bank official said, "First, the bank sends a team of economists to the country and opens lines of communications. Then, the bank makes what it calls sectoral studies on the country's agriculture, transport system, and other possible candidates for World Bank assistance. Only when the paper work has advanced sufficiently can we seriously talk loans."[128]

The first World Bank loan to China, however, was signed shortly after China's reseating. Working with "unusual speed,"[129] a $200 million loan package was agreed upon in mid-1981. The package, half with a 9.6 percent interest rate from the World Bank and the other half in nearly interest-free funds from the bank's affiliate, the IDA, would be used to finance science and engineering training at 26 Chinese universities.[130] Shortly after, a $60 million loan was signed for an agricultural project to reduce the salinity of the North China Plain.[131]

In November 2, 1982, the World Bank approved another $200 million loan credit to assist port, education, and agriculture projects in China. Of the loan, $124 million would be used to help modernize and expand port facilities in the cities of Shanghai and Tianjin. In addition, the bank decided to provide China with $75.4 million through its affiliate institution, the IDA. These credits would be used to support programs of higher education and for research in agricultural science.[132] The World Bank's loan is for 20 years and carries an interest rate of 11.6 percent. The IDA's credits are for 50 years and have a fee for administrative costs of 1 percent per year.[133]

As far as World Bank group loans are concerned, China is particularly interested in IDA credits. Although it has the right and need to borrow, the timing is not favorable. "When we joined," said Ge Fucun, director of the Ministry of Finance's External Finance

Department, "IDA 6 [Funds of IDA contributed by its members are replenished at three-year intervals. IDA 6 refers to the period between 1981 and 1983] already had been distributed, and we only got a few hundred million. If we had joined earlier, we would have gotten a lot more."[134] As a result, only a small portion of the loans China has borrowed from the World Bank group is from the IDA.

Although the direct benefits conferred upon China by the World Bank loans have already been felt, a "significant share of the money appears destined for the US."[135] This view was shared by Caio Kock-Weser, chief of the World Bank's China division.[136] For example, about half of the $43 million worth of contracts financed by the first World Bank loan to China was awarded in the first round to US companies.[137]

Owing to the potentiality of using the funds,[138] China may eventually become a main beneficiary member of the World Bank. Commenting on the work of the World Bank relating to China, Kock-Weser said, "It is a very large program we're working on, some 20 projects for lending in the coming years, though some are just ideas. We are hoping to lend to China between $1 billion and $2 billion a year by the mid-1980s."[139]

Although China's potential borrowing from the World Bank is great and the loans are beneficial to both China and the United States, some difficulties are still pending solution. Ironically, the United States reduced its commitment to the IDA when the first World Bank loan to China had demonstrated the beneficial relationship between the bank's lending and US exports. The United States refused, at the World Bank annual meeting of 1982, held in Toronto, Canada, to commit itself to bridging the gap between the end of IDA 6 and the beginning of IDA 7, which covers the years 1985 through 1987. Thirty-one member countries agreed to contribute an extra $2 billion to the IDA at the meeting.

The direct negative effect of the US refusal on its possible exports to China financed by IDA credit is from a special technical account to be established with IDA. Under the terms of the proposed account, procurements will be from donor countries only.[140] Since the United States is not a donor country, US exporters will not be eligible. Thus, China had to exclude US companies from bidding for $60 million worth of fertilizers and other products destined for a rubber development project financed by the IDA.[141]

To conclude, China has shown an increased willingness to use foreign capital to spur economic development. Being a country with a capital-intensive economy, the United States is in a good position to cooperate with China in its economic development programs. The cooperation can be carried out at either the bilateral or the multilateral level, such as the World Bank and the Asian Development Bank.[142] The United States, however, is not in such good positions with Western European countries and Japan. Governments of these countries have financial aid programs that subsidize domestic commercial banks making loans to China. Quite a few have signed long-term loan agreements with China, under which low-interest loans are available to the latter. The United States does not have large financial aid programs and has no loan agreement with China. Since the proceeds of most of the loans are attached to exports, the lack of a financial aid program and a loan agreement may prohibit some potential transactions between the two countries. Large foreign exchange reserves that China possesses make the country reluctant to borrow foreign loans at commercial rates, which in turn puts the United States in a much less competitive position compared with other industrialized countries.

In order to increase the cooperation of the two countries in the financial area, it seems that the US government needs to establish some government-subsidized loan programs for commercial banks. It may also be necessary to enlarge the funds of the Ex-Im Bank in order to increase US banks' participation in the Chinese financial market and their competitiveness at the international market.

NOTES

1. Advanced technology from abroad is also indispensable for a country's economic development. Since this chapter is designed to discuss financial issues, the issue of the transfer of technology will not be dealt with.

2. Michael J. Moser, "Documentation for Commercial Bank Loans to Chinese Borrowers: Some Legal and Practical Issues," in *Legal Aspects of Doing Business in China* (New York, Practicing Law Institute, 1983), p. 254.

3. See the World Bank Report on China, Report No. 3391-CHA, Annex H: External Trade and Finance (1982), p. 51. The first foreign loan formally signed was from the First National Bank of Chicago. See *Asian Wall Street Journal*, June 11, 1979. Chase Manhattan signed a preliminary loan contract in early 1979 for the construction of a business center in Peking. That loan, however, was canceled by China later on.

4. See Chongwei Ji, "Questions Concerning China's Utilization of Foreign Investment and Relevant Economic Laws," A speech delivered at a seminar on China's New Economic Development Trends held in 1981 in Europe.

5. See Chongwei Ji, "China's Utilization of Foreign Funds and Relevant Policies," 16 *Beijing Review* 15 (1981).

6. See Yuming Wei, "China's Absorption of Foreign Funds and Relevant policies." A speech delivered on March 31, 1981, in Brussels, Belgium. The material can be found in *China Economic News*, Suppl. No. 3 (edited and published by Economic Information & Consultancy Co., Hong Kong), April 4, 1981.

7. Moser, "Documentation for Loans," p. 255.

8. See *Asian Wall Street Journal*, May 14, 1979.

9. Moser, "Documentation for Loans," p. 255.

10. See *Asian Wall Street Journal*, August 6, 1981.

11. Premier Zhao Ziyang, in a meeting with a US businessman, said that China would borrow more loans from foreign countries and foreign banks if the conditions were favorable. See *People's Daily*, December 8, 1982.

12. At the beginning of 1983, the Bank of China was reported as saying that it would consider taking the Chinese seat at the Asian Development Bank. See *Asian Wall Street Journal*, January 13 and March 14, 1983.

13. See Wei, "China's Absorption of Foreign Funds."

14. Ibid.

15. 16 *Beijing Review* (1981).

16. See Enhua Zhang, "On Banking Reform," 29 *Beijing Review* (1981).

17. Under the previous system, recipient enterprises did not have to repay the funds or pay any interest. As a result, they tended to be more interested in absorbing funds rather than in economic results, which in turn resulted in tremendous waste. Statistics between 1952 and 1978 show that capital construction investments in that period amounted to 600 billion yuan, whereas only 400 billion yuan were incorporated in fixed assets. See Ibid.

18. *Beijing Review*, October 17, 1983, p. 7.

19. Ibid. The specialized banks and other monetary institutions function independently within the business scope set by the state. Their regular business and administrative affairs are not to be interfered with by the central bank.

20. Ibid.

21. The Industrial and Commercial Bank of China was founded on January 1, 1984.

22. *Beijing Review*, April 9, 1984, p. 17.

23. *Beijing Review*, October 17, 1983, p. 7.

24. See "The Charter of the Bank of China," *People's Daily*, September 3, 1982.

25. Ibid.

26. See *Beijing Review*, March 5, 1984, p. 22.

27. *People's Daily*, January 5, 1983.

28. *Asian Wall Street Journal,* May 17, 1982, p. 5.

29. Ibid.

30. *Asian Wall Street Journal*, March 22, 1982.

31. *China Business Review*, September-October 1982, p. 24.

32. Ibid.

33. Ibid.

34. Ibid.

35. "Bank of China to Help Finance US Hotel Venture," *Asian Wall Street Journal*, January 17, 1983.

36. Ibid.

37. "Bank of China Takes Lead in Arranging $98.7 Million Loan for Hotel in Canton," *Asian Wall Street Journal*, June 27, 1983.

38. Ibid.

39. *Asian Wall Street Journal*, November 16, 1981.

40. See Vigor Keung Fung, "China, Cool to Foreign Joint Ventures, Looks to Overseas Loans for Its Projects," *Asian Wall Street Journal*, August 24, 1981.

41. See *People's Daily*, February 6, 1983.

42. *China Business Review*, January-February 1982, p. 5.

43. See 50 *Beijing Review* (1980).

44. Ibid.

45. *China Business Review*, January-February 1982, p. 5.

46. 25 *Beijing Review* 6 (1982).

47. Ibid.

48. *People's Daily*, December 28, 1982.

49. Ibid.

50. For instance, the Ministry of Agriculture, Forestry, and Animal Husbandry has entrusted the bank to allocate the loans the Ministry borrowed from the International Fund for Agricultural Development of the United Nations and the World Bank. See *Center Daily News*, October 11, 1982, p. 9.

51. *New York Times*, December 13, 1983, p. D30.

52. *China Business Review*, September-October 1982, p. 26.

53. The World Bank Report on China, Report No. 3391-CHA, Annex H: External Trade Finance (1982), p. 53.

54. E.S. Browning, "China Turns to Syndicate to Pay for Italian Imports," *Asian Wall Street Journal*, July 13, 1981, p. 6.

55. Ibid. The total interest rate paid to the banks would float at 0.875 percentage point above the London interbank rate, which was then nearly 18 percent.

56. Moser, "Documentation for Loans," p. 272.

57. See Paul D. Reynolds, "The Bank of China as Borrower and Guarantor: Its Record and Prospects," *East Asian Executive Reports*, July 1982.

58. See *Asian Wall Street Journal*, June 11, 1979.

59 Moser, "Documentation of Loans," p. 272.

60. *Asian Wall Street Journal*, July 13, 1981, p. 6.

61. See *Asian Wall Street Journal*, May 14, 1979.

62. On February 2, 1934, President Roosevelt issued Executive Order No. 6581, directing the secretaries of commerce and state to incorporate a banking concern under the laws of the District of Columbia. The bank was first known as the "Ex-Im Bank of Washington."

63. See Export-Import Bank Act of 1945, Ch. 341, 79th Congress, 59 Stat. 526.

64. Export-Import Bank Act of 1945, Section 3(a), as amended, 12 USC Section 635a (Suppl. V, 1975).

65. Export-Import Bank Act, Section 2(a)(1), 12 USC Section 635a(1).

66. The trade representative and the secretary of commerce serve, ex officio and without vote, as additional board members. See 1979 Reorganization Plan No. 3, Section 3.

67. See Robert S. Rendell, "Export Financing and the Role of the Export-Import Bank of the United States," 11 *Journal of International Law and Economics* 91, 119 (1976).

68. See Paul H. Wishny, "Import and Export Financing," 3 *Banking and Commercial Lending Law* 433 (1982).

69. Oversight Hearings on the Export-Import Bank: Hearings Before the Subcommittee on International Trade, Investment, and Monetary Policy of the Committee on Banking, Finance, and Urban Affairs, House of Representatives, 96th Congress, 2nd Sess., June 12 and 19, 1980.

70. Ibid.

71. Ibid., Article 3.

72. The Foreign Credit Insurance Association is a private organization established in 1961 to provide for insurance by private insurers of US exports against commercial and political risks. Normally, the association works in cooperation with the Ex-Im Bank. It usually insures the commercial risks, while the Ex-Im Bank insures the political risks.

73. At an interview held in early 1979, W. Michael Blumenthal, the former secretary of the treasury, discussed the possibility and difficulty of providing Ex-Im Bank credits for exports to China. See *China Business Review*, January-February 1979, p. 20.

74. See the Trade Act of 1974, 19 USC 2101, Section 402(b), 88 Stat. 2057.

75. Ibid., Section 402(c).

76. See *Asian Wall Street Journal*, January 28, 1980.

77. The remaining restriction set out in the statute is that each loan of $50 million or more to a Communist country requires a separate determination by the president that the credit is in the US national interest. See the Export-Import Bank Act, Section 2(b)(2), 12 USC Section 635(b)(2).

78. *Asian Wall Street Journal*, November 24, 1980, p. 16.

79. Ibid. This preliminary commitment was canceled by the US Ex-Im Bank in early 1981. According to bank officials, the commitment was allowed to expire at the end of 1980. See *Asian Wall Street Journal*, December 21, 1981, p. 20.

80. See "Ex-Im Bank Clears Two Loan Guarantees to Aid Sales to China," *Asian Wall Street Journal*, June 13, 1983.

81. Export-Import Bank Act, 12 USC Section 84.

82. Ibid.

83. 12 CFR Section 7.1100(b).

84. Ibid., Section 7.1160.

85. See comptroller of the currency, staff interpretive letter, September 24, 1976.

86. 12 CFR Section 7.1330(a).

87. In his interpretive ruling, the comptroller of the currency did not give a clear definition of government agencies and instrumentalities. He said that as far as the definition is concerned, "at one extreme, if there is no direct or indirect government ownership, the borrower is a private entity . . . . At the other extreme, if the borrower is a central bank or a government ministry or department which functions only as such, it is part of the government and can never be treated as a distinct borrowing entity." See 44(No. 75) *Federal Register* (1979).

88. 12 CFR Section 7.1330(a).
89. Ibid.
90. Ibid.
91. Ibid.
92. The Income Tax Law of the People's Republic of China Concerning Foreign Enterprises was passed at the fourth session of the Fifth National People's Congress and promulgated on December 13, 1981. The Detailed Rules and Regulations for the Implementation of the Income Tax Law of the People's Republic of China Concerning Foreign Enterprises were approved by the State Council on February 17, 1982, and promulgated by the Ministry of Finance on February 21, 1982. Both statutes came into effect on January 1, 1981.
93. Income Tax Law for Foreign Enterprise, Article 11.
94. Ibid.; also the Detailed Rules and Regulations, Article 31. There is a tension in the stated policies of China and the United States: The United States generally prefers loans to private enterprises, whereas China generally imposes higher taxes on private loan transactions. What is needed is a loan trust that is "private" from the US perspective but "public" or "state" from the perspective of China. This requires a subtle legal accommodation.
95. The Detailed Rules and Regulations, Article 30.
96. Ibid., Article 29.
97. Ibid.
98. As discussed earlier, this kind of arrangement may eventually make US commercial banks violate the lending limit prescribed by the US National Bank Act.
99. Apparently, these techniques are very successful.
100. See *Asian Wall Street Journal*, December 28, 1981.
101. Ibid.
102. *Hong Kong Standard*, May 19, 1982
103. See Chongwei Ji, "China's Utilization of Foreign Funds."
104. *Asian Wall Street Journal*, March 29, 1982, p. 6.
105. Ibid.
106. Ji, "China's Utilization of Foreign Funds."
107. Ibid.
108. Ibid.
109. See *Asian Wall Street Journal*, March 29, 1982, p. 6.
110. Deirdra D. Deamer, "Financing Plant and Equipment Exports to China," *China Business Review*, January-February 1979, p. 42.
111. *New York Times*, December 13, 1983, p. D30.
112. *Beijing Review*, March 5, 1984, p. 22.
113. *Asian Wall Street Journal*, December 13, 1982.
114. Ibid.
115. It was reported that President Reagan would propose bolstering the Ex-Im Bank in his budget for 1984. He was expected to ask for an additional \$2 billion in loan guarantee authority for the bank and to seek \$2.7 billion more in the bank's direct lending authority. If the budget is approved by Congress, the Ex-Im Bank's current problem may be solved eventually and its competitiveness may be strengthened. See *New York Times*, January 27, 1983, p. D2.

116. The Private Export Funding Corporation was established in 1970 and engages in making medium-and long-term loans to borrowers outside the United States to finance the purchase of US goods and services.

117. China's quota in the fund was $550 million special drawing rights, the equivalent of about $720 million.

118. See "Two Agencies Act to Enlarge Role of China," *Wall Street Journal*, August 11, 1980.

119. According to the Articles of Agreement of the International Monetary Fund, Article 3 (3)(a), members are required to pay 25 percent of the increased quota in special drawing rights, but the board of governors may decide that the payment may be made in other currencies or in the members' own currency. The document of Articles of Agreement of the IMF can be found in A.F. Lowenfeld, *International Economic Law*, Vol. 4 (New York, Matthew Bender, 1977).

120. The World Bank's callable capital, unlike the paid-in capital, may not be used in its operations for disbursements or for administrative expenses. It is used solely for the protection of the bond holders of the bank.

121. In the IMF, each member has 250 votes plus one additional vote for 100,000 special drawing rights [Articles of Agreement, Article 12 (5)(a)]. Each World Bank member has 250 votes plus one additional vote for each share of stock held [Article 5 (3)(a)].

122. See Articles of Agreement of the IMF, Article 8 (5)(a).

123. Ibid., Article 8 (2)(a).

124. Ibid., Article 8 (3).

125. Joseph Gold, *The Legal Character of the Fund's Stand-By Arrangements and Why It Matters* (Washington, DC, IMF, 1980), p. 16.

126. Frank Ching, "China Losing Hope of Big Loans from World Bank," *Asian Wall Street Journal*, September 20, 1982.

127. "Nature of Relationship Between China and the World Bank May Evolve Gradually," *Asian Wall Street Journal*, April 28, 1980.

128. Ibid.

129. "World Bank Acts Quickly on First Loan to China," *Asian Wall Street Journal*, June 29, 1981.

130. Ibid.

131. *Asian Wall Street Journal*, September 20, 1982.

132. "China Aid Set by World Bank," *New York Times*, November 3, 1982.

133. Ibid.

134. Ching, "China Losing Hope."

135. Nicholas H. Ludlow, "China and the World Bank," *China Business Review*, November-December 1982, p. 12.

136. He said that "the World Bank [had] a bearing on the West's commercial interests in China." See Ching, "China Losing Hope."

137. Ludlow, "China and the World Bank."

138. A study concluded, "Indeed, the People's Republic of China promises to become a model beneficiary nation," Ibid. China's evaluation of the first round of bidding on its education projects was organized in 2 months, while normally it takes 8 to 13 months for similar projects.

139. Ching, "China Losing Hope."

140. Ludlow, "China and the World Bank."

141. *New York Times*, December 6, 1983, p. D2.

142. The head of the Information Department of the Chinese Foreign Ministry, Qui Huaiyuan, revealed China's interest in reseating at the Asian Development Bank (ADB) at a news briefing held on March 8, 1983, in Peking. See *People's Daily*, March 9, 1983.

Chapter 5 High-Technology Sales to China

> China has always regarded the issue of technology transfer not just as a simple technical question, but as a question of whether mutual trust can be established between the two countries.
>
> – **Zhao Ziyang**

The basic features of international economic exchanges include the import and export of commercial products and the transfer of technology, e.g. high-technology sales of hardware, advanced industrial products and equipment, and software, blueprint, know-how, etc. The Export Control Act of the United States was adopted after the second world war.[1] With changes taking place in the political, economic, and military environments in the international community, changes in relations between East and West, and among allies, and especially changes in the domestic economy in the United States, the Export Control Act itself evolved. Certain revisions, some of which are significant, have been made. The United States still uses export controls to further its foreign policy. In fact, they have been used time and time again in its history as sanctions against certain countries. At the same time, they can be employed as a friendly gesture in certain cases. To the extent necessary, the executive branch of the government enjoys considerable discretion in imposing controls on export.

China-US economic relations are directly affected by the Export Control Act and implementing regulations. The controls on the sale of high technology became more significant and sensitive when China started its modernization program. China needs advanced technology to realize industrialization. The United States possesses the world's most advanced technology. Nevertheless, owing to a lack of mutual understanding and trust, the two countries have had difficulties on some occasions in the transfer of high technology, which in turn has had a significant impact on the overall bilateral economic relationship. Since the transfer of technology has a great impact on bilateral relations, it is very worthwhile for both countries to understand the whole series of export control laws, their background, how they are implemented, etc. This chapter will try to briefly review the US export control laws.

EVOLUTION OF EXPORT CONTROLS

The Export Control Act of 1949

The end of World War II saw the start of a confrontation between the East and West, which led to an embargo of goods to the East. The reason for this dramatic change was at least twofold. With the defeat of the common enemy, ideological differences between the East and West came to the fore. There was a general fear of Communist domination among the Western allies. They were afraid of the spread of Communism and felt the need to curb it by the embargo of goods. Another factor was the postwar short supply of goods. Under these circumstances, wartime controls on export by the United States continued despite the end of the war.

On February 28, 1949, the Congress enacted the Export Control Act.[2] It was the first comprehensive law in the legislative history on export control in peacetime.[3] This act, which was designed to expire in 1951, gave the president vast power to regulate foreign trade. It declared that to use export controls as a weapon to protect the national economy, further foreign policy, and exercise vigilance over national security was the policy of the United States.[4] It further provided that to effectuate the policies set forth, "the president may prohibit or curtail the exportation from its territories and possessions, of any articles, materials, or supplies, including technical data, except under such rules and regulations as he shall prescribe".[5] The president, under this act, secured virtually unlimited power to control exports in the name of foreign policy, national security, or domestic economy. The Export Control Act of 1949 transformed export from a right to a privilege.[6] This presumption was based on the fact that the world had not yet recovered from the devastation of World War II. Under the pressure of the shortage of supplies, export from one country to another was at least a friendly action, if not a privilege.

The act authorized the president's delegation of the power of export controls. As a result, the Department of Commerce, instead of the Department of State, took on the function of export controls, created the organization, and enacted enforcement and regulations on its own.

The 1949 Act required exporters to obtain either a "general" or a "validated" license when export was planned. The type of license required depended upon the nature and destination country of the goods to be exported. A general license was a general authorization to export certain types of commodities to certain destinations without the necessity of filing an application for export.[7] It was in fact a regulation granting permission to export without a specially issued document specifically authorizing it. A validated license was a document issued to an exporter by the Department of Commerce, authorizing the exportation of a particular commodity (or technical data) to a particular consignee in a particular country for a particular use.[8] Under this act, neither a general nor a validated license was available for exports to China.

The Export Control Act was renewed in 1951, and again in 1953, 1956, 1958, 1960, 1962, and 1965. The 1965 version was to be reviewed by the Congress in 1969. The renewals of the act reflected the deterioration of the relations between the United States and its allies, on the one side, and Communist countries, on the other, marked by the Korean War.

In addition to the Export Control Act, the president was equipped with the Trading with the Enemy Act of 1917.[9] Under this act, the president may impose controls on export, by persons subject to the jurisdiction of the United States, of goods produced outside the United States. The president was also authorized to prohibit imports from certain countries and even to block assets of the said countries. In 1950, President Truman used this power to stop imports from China and to freeze Chinese property in the United States.[10] In 1953, a set of regulations was issued controlling export to Communist countries by its nationals of goods manufactured outside the territories of the United States. While the short supply throughout the world was the reason advanced by the executive branch for the continuation of the export controls, these controls have been used very often for foreign policy purposes. This was witnessed by Francis McIntyre, assistant director of the Office of International Trade. He stated that at the time that the Export Control Act was passed, shortages of supply accounted for only about one-third of the export licensing activities of the office.[11] The export controls were in fact imposed on export to Communist countries.

The Coordinating Group and the Battle Act

Tempted by the economic advantages of foreign trade and of sharing the foreign market, Western European countries tended to liberalize their trade with Communist countries. Domestic economic necessity and pressure from exporters made the liberalization of trade inevitable. Faced with the growing ineffectiveness of the unilateral imposition of export controls, the United States sought international cooperation from its allies.

In November 1949, the United States, Britain, France, Italy, the Netherlands, Belgium, and Luxembourg formed a secret "Consultative Group," a multilateral system of strategic controls on trade with the "Sino-Soviet bloc." This body, which was composed of officials from member countries, worked out a series of embargo lists. The number of members in this Consultative Group was expanded subsequently. Today, it includes all North Atlantic Treaty Organization (NATO) members except Iceland, and Japan. Thus, its membership is 15.

The Consultative Group created two permanent committees, namely, the Coordinating Committee (COCOM) and the China Committee (CHINCOM), in 1950 and 1952, respectively. COCOM was charged with the administration and supervision of trade with East Europe. CHINCOM was concerned with trade with China. Four secret lists were promulgated: (1) items totally embargoed; (2) items for which a quota had been found appropriate; (3) items to be carefully watched; and (4) additional items to be denied to China and North Korea (the China List). These lists contained only a minimal level of export control to Communist countries. Each member was free to impose more restrictive controls on its export, which was and is the case with the United States. It is reported, however, that in general the United States restricts exports of more products than does COCOM.[12]

With the improvement of the relations between China and Western European countries, the China list was abolished in 1957. From then on, trade with China has been under the scrutiny of COCOM. The COCOM lists were likewise reduced to three categories. Nevertheless, the second and the third categories were replaced by a new list (the watch list). Thus, COCOM has two sets of lists, namely, the embargo list and the watch list.

COCOM was not established by international treaty, and thus it is not an organization.[13] The overall framework of COCOM is to provide a consensus decision-making body to make sure that embargoes imposed upon exports to Communist countries work effectively. The implementation of COCOM decisions is voluntary and through domestic legislation. Although the work of COCOM has been seldom reported, it appears that once decisions are made, member countries will carry them out.

Although there are embargo and watch lists, exceptions can be made with regard to exports. A member country is required to file an application to COCOM based in Paris. The decision to grant exceptions is usually made by consensus. On certain occasions, however, a decision may be made by compromise among the member countries, or between COCOM and a nonmember country, or both. The COCOM approval for the export of computers manufactured by Hitachi, a Japanese company, and IBM, a US company, to China illustrated a compromise.[14] This case, as it was reported, reflected the subtle relation between China and the United States. The United States at first rejected the application by Hitachi, which resulted in a Japanese objection to a similar transaction by IBM. The United States plays a leading role in COCOM, for it is the chief supplier of economic and military assistance to Western Europe and possesses the most advanced technology.[15]

COCOM did not have an effective implementation system. To supplement it, Congress enacted the Mutual Defense Assistance Control Act (the Battle Act) in 1951.[16] This act was designed to induce cooperation from its allies by reducing foreign aid to a certain country under certain circumstances. Under this act, a country that exports strategic items to Communist countries will not be considered qualified for US aid. There is, within the Department of State, a Battle Act administrator working in conjunction with the Consultative Group. The Battle Act administrator is required under Title I to prepare two lists. The first includes "arms, ammunition, implements of war, and atomic energy material," or items that can be defined as strategic. The act provides that whichever country permits the shipments of items on this list must be deprived of US aid – economic, military, or financial. The second list contains items that can be incorporated into the manufacture of military material. A country allowing the export of items on the second list is also punishable by the denial of

US aid, unless the president determines that such a cut-off will be clearly detrimental to the security of the United States.

The effectiveness of the act and COCOM has been diminishing as European countries have become less dependent on aid and as the technological superiority of the United States vis-à-vis both Western European countries and other countries has narrowed.[17] Another major factor that has made both COCOM and the Battle Act less effective is that international and domestic difficulty among and within industrialized countries has been mounting. The independence of former colonies has resulted in the loss of some markets and raw material supply for the West. Growing world economic interdependence coupled with economic crises, inflation, and unemployment at home has caused most European countries to become more and more involved in the economic development of newly independent countries and the Communist world. As a result, the COCOM restrictions have become less effective. The United States, the leader of the industrialized world, has received pressure from its allies and domestic industries to liberalize export controls. Thus, a somewhat more realistic strategy became inevitable.

The Export Control Act of 1969

By the late 1960s and early 1970s, everyone was obliged to take account of the new level of the interdependent international economic structure. Both industrialized and industrializing countries felt the need and showed the desire to promote international trade. With less restrictive controls, US allies took the lead in trading with Communist and other newly independent countries.

Tempted by profits made and advantages secured in international trade by other industrialized countries, US businesses began to put more pressure on Congress to liberalize export controls to match less restrictive allied controls.[18] The Congress, under heavy pressure from the business sector and from the executive branch's desire to reshape its foreign policy,[19] amended the 1949 Export Control Act in 1969. The new act, which was called the Export Administration Act, made a few policy changes regarding export control. It marked the end of the trade embargo era and the start of the qualified promotion of exports.

It was declared that the US policy was: (1) to encourage trade with all countries with which the United States had diplomatic or trading relations, unless the trade was determined by the president to be detrimental to the national interest; (2) to restrict the export of goods and technology that would make a significant contribution to the military potential against the US security interests; (3) to protect the domestic economy, further foreign policy, and exercise vigilance over exports for the purpose of national security; and (4) to formulate and apply any necessary controls to the maximum extent possible in cooperation with those nations with which the United States has defense treaty commitments.[20]

These policy objectives reflected conflicting interests among different sectors in the United States. Promotion of international trade would benefit the exporters and the national economy as a whole. It was the best way to earn profits from abroad. Restrictive controls on export might contribute to the safeguards of national security while affecting the balance of trade. These were only part of the problems facing the administration of the act. There were also conflicting interests within each sector. It was not surprising that the Commerce Department received pressure from all sides. No wonder a former secretary of commerce remarked that "I would be very glad if some other department would take it all over."[21] Export controls in fact have long been a contentious political issue rather than a pure legal issue.[22]

The allocation of the power to regulate export controls prescribed in this act was important. Under this act, the secretary of commerce was charged with instituting organizational and procedural changes in any office or division of the department relating to the control of exports. When the secretary made the decision, the changes should necessarily facilitate and effectuate the fullest implementation of the policy set forth by Congress.[23] Promotion of trade was set out as an important policy in the act. This authority of the secretary of commerce was not vested in the 1949 Export Control Act. The power, however, was not complete, for the entire administration of export controls was still in the hands of the president.[24] It was stated that to effectuate the policies set forth in this act, the president might prohibit or curtail the exportation from the United States, its territories, and possessions of any article, material, or supply, including technical data or any other information, except under such rules and regulations as the president shall prescribe. These rules and regulations might provide for the denial of any export application or request when the president determined that the export would prove detrimental to the security of the United States.[25] This national security provision apparently referred to items and technical data that could be adapted to military use or the so-called "dual-use" materials, for export of arms and military equipment was regulated by the Arms Export Control Act of 1968.[26] The act gave the president vast power to impose controls on exports without regard to destination, based on national security or foreign policy grounds.

In any event, the 1969 Export Administration Act at least was a step forward toward the liberalization of trade. Coincidentally, restrictions that had been imposed unilaterally on relations with China began to be lifted in 1969. Trade with China was again allowed. In February 1972, China started to be treated on an equal footing with the Soviet Union by the United States.

Although subsequent amendments were made to the Export Administration Act of 1969 in 1974, 1977, and 1978, much of the legislation enacted in 1969 remained in force until 1979 when the 1979 Act was implemented.

The Export Administration Act of 1979

The Export Administration Act of 1979 shows an increasing desire by the United States to promote export trade and impose less control. In its findings, the act recognizes the significant contribution to the US well-being by the export of trade. The serious adverse effects on the balance of payments and the domestic economy caused by export controls have been realized, and exports are encouraged and to be given a high priority.[27] The US policy is defined to minimize uncertainties in export control policy, to use export controls only after full consideration of their impact on the economy of the United States, and only to the extent necessary.[28] These provisions illustrate the displeasure of Congress and businesses toward the export controls previously imposed. During the 1979 congressional review of the Export Administration Act of 1969, the advisability of the use of export control for foreign policy purposes was questioned. George Ball, speaking before the House Committee on Foreign Affairs, stated that using export control as a weapon to influence other nations' policy had proved ineffective. He said that it had not served US foreign policy while serving its domestic economy, for other allied nations were unwilling to go along with the United States.[29] In fact, one can hardly find a case in history in which export control helped realize foreign policy objectives effectively, for export controls as well as other economic actions are always two edged: In an interdependent world, each economic deprivation can be matched by a comparable response on the part of the target.[30] The effectiveness of export control depends on the enforcer's ability to control and its willingness and readiness to pay the price of the control. During the debate over the Export Administration Act of 1979, many attributed the declined domestic economy to the application of export controls and appealed to confine the application of foreign policy controls on exports to the unavailability of foreign sources.[31]

Consequently, national security control and foreign policy control are treated in separate sections. This separate treatment illustrates the previous debate over the uncertainty of export controls. The executive may use foreign policy and national security controls interchangeably. This may frustrate exporters as well as the public, for the objectives of foreign policy have never been made clear to the public. Thus, an exporter can hardly figure out whether an item is prohibited for export or not.

Essentially, the act recognized that trade relationships with China involved very different considerations from those with the Soviet Union. Under the heading of national security control, Congress abolished the distinction between Communist and non-Communist country status in imposing export controls. The basis for control is a nation's present and potential relationship with the United States and its ability and willingness to control retransfers.[32] Enacting this provision, the United States has realized the fact that a country's relationship with the United States has little to do with its Communist or non-Communist character. The establishment and maintenance of a friendly relationship depend basically on common interest. The argument can be made by invoking the second world war in which Communist and non-Communist countries formed an alliance against the common enemy.[33]

Owing to the rapid development of technology, the act attached great importance to foreign availability and instructed the secretary of commerce to review the matter on a continuing basis.[34] Read together with other provisions, it is clear that unless adequate evidence can be gathered that noncontrol of the export would prove detrimental to the foreign policy or national security of the United States, export control should not be imposed.[35]

In order to carry out this review, and taking into account the sophisticated and complex nature of developing technology, the secretary is empowered and authorized to set up technical advisory committees to examine the matter of foreign availability.[36]

To be distinguished from foreign policy control, a commodity control list (CCL) on national security grounds should be established and maintained by the secretary of commerce.[37] Obviously, this provision is to give exporters some certainty of export control policy and to restrain the use of export control by the president.

Another noteworthy provision is the creation of a new type of license – a qualified general license.[38] The act urged the secretary of commerce to use a qualified general license, in lieu of a validated license, to the maximum extent practicable.[39]

According to the changes made in the act, the president must consider a number of factors before export control can be imposed on foreign policy grounds. The criteria are as follows: (1) the probability of achieving the intended objectives; (2) the compatibility of the proposed control with other foreign policy objectives; (3) the likely effects of the proposed controls on the export performance of the United States, on the competitive position of the United States in the international economy, on the international reputation of the United States as a supplier of goods and technology, and on individual US companies and their employees and communities, including the effects of the controls on existing contracts; (4) the ability of the United States to enforce the proposed controls effectively; and (5) the policy consequences of not imposing controls.[40] As mentioned earlier, the separate treatment of national security and foreign policy controls is to provide the public with some certainty, for national security interest is more stable and predictable than foreign policy purposes. The criteria requirement is another step forward to limit the use of foreign policy control. Under the current law, the president is given a full hand but is also exposed to the political risks of the policy.

Another action was taken by the Congress to circumscribe executive discretion in the use of export controls for foreign policy purposes: The president is required to make reasonable efforts to achieve the purposes of the controls through negotiation or other alternative means, before resorting to the imposition of control.[41] Unless other alternative means are determined to be exhausted, export control should not be employed.

Finally, the secretary of commerce is required to consult regularly with the business sectors for the purpose of obtaining their views on export control policy and the foreign availability of goods and technology.[42] The consultation provision gives businesses additional opportunity to influence the governmental decision-making process.

Now, they can influence the Commerce Department and the president on a regular and periodic basis. Nevertheless, the secretary of commerce has the freedom to consult or not to consult those business sectors.

All in all, even though Congress tried hard to limit the president's power, the executive still has vast discretion over the imposition of controls on exports. Even decisions and rules not in conformity with the act may still be adopted.

ADMINISTRATIVE STRUCTURE OF EXPORT CONTROLS

In the trade system of the United States, the license is the basic device for the exportation of goods. Nothing can be shipped out of the country without an appropriate license. Export licenses are granted or denied by the Office of Export Administration under the Commerce Department.[43]

The Department of Commerce's licensing jurisdiction is over all commodities and unclassified technical data exported from the United States except certain specialized items handled by other government agencies. For example, defense articles and defense services are licensed by the Office of Munitions Control, under the Department of State; exports of nuclear equipment, facilities, and materials are licensed by the US Nuclear Regulatory Commission; reexports of nuclear equipment and materials are licensed by the Department of Energy; narcotics and dangerous drugs are licensed by the US Department of Justice; natural gas and electric energy are licensed by the US Department of Energy; endangered species of fish and wildlife are licensed by the US Department of Interior, etc. The Departments of State and Energy have further responsibilities for the control of exports of classified and unclassified technical data relating to commodities under their jurisdiction.[44]

The export licensing controls administered by the Department of Commerce apply to: (1) exports of commodities and technical data from the United States; (2) reexports of US-origin commodities and technical data from a foreign destination; (3) US-origin parts and components used in a foreign country in the manufacture of a foreign end-product for export; and (4) in some instances, the foreign-produced direct product of US-origin technical data. Although the Export Administration Act authorizes the control of non-US-origin exports by US subsidiaries, affiliates, or branches in foreign countries, the regulations do not generally extend to such exports if the commodities exported are of foreign manufacture, contain no US materials, and are not based on restricted US technology.[45]

In order to administrate export controls, an Office of Export Administration (OEA) was created in the Commerce Department. The principal function of the OEA is to issue export regulations, grant or deny licenses, and investigate violations of the Export Administration Act and its own regulations. It has been able to operate export controls with quite a free hand. Violations of the regulations issued by the OEA and of the Export Administration Act can be punished with civil, administrative, and criminal penalties.

Export license applications must go through all procedures. They should first be sent to the Operations Division of the OEA, where they are checked for completeness and to determine if any party to the transaction has been previously denied an export license.[46] If an application does not involve a Communist destination, it may be decided by the division in a single day. If it does not qualify for the quick treatment, the application should go to the Compliance Division, and then to the Policy Planning Division. Apparently non-Communist destination applications can skip the former and go straight to the latter.[47] The Policy Planning Division reviews license applications and prepares documentations on those applications to be forwarded to a higher reviewing body. In practice, the OEA handles most of the export applications. Only in extraordinary cases are higher review bodies involved.

At the higher level, there is an interagency body called the Advisory Committee for Export Policy (ACEP), in which are represented the Commerce, State, Defense, Treasury, and other departments. Applications with national security implications are subject to the ACEP's review. Within the ACEP, an Operating Committee has been set up. The committee meets weekly to review exceptional license applications.[48] This committee is chaired by the OEA's assistant director of policy planning.

Cases that cannot be solved at the Operating Committee level are passed to the sub-ACEP composed of the deputy assistant secretaries of various departments. Above the sub-ACEP is the ACEP itself, which is an organ at the assistant secretary level. All these committees are chaired by the Commerce Department.

As mentioned previously, the Export Control Review Board created by Kennedy, consisting of the secretaries of various departments, is the highest-level consideration of trade control policies and actions, and is chaired by the secretary of commerce.[49] Nevertheless, this organ if responsible to the president and the cabinet. When it becomes necessary, an application may be reviewed by the cabinet members or the president.

In granting a license for the export of high technology, the Defense Department plays a crucial role. The secretary of defense is authorized to review the proposed export of any goods or technology to any country to which such exports are controlled for national security purposes. Whenever the secretary finds that the proposed export will make a significant contribution to the military potential of such country and will prove detrimental to the national security of the United States, it is recommended that the president disapprove such an export.[50] The president is the only person who can override a recommendation by the secretary of defense. In doing so, the president must then report this decision to Congress.[51] The Defense Department has been categorized as most conservative in granting licenses among the government circle.[52]

The United States is represented by the State Department in COCOM. When other nations apply for export exceptions from the COCOM list, the applications are considered in the State Department in the United States.

EXPORT ADMINISTRATION REGULATIONS

Country Groups

The export control of the United States is based on the commodity and the country of destination. Certain products are allowed to certain countries but not others.

For the purposes of export control, all country destinations are divided into seven groups: country group Q, Rumania; country group T, all nations in the Western Hemisphere, except Cuba and Canada; country group V, all countries not included in any other country group (except Canada); country group W, Hungary and Poland; country group Y, the Soviet Union, Albania, Bulgaria, Czechoslovakia, East Germany, Mongolia, and Laos; and country group Z, Kampuchea, Cuba, North Korea, and Vietnam.[53] Canada is not included in any country group because exports to that country are normally controlled only in specific short supply or nuclear nonproliferation situations.

China was originally the sole member of country group P. It was shifted from group P to V by an amendment to the Export

Administration Regulations in November 1983.[54] Although China has been placed in this group, certain restraints are retained regarding exports to this country. Exports that would make a direct and significant contribution to nuclear weapons and their delivery systems, electronic and antisubmarine warfare, intelligence gathering, power projection, and air superiority are still restricted.[55]

Most commodities can be exported to Canada and country groups T and V under general licenses. Exports to country group Z, however, usually require validated licenses. Commodities that are essentially peaceful in nature or for civilian use only may be exported to country group Y under general licenses. Other commodities and technical data require validated licenses.

Exports under validated licenses are reviewed by the Department of Commerce on a case-by-case basis. The review generally includes an analysis of the kinds and qualities of commodities or technologies to be shipped; their military or civilian uses; the unrestricted availability abroad of the same or comparable items; the country of destination; the ultimate end-users in the country of destination; and intended end-use.[56] Country groups Q and W are treated indifferently in the Export Administration Regulations. The restrictions imposed upon export to those countries are less severe than for exports to other East European countries. Since the Soviet invasion of Afghanistan, exports to that country require severe scrutiny. Because of the nature of Afghanistanian government, the country is now being treated like the Soviet Union.

In conformity with United Nations resolutions and US foreign policy, exports to South Africa and Namibia of arms, munitions, military equipment and materials, machinery and materials for their manufacture and maintenance, and related unpublished data are prohibited. Exports for military or police end-use are also denied. Otherwise, export controls for these countries are generally the same as for country groups T and V.[57]

Licensing System

Except for most commodities and data shipping to Canada, no export to any country can be made without either a general or validated license.[58]

A general license is a license established by the US Department of Commerce permitting export within the provisions thereof. No application is required for its use and no document issued. A general license is not applicable to the export of commodities or technical data under the licensing jurisdiction of agencies other than the Department of Commerce.[59] An exporter must present to the Customs Office at the port of export a Shipper's Export Declaration describing the commodities to be exported.[60] When an export is made under a general license and no validated license is required, the declaration is the only export control document.[61] In the event that part of the declaration is not true, the exporter may be punished for violation of the regulations. So the declaration must conform in all respects with the provisions of a general license and must correctly describe the commodities in terms of the CCL. It must contain the names and addresses of all parties to the transaction, the seven-digit Schedule B number, and a sufficiently detailed commodity description to allow verification of the number and appropriate general license designation.

A validated license is a document issued by, or under the authority of, the OEA, authorizing a specific export. The validated license is subcategorized into five categories, namely, individual license, project license, distribution license, qualified general license, and service supply license. The individual license is a general description of any validated license, except the other four mentioned above. It authorizes an export of machinery, technology, or technical data to a designated consignee. A project license authorizes the export of commodities required for a specified activity for a period of approximately one year from the issuance of the license.[62] It may be applied where an exporter is involved in multiple transactions with a single foreign importer, as, for example, in supplying goods for a capital expansion or renovation. The qualified general license was created by the Export Administration Act of 1979. It authorizes the multiple export of certain commodities to approved consignees in country groups Q, W, and Y for a period of one year. The validity of this period may be extended. The consignees must be actual or prospective users of the licensed commodity.[63] Applications for this license may be approved when the proposed commodities or technical data are relatively low-technology items that would be approved routinely under the validated license procedure. An end-user who proposes to sell or distribute commodities may not qualify for a qualified general license. Nevertheless, when the commodities are associated with equipment licenses under a qualified general license, they may be exported, if permissible, under general license.

In order to file an application for validated licenses, the applicant must be subject to US jurisdiction. Otherwise, an agent in the United States must be appointed to act in the applicant's behalf. The applicant or agent must disclose fully all parties with interest in the transaction. This includes all parties participating on their own account, the intermediate consignee, and the purchaser.

An application for export must be based on an order from the foreign consignee, which is defined as something more than a mere business inquiry.[64] In other words, although an order is less than an offer, there should be adequate evidence that the transaction will be concluded once the export license is secured. An application should be accompanied by the following information: country of ultimate destination, names and addresses of the parties, quality, value and description of the items to be exported, and end-use of the exports.[65]

When a shipment is made, the exporter in addition to the requirement under general license must submit the validated license to the Customs Office.

A CCL has been established in the Export Administration Regulations.[66] The CCL contains all commodities subject to licensing control by the OEA. It is the key to determining whether a specific shipment may be exported under an established general license authorization, or whether a validated license is needed. For all of the commodities licensed by the OEA, the CCL shows the destinations for which each commodity requires a license document, the reason for control, the unit of control, and GLV dollar value limit. Opposite each item on the CCL, there are listed country groups, symbolized by the letters, Q, T, V, W, Y, or Z, to which the products may be exported without a validated license. The establishment of the CCL is to help exporters be certain of whether or not a validated license is required for a particular foreign importer.

Technical Data

One of the new trends in international trade is the transfer of technology and know-how. In fact, there are two types of transfer. One is the pure transaction of technology sales. The other is the transaction of technology associated with the purchase of products and equipment. For instance, when buyers purchase a computer, they must at the same time buy the software. Otherwise, they may not be able to operate it. This is especially the case in a turn-key transaction.

In these transactions, a transfer of technology and know-how may be inevitably involved. The provisions of the Export Administration Regulations are generally applicable to technical data transactions. At the same time, a special set of rules was created in the regulations for exports of technical data.

Technical data, as defined by the regulations, means information of any kind that can be used, or adapted for use, in the design, production, manufacture, utilization, or reconstruction of articles or materials. The data may take a tangible form, such as a model, prototype, blueprint, or operating manual; or they may take an intangible form such as technical service.[67] The export of data is defined as an actual shipment or transmission of technical data out of the United States; any release of technical data in the United States with the knowledge or intent that the data will be shipped or transmitted from the United States to a foreign country; or any release of technical data of US origin in a foreign country. It is further specified that a release may be made through visual inspection by foreign nationals of US-origin equipment and facilities; oral exchanges of information in the United States or abroad; or the application to situations abroad of personal knowledge or technical experience acquired in the United States.[68]

The export of technical data as defined in the regulations can be as significant as the export of goods and equipment. At the same time, it is particularly difficult to control the exportation of data because of its complex nature. Being aware of the potential difficulty that the regulations may cause if a too strict control is imposed, the OEA made important exceptions. A general license designated GTDA is applicable to the following cases: (1) data that have been made generally available in any form, such as in lectures, conferences, trade shows, publications, and so on; (2) dissemination of information not directly and significantly related to the design, production, or utilization in industrial processes; (3) instruction in academic institutions and academic laboratories; and (4) patent applications.[69] Thus, the OEA's licensing authority extends to data that are either unpublished or not generally available in published form, except for scientific and educational data not directly and significantly related to the industrial process. Exports of technical data to Communist countries require validated licenses in general.[70]

Country groups T and V, except China and plus Canada, qualify for a general license GTDR.[71] In order to prevent exported technical data from being retransferred, a US exporter must obtain written assurance from the foreign importer that neither the technical data nor the direct product thereof is intended to be shipped, either directly or indirectly, to country groups Q, W, Y, or Z, Afghanistan, or the People's Republic of China.[72] The written assurance can be in the form of either a letter or other communication from the importer evidencing such intention. A licensing agreement with provisions to this effect is accepted as a written assurance.

Enforcement

If an export is not properly licensed, or if a licensed export is later diverted from the approved destination to one that is not approved, the Department of Commerce will investigate to determine the facts and appropriate action to be taken. Other violations of the regulations will be followed by the same procedure.[73] Depending on the seriousness of and circumstances surrounding the violation, the sanction may be a warning letter, a civil penalty of up to $10,000 for each violation, administrative action denying the US or foreign firm the right to participate in specified US export transactions for a certain period of time, or a criminal punishment through the courts.[74] Knowing violations are punishable by a fine of not more than five times the value of the exports involved or $50,000, whichever is greater, or imprisonment up to five years, or both. Willful violations with a country to which exports are restricted are punishable by a fine of not more than five times the value of the exports involved or $100,000, whichever is greater, or imprisonment for ten years, or both.[75] Persons who export to a controlled country goods for military or intelligence-gathering purposes contrary to the license conditions, with knowledge, commit a willful violation. Therefore, they are punishable to the extent described above. False statements of fact are punishable too.[76]

Under these severe punishments, and especially owing to the efforts made by the Investigation Division of the OEA, the Export Administration Regulations have been carried out fairly well.

POLICY VERSUS LAW

The transfer of technology has always been a sensitive issue in Sino-American economic relations. The United States has repeatedly stated that a strategic relationship with the People's Republic of China will be central to US foreign policy, and that China is to be treated as "a friendly nation with which the United States is not allied but with which it shares many interests."[77] Exports of advanced technology to China, however, have been approved slowly. This is due to several factors. First, the governments of the two countries have different expectations: After the normalization process, China placed too much hope on the United States without understanding its domestic politics and foreign policy direction. Second, different views are held by various US groups and lobbies regarding the development of Sino-American relations. Third, there has been bureaucratic delay in translating the policy toward China into actual technology transfer. This was particularly true in the first part of the Reagan Administration's term in office. In this period, the US government rejected a few large potential exports to China. In addition, somewhat severer measures were taken regarding exports to companies in Hong Kong.

In the summer of 1982, shortly after Assistant Secretary Lawrence J. Brady announced that the United States was willing to sell items adaptable to military use to China, the Commerce Department denied export licenses to Hong Kong companies. The best-known case is that of Hua Ko.

Hua Ko Electronic Company, which is a Hong Kong company, started to build a plant to manufacture semiconductor chips in Hong Kong early in 1984. The company put orders to purchase some $1.2 million worth of US equipment. Export licenses, which are absolutely necessary, were denied by the US Department of Commerce. The denials included ion implantation equipment from Varian Associates, testing equipment from Fairchild Test System Group, and other equipment from Thermo Products Corporation. Almost at the same time of the denial, agents of the US Customs Service raided San Jose, Inc., a subsidiary of Hua Ko Electronic Company, and seized its records. It was said that the federal agents acted under a court-authorized search warrant and that the raid was the result of a Customs Service investigation into the alleged shipment of restricted US technology to China. Whether the alleged shipment actually occurred or not was not reported. This at least shows that the United States is very much concerned about technology going to China.

The denial of export to Hua Ko was reported as a result of its strong link to mainland China. Bohdan Denysky, deputy assistant secretary for export administration of the Commerce Department, said "Our policy is that it's not so much the place you're sending it to. It's what nationality [people] are using it." He said that some export licenses approved before the Reagan administration came into office should have been denied, because the Hong Kong companies receiving the equipment had strong links to the mainland.[78]

By 1982, two other Hong Kong companies had been producing the same product in the same area in which Hua Ko planned to produce: RCL Semiconductors Ltd. and Elcap Electronics LTD. It is said that both have connections with the mainland and have employed engineers from the mainland in their plants. In addition, Elcap's president, Larry Yung, is the son of Rong Yiren, who heads the CITIC. Nevertheless, both companies imported equipment and machines from the United States during the Carter administration. The machines and equipment employed in these factories are the same as those denied to Hua Ko and other companies. Even the producers of the equipment are the same. For instance, Elcap's ion implanter, which is similar to that denied to Hua Ko, was also manufactured by Varian Associates. In 1978, Fairchild sold four $350,000 semiconductor testing systems to Elcap. But after four years, the same system cannot be exported to Hua Ko, another Hong Kong company. These facts illustrate that the Reagan administration in the first part of their term in office imposed very strict controls on exports to China and China-related companies in Hong Kong.

Another Hong Kong company that was reported as having no Chinese backing, System Data Semiconductor Ltd., has had delivery of another Fairchild testing system delayed for almost two years because the Commerce Department does not believe it needs such a machine. The department suspects that the machine may be re-exported to China.

Before those denials, there were few restrictions on exports of US machinery and equipment or technology bound for Hong Kong, which the United States labeled a "free world" destination. Bohdan Denysky frankly admitted that the policy has changed under the Reagan administration. He said, "One can make the argument that Hong Kong is not on the list of countries we are worrying about, and we should approve all commodity licenses to it. That has been pretty much the policy in the past."[79] Perhaps he referred to the Carter administration when he mentioned "the past." Under the changed policy, electronic machinery that makes or tests integrated circuits smaller than the four- to five-micron level cannot be exported from the United States to a company in Hong Kong presumably having ties with the mainland. This level of technology is about five or six years old. The Commerce Department has decided to treat those companies in Hong Kong the same as companies in the mainland with regard to the exportation of commodities. Although the age of technology does not reflect the level of technology, this policy does imply that the United States is very much concerned with the transfer of high-level technology to China.

The difficulty with this policy is, what is a tie to the mainland and what is a "strong link?" As one businessman from Hong Kong said, "The situation can be very complex and certain businessmen have to be involved with the mainland."[80] Should all the companies in Hong Kong having anything to do with the mainland be denied export license? What standard does the Commerce Department employ in deciding a particular case?

The United States used to worry that the "China-linked" companies in Hong Kong would reexport the equipment to the mainland. Now the concern has broadened. Even if the machines stay in Hong Kong, the United States may not want Chinese engineers learning advanced technology from them.

In fact, Hua Ko was not the only case in which an export license was denied. The Commerce Department denied "several more" cases in the first six months of 1982, because of their strong ties to the mainland.[81] Denysky openly stated, "We are looking very closely at Hong Kong applications. If we find the company could be owned or controlled or have strong ties with China, we treat these companies as if we were dealing with the People's Republic of China".[82]

Upon learning of this outcome of the new policy to liberalize exports to China, neither the Chinese government nor the US exporters have much enthusiasm for the policy. President Reagan promised to increase sales of high-technology equipment to China in 1981. The proposed change, however, was said to be held up because of reluctance on the part of the Defense Department.[83] Although Reagan is said to "mean business" this time, both US exporters and the Chinese government are waiting to see the actual effect.

Under the new regulations, exports of advanced technology will be basically divided into three categories, namely, green, intermediate, and red. The green category covers roughly seven areas: computers, computerized instruments, microcircuits, electronic instruments, recording equipment, semiconductor production equipment, and oscilloscopes. Exports falling in this category will generally be approved by the Department of Commerce without interagency review, whereas exports within the intermediate category will be reviewed case by case. Exports in the red category are presumably denied, because of their strategic implication as decided by the administration.

A remaining question will be interagency reviews, or how the United States will define its security interest vis-à-vis China. One criterion recommended by the Export Controls Working Group of the National Council for US-China Trade was to base export control decisions on a comparison of the relative risk of making the same sale to other friendly countries.[84] In other words, exports to China should not be restricted unless possession of the technology or equipment by China presents more risk to the security of the United States. At the same time, how to balance this security issue with the US policy of "support for China's modernization and . . . encouraging participation by US firms in that modernization effort" is another question to be answered.[85]

In any event, these newly adopted regulations will provide US exporters with some certainty as to what they will be allowed to export to China. Although the actual effect of these regulations on future transactions is difficult to determine, they are welcomed by both the Chinese government and US exporters.

To conclude, export controls have a significant impact on Sino-American economic relations. First, the Chinese government has always treated the issue of export control as a test of its relationship with the United States. The easing of controls may strengthen mutual trust, which will in turn lead to growing economic exchange. Second, substantial loosening of export controls will increase US exports to China. Also, it will enlarge US participation in China's economic development by joint ventures, cooperative ventures, and wholly US-owned concerns, which may use advanced US-made technology and equipment. It may also balance, at least to some extent, the Chinese grievance on its trade deficit with the United States.

Since the establishment of diplomatic relations between China and the United States in 1979, China has been receiving more favorable treatment than the Eastern European countries. It was singled out by the Carter administration as the sole member of a special country group – group P. Under the policy of the Reagan administration, China is being treated as a special member of a general country group – group V. Although improvements have been made, a more realistic policy to liberalize controls may be necessary. For instance, it is not wise for the United States to impose any control on merchandise that can be purchased from other sources. Also, since the United States treats China as a friendly country, it should give China a real country group V status. In addition, still complicated licensing procedures should be further simplified to realize a substantive improvement in transfers, for some of the reviews may well delay, if not preclude, transactions.

NOTES

1. The Export Control Act of 1949 was adopted on February 28, 1949. Before its adoption, the wartime controls on export were in force.

2. Export Control Act of February 28, 1949, Ch. 11, 63 Stat. 7, as amended, 50 USC App. 2021-32 (64).

3. Harold J. Berman and John R. Garson, "United States Export Controls – Past, Present, and Future," 67 *Columbia Law Review* 792 (1967).

4. Export Control Act, Ch. 11, Section 2, 63 Stat. 7 (1949).

5. Ibid., Section 3.

6. Gary K Bertsch, "US Export Controls: The 1970s and Beyond," 15 *Journal of World Trade Law* 67-68 (1981).

7. Berman and Garson, "United States Export Controls," p. 814.

8. Ibid., p. 815

9. Trading with the Enemy Act, Ch. 106, 40 Stat. 411 (1917), as amended, 50 USC App. 1-44 (1970). On December 28, 1977, Congress adopted the International Emergency Economic Powers Act [see 50 USC Section 1701-1706 (Supp. I 1977)]. This act, which replaced the 1917 Trading with the Enemy Act, provides the sole statutory authority for the imposition of embargoes by the president in peacetime.

10. In order for the Department of the Treasury to take actions regarding China, President Truman declared that an emergency existed with respect to Korea on December 16, 1950, when the Chinese army was sent to Korea [see Proclamation No. 2419 of December 16, 1950. The document can be found in Lowenfeld, *International Economic Law*, Part 3, document supplement, p. 383 (New York, Matthew Bender, 1977)]. The next day, the Treasury Department promulgated the Foreign Assets Control Regulations [see 31 CFR Section 500.101-500.809 (1970)]. These regulations prohibited imports from China and blocked all bank accounts and assets in the United States owned by China and its nationals.

11. *New York Times*, March 5, 1949.

12. See Richard H. Solomon (ed.), *The China Factor* (Englewood Cliffs, Prentice-Hall, 1981) in general. Also see *China Business Review*. (Washington, DC, National Council for U.S.-China Trade). It seems that the United States has more restrictive controls on exports than any other industrialized country.

13. US Department of State, the Battle Act Report, 19th Report to the Congress 1-3 (1966). See also Andreas F. Lowenfeld, 3 *International Economic Law* 11 (1977).

14. *Asian Wall Street Journal*, May 31, 1982.

15. Lowenfeld, *International Economic Law*, p. 12.

16. 22 USC 1611-13 d (1964).

17. Lowenfeld, *International Economic Law*, p. 13.

18. Bertsch, "US Export Controls," p. 69.

19. By the late 1960s, newly independent countries had become an important force in the international forum. They defeated the traditional control by

the United States of the United Nations and frequently used oil as a weapon to bargain with industrialized countries. With these changed situations in the international community, the US government changed its previous position.

20. Public Law 91-184, 83 Stat. 841 (1969).

21. Berman and Garson, "United States Export Controls," pp. 305-306.

22. Bertsch, "US Export Controls," p. 70.

23. Public Law 91-184, 83 Stat. 841 (1969).

24. Under the Constitution of the United States, the president is in charge of foreign relations. Since export control is directly related to foreign affairs, the president cannot avoid the responsibility.

25. Ibid.

26. 22 USC 2751-1794 (1976 and Supp. III 1979).

27. The Export Administration Act of 1979, 50 USC App. 2401 (1979).

28. Ibid., App. 2402.

29. Extension and Revision of the Export Administration Act of 1969; Hearings and Markup Before the Subcommittee on International Economic Policy and Trade of the House Committee on Foreign Affairs, 96th Congress, 1st Sess. (1979) (statement of George W. Ball, former undersecretary of state).

30. See Michael W. Reisman, "Sanctions and Enforcement," edited by Cyril E. Black and Richard A. Falk in *The Future of the International Legal Order* (Princeton, Princeton University Press, 1971), pp. 330-331.

31. S. Rep. No. 169, 96th Congress, 1st Sess. 7 reprinted in 1979 US Code Cong. and Ad. News 1147.

32. Export Administration Act of 1979, App. 2404.

33. The alliance was broken as soon as the war was over. Nevertheless, it does prove that when countries of different legal and political systems have common interests – economic, military, and political – they can cooperate fairly well.

34. Export Administration Act of 1979, App. 2404.

35. Ibid., Section 2403.

36. Ibid., Section 2404.

37. Ibid.

38. Ibid., Section 2403.

39. Ibid., Section 2404.

40. Ibid., Section 2405.

41. Ibid.

42. Ibid., Section 2403.

43. From the early 1940s on, export controls have been administered by the Office of Export Administration, formerly the Office of Export Control, before that the Office of Export Supply. In 1945, the Department of Commerce was empowered to operate export control. This authority was delegated by the president to the secretary of commerce under the 1949 Export Control Act. The Commerce Department from then on created organizations and rules to carry out the act.

44. Export Administration Regulations, 15 CFR 370.10 (1980).

45. Ibid., 370.3, 379.2, 374.1, 374.2, 376.12, and 379.8.

46. Richard S. Elliott, "The Export Administration Act of 1879: Latest Statutory Resolution of the Right to Export versus National Security and Foreign Policy Controls," 19 *Columbia Journal of Transatlantic Law*, p. 270 (1881).

47. Ibid.
48. Bertsch, "US Export Controls," p. 71.
49. Executive Order No. 10945, May 24, 1961, 26 Fed. Reg. 4487 (1961).
50. Export Administration Act of 1979, App. 2409
51. Ibid.
52. Many companies have complained about the Department of Defense's conservative attitude. See 9(2) *China Business Review* 20-23 (1982).
53. Export Administration Regulations, 385.
54. See *Federal Register*, November 23, 1983, p. 53064.
55. Export Administration Regulations, 385.4.
56. Ibid., 385.2.
57. Ibid., 385.4.
58. There are currently six types of validated licenses: individual, project, distribution, qualified general, and service supply. The distribution license is available only to countries in country groups T and V, except China.
59. Export Administration Regulations, 371.1.
60. Ibid., 371.2.
61. Ibid., 386.3.
62. Ibid., 372.2.
63. Ibid.
64. Ibid., 372.6.
65. Ibid.
66. Ibid., 399.1.
67. Ibid., 379.1.
68. Ibid.
69. Ibid., 379.3.
70. Ibid., 379.4.
71. Ibid.
72. Ibid.
73. Ibid., 385.
74. Ibid.
75. Ibid.
76. Ibid.
77. *New York Times*, June 21, 1981, p. D1.
78. *Asian Wall Street Journal*, July 5, 1982.
79. Ibid.
80. Ibid.
81. "US Lowers Barriers to High Tech Sales to China," *China Daily*, June 23, 1983. The news was released by the Commerce Department itself.
82. *Asian Wall Street Journal*, July 5, 1982.
83. "Reagan Permits Chinese Access to Technology," *Asian Wall Street Journal*, June 27, 1983.
84. *China Business Review*, July-August 1983, p. 9.
85. "US Lowers Barriers to High Tech Sales."

Chapter 6 Antidumping Laws and Mushrooms under 406

> Optimal government intervention would take the form of temporary subsidies to the ailing industry to encourage the appropriate adjustment, thus allowing consumers to continue to enjoy cheap imports. For fiscal, administrative, and political reasons, however, governments often opt for increased trade barriers instead.
>
> **– John J. Barcelo III (1980)**

Dumping is a technical term that originally described an international trade practice whereby a product from one country was sold in another at a price less than that in its own country. A recent definition of dumping declares that it occurs when an exporter sells a product in another country at less than the normal value in the exporting country, as measured in the ordinary course of trade for a like product.[1] Whatever the definition, dumping is used to describe unfair international trade, which can be traced back to the days of Elizabethan England.[2] Efforts were not made to prevent dumping, however, until the 1900s.

From the beginning of this century, trade issues emerged onto the surface of relations between the United States and Europe. The United States was afraid that European countries might flood the US market with their cheap merchandise, thus hurting the US domestic industry. The Europeans could compete very successfully with US producers, for labor and raw material in the countries of Europe were comparatively cheaper than in the United States. In order to protect domestic industry, the United States began for the first time to enforce its antidumping law.[3]

After World War II, international trade became more diversified and complicated. First, Communist governments were established in several countries. This brought about changes in the economic systems in those countries. Their state-controlled economies are distinguishable from the traditional capitalist economy, which is often referred to as a "market economy." There was, and is, a fear among Western countries that these Communist countries may compete with Western domestic industry by exporting large quantities of cheap commodities. Second, the decolonization process brought the independence of many former colonies. Cheap labor and raw materials make these countries good competitors in the international market, although almost all they can offer are light industrial products, such as textiles and agricultural products, and other raw materials. Third, in addition to the state-controlled economy in Communist countries, state-owned companies have been created in Western countries. Also, all industrialized countries have full employment policies, and thus are highly sensitive to the effects of imports in dislocating domestic employment. As a result, frequent state or government interference in trade has become an inevitable international trend.

One final point is that the executive authority does not follow economists' theory in deciding antidumping or price discrimination cases. For economists, if a certain product costs less for the producer to serve country A than to serve country B, country A will be afforded the benefit of the producer's cost savings and thus will pay a lower price. Unless the exporter sells this product to country A at a lower price than that charged to country B, the exporter may be accused of discrimination against country A. Under legal theory, however, discrimination does not exist when all countries, or customers, at the same functional level are paying the same price.[4]

Facing the developing phenomena of international economic relations, the United States has made efforts to update its laws relating to foreign trade. Antidumping law is no exception. Congress enacted major changes in the antidumping and countervailing duty laws in the Trade Act of 1974 and the Trade Agreements Act of 1979.[5,6] The US antidumping statutes are concerned primarily with the protection of US industries from foreign competition without damaging the US position as a world exporter. The statutes were intended to prevent encroachment on the US domestic market by foreign countries or entities. They attempt to minimize possible retaliations by foreign governments. In addition to the increasingly protectionist nature of antidumping law, the differential treatment of products from Communist countries is another visible feature of the statutes.

This chapter will discuss the US antidumping duty laws and their implementation, including the procedures for filing a petition.

Since the same procedures and criteria are applied in countervailing duty lawsuits, and since no such cases had been brought up against a socialist country before September 1983, countervailing duty laws will not be discussed in this study. Because Section 406 of the Trade Act of 1974 is a special statute that concerns solely merchandise from Communist countries and because there is no dumping consideration in it, it will be examined in a separate part of this chapter.

INSTITUTIONAL SCHEME RELATING TO DUMPING

The Antidumping Act of 1916

Fearing the potential flood of inexpensive European products into the US market, Congress enacted Section 801 of the Revenue Act of 1916, the first antidumping law in history. Dominated by the free-trade-oriented Democratic party, Congress gave the statute the form of an unfair competition law. It was designed to prevent only predatory dumping, As a criminal statute, it makes it unlawful for any person importing any article into the United States, commonly or systematically, to sell at a price "substantially less than the actual market value or wholesale price" of such article, in the principal markets of the country of production, if the importation is done "with the intention to destroy or injure an industry in the United States, or to prevent the establishment of an industry in the United States." It is unlawful if the importation is done with the intent of restraining or monopolizing any part of the trade or commerce in such articles in the United States.[7] Any person who is injured by the importation of dumped goods can sue in district court for relief under this law. In order to win a case, the plaintiff must prove the intent of the importer, although actual injury is not required by the statute.[8] In the case of successful litigation, civil as well as criminal remedies may be granted by the court. The former include treble damages, costs, and attorney's fees, whereas the latter include a criminal fine of up to $5,000 and imprisonment of the violator for one year.[9]

Although this law is still in effect, it has been seldom used, and never successfully.[10] The most difficult problem with this statute is the proof of intent. The cost of litigation coupled with the unlikelihood of successfully proving intent may have limited the number of cases under this statute. Another reason seems to have been the adoption of the 1921 Antidumping Act, which provided more attractive methods of civil remedies.

The Antidumping Act of 1921

Five years after the enactment of the 1916 Act, Congress passed a new law, the 1921 Antidumping Act, to protect domestic industry in the United States. This was the result of post-World War I international trade and the resurgence of commercial trade with Europe. During the war, European industries were closed and exportation was impossible, for merchant ships were turned into war service. The end of the war provided Europe with opportunities to export its stockpiled goods to the United States, which was a vast market for competitive European products. The dramatic growth of international trade made the weaknesses of the 1916 Act visible. More effective efforts were evidently necessary to protect domestic industry.

The protectionist nature of the 1921 Antidumping Act was the same as that of the 1916 Act. Congress, however, has never admitted the protectionist nature of US antidumping law. In a subcommittee report, it was stated that the antidumping law was not a "protectionist statute designed to bar or restrict US imports; rather, it [was] a statute designed to free US imports from unfair price discrimination practices."[11]

There were, however, two major differences between the two statutes. First, the 1921 Act did not require willful intent of the dumper. The new legislation embodied a broad injury standard to measure the adverse impact the dumped goods might have upon domestic industries. Whenever it was found that "an industry in the United States [was] prevented from being or [was] likely to be injured, or [was] prevented from being established, by reason of the importation into the United States of a class or kind of foreign merchandise . . . [that was] being sold or [was] likely to be sold in the United States or elsewhere at less than its fair value, relief should be granted to the petitioner." The standards and methods to be used in deciding injury to a domestic industry were not specified in the statute. This left the secretary of the treasury with discretion in this decision. Once sales at less than fair value and an injury were determined, an antidumping duty could be imposed on the importation of the dumped goods.

Second, the 1921 Act transferred the administration of the law from the judicial branch to the Treasury Department in the executive branch of the government.[12] The penalty for dumping under this law was likewise a civil remedy of the imposition of high duties instead of a criminal sanction.[13]

Although the 1921 Act was more effective than its predecessor, private complainants could not receive any direct remedies, for the only sanction under the law was higher antidumping duties.

The Tariff Act of 1930

Section 337 of the Tariff Act, as amended,[14] is another relief mechanism for the domestic industry. This section makes it unlawful for anyone to use "unfair methods of competition and unfair acts in the importation of articles into the United States, or in their sale when the effect or tendency of which is to destroy or substantially injure" an effectively and economically operated domestic industry, or to prevent the establishment of such an industry, or to restrain or monopolize trade and commerce in the United States.[15]

This law authorizes the Tariff Commission [later renamed the International Trade Commission (ITC)] to administer investigations under Section 337. When a Section 337 violation is established, the commission may issue an exclusion or a cease-and-desist order.[16] Subsection (d) reads, "If the Commission determines, as a result of an investigation under this section, that there is violation of this section, it shall direct that the articles concerned, imported by any person, violating the provision of this section, be excluded from entry into the United States. . . ." Subsection (f) provides that "in lieu of taking action under subsection (d) or (e) of this section, the Commission may issue and cause to be served on any person violating this section, or believed to be violating this section, as the case may be, an order directing such person to cease and desist from engaging in the unfair methods or acts involved. . . ." In order to secure relief under the Tariff Act, the complainant must show that the practice has the tendency to injure or destroy a domestic industry or prevent the establishment of one. Unless this causation requirement is satisfied, no remedy will be granted.

During the early period of the history of the statute, the enforcement was limited to patent violations.[17]

In 1978, the ITC issued its first cease-and-desist order against a predatory pricing practice in its investigation of the Certain Welded Stainless Steel Pipe and Tube case under Section 337.[18,19] The commission ordered the manufacturer not to export the relevant goods to the United States at a price "below the reasonably anticipated marginal cost."[20] The commission's decision was finally vetoed by the president of the United States. Subsequent attempts to use Section 337 for antitrust, antidumping, or countervailing duties also proved fruitless.

The Trade Agreements Act of 1979

The Trade Agreements Act of 1979 was written to incorporate the Tokyo Round Agreements into US law.[21] The law, which came into effect on January 1, 1980, represents the most comprehensive procedural overhaul of US antidumping law in its history. Title I of the 1979 Act repealed the Antidumping Act of 1921 and amended the Tariff Act of 1930 by adding Title VII thereto.[22,23] It divides the determination of injury by the ITC into two stages: the preliminary 45 days after filing and the final determination at the end. At the same time, it defines "material injury" and requires proof of injury before antidumping duties may be imposed.[24]

Under the new law, material injury is defined as a harm that "is not inconsequential, immaterial, or unimportant." Needless to say, this definition is vague and requires refinement. The ITC is still left with a great deal of discretion in the determination of whether an injury has occurred.[25] The act, however, does require that the ITC take into account the following factors: (1) the volume of imports of the merchandise; (2) the effect of imports of that merchandise on prices in the United States for like products; and (3) the impact of imports of such merchandise on domestic producers of like products.[26] The ITC should consider if the increase of the volume of import is significant, and whether there is significant price undercutting.[27] In evaluating the impact of the import on domestic industry, all relevant economic factors are to be considered: output, sales, market share, profits, productivity, and utilization of capacity.[28] Industry is defined in the 1979 Act as "domestic producers as a whole of a like product which constitutes a major proportion of the total domestic production of that product."[29] The legislative history shows that the term "like product" should not "be interpreted in such a fashion as to prevent consideration of an industry adversely affected by the imports under investigation."[30] There are, however, three exceptions to the above general definition: (1) Domestic producers that are related to the exporters or importers, or are themselves importers of the products under investigation, are excluded in delineating the industry.[31] (2) A domestic industry may be divided into two or more regional markets and may be treated as if they were a separate industry.[32] (3) When there is a lack of sufficient data to identify the domestic production of a like product, then the effect of the import is assessed by examining the production of the narrowest group or range of products, including the like product, for which the necessary information can be secured.[33] Although the protectionist intent of the law is clear, there may be a conflict in its application. According to the above-cited committee report language, the scope of possible complainants will be expanded, while the exception clauses of the statute have the effect of narrowing the scope. The term "like product," in fact, is always double edged. When it is interpreted to enlarge the scope of complaints, the likelihood of finding injury to an industry is reduced.

The enactment of procedural changes is another accomplishment of the 1979 Act. According to the new version of the law, an antidumping investigation may be initiated by the secretary of commerce or via petition by an interested party.[34] When interested parties file a petition, they must file it concurrently with both the Commerce Department and the ITC.

The Commerce Department is required by the law to determine whether the petition proceeding alleges that a sale of an imported product at less than fair value has occurred, whether there is material injury or the threat thereof to domestic industry, or whether the importation in question has materially retarded the establishment of an industry in the United States.[35] If the determination is positive, the Commerce Department will begin an antidumping proceeding. The decision must be made within 20 days from the filing of the petition. If the Commerce decision is negative, the petition will be terminated.[36]

The ITC is charged with the determination of a reasonable indication that a domestic industry has been injured by the importation of the products under investigation. This investigation must be made within 45 days after the initiation of the investigation.[37] After the ITC determination is established, the Commerce Department will also make a preliminary determination with regard to whether there exists good reason to believe that the specified products are sold at less than fair value.[38] If the Commerce Department's determination is affirmative, the secretary of commerce must suspend the liquidation of duties on the goods imported.[39]

The secretary of commerce is required to make a final determination within 75 days after the preliminary decision is made. In case of complicated pleadings or upon request by the exporters, the period may be extended to 135 days. If the final determination by the Commerce Department is negative, however, investigations at both the Commerce Department and the ITC shall be terminated.[40]

The ITC must make its own final determination within 120 days after an affirmative preliminary determination or 45 days after an affirmative final determination by the Commerce Department. If the Commerce Department's decision is negative, then the ITC's own investigation is halted. Otherwise, a separate final decision must be made by the ITC.[41] If the determinations of the Commerce Department and the ITC are both affirmative, then the former should issue an antidumping duty order.[42] Whenever one of the final determinations is negative, the investigation is terminated.[43]

An investigation of an antidumping petition may be suspended by the Commerce Department upon receipt of an agreement from the exporter of the merchandise in question. The agreement will normally include: (1) cessation of the exports to the United States within six months after the date of the suspension; or (2) revision of the prices of the allegedly dumped products to eliminate completely any difference between the foreign market value of the merchandise and the US price of that merchandise.[44]

In addition to making preliminary and final determinations, the Commerce Department reviews orders annually and the ITC does so upon request.[45]

Under the present law, administrative decisions can be reviewed by the judiciary. The initial forum for judicial review is the Court of International Trade with subsequent recourse to the Court of Customs and Patent Appeals.[46,47] Interested parties to an antidumping investigation may file a summons and complaint with the court, if they do not agree with the decision of either the Commerce Department or the ITC. The jurisdiction of the court is broad. It may review the decision to initiate an investigation and the preliminary and final determinations made by administrative agencies, whether these be positive or negative.

DETERMINATIONS OF AGENCIES

Fair Value

In determining whether certain imported merchandise is sold at less than fair value, the Commerce Department must define what the fair value is. The law does not define the term. It has been, however, deemed an "intelligible principle"[48] or an "estimate of foreign market value."[49] In fact, this fair value concept is a comparison between the price of a good in the US market and in a foreign market. As far as the US market is concerned, the antidumping statute is concerned with the purchase price and the exporter's sales price.[50,51] It is not difficult to apply the law universally when the merchandise is sold to an unrelated purchaser in the United States. Nevertheless, in complex situations, the Commerce Department has to set up its own standard in deciding US prices. For instance, when an exporter has a subsidiary in the United States, or is a subsidiary of the importer, the price may be set up artificially, regardless of the actual costs. To complicate the case, an exporter may in fact sell merchandise to both related and unrelated parties. In such a situation, the Commerce Department normally regards the price from the foreign manufacturer to the unrelated trading partner as a reliable price, for there is less incentive for a trading company to sell merchandise below its own cost of acquisition and marketing.[52] Thus, the determination of whether a party is related or not is critical to the determination of price.

More complex circumstances may occur; for example, the related or unrelated purchaser in the United States may further process the item before selling. In such a case, the law states that the increased value of merchandise must be deducted from the exporter's sale price.[53] In other words, the fair value in the US market would reflect the home market price for export to the United States plus the cost of all containers and coverings as well as packing costs.[54]

Foreign Market Value

Foreign market value is usually considered to be the home market price. It is the price at which the imported merchandise or similar product is sold or offered for sale in the principal market of the home country, in the usual wholesale quantities and in the ordinary course of trade for home consumption.[55] Nevertheless, in certain cases, a home market price cannot be ascertained; for instance, when the home market is too small, or the quantity of the sale of the merchandise is too small to be sufficient basis determining the home market price. In other situations, the product may not be sold in the home market at all or at a price below cost. Anticipating these problems, the statute provides that in these and other situations, administrative agencies should resort to the price of the item in a third country or construct a price.[56]

Whenever possible, the Commerce Department should make reference to the price of such or similar merchandise sold to a third country, which is exported to the United States. Unless adequate information is not available or cannot be verified by the department, this third country method should be the preferred method by which fair value is determined.[57] In fact, this method is similar to that of the home market value, for both focus on the price at market.

Constructed Value

Concerning the determination of constructed value, the statute provides that

> the constructed value of imported merchandise shall be the sum of (A) the cost of materials. . . and of fabrication or other processing of any kind employed in producing such or similar merchandise. . . which would ordinarily permit the production of that particular merchandise in the ordinary course of business; (B) an amount for general expenses and profit equal to that usually reflected in sales of merchandise of the same class or kind as the merchandise under consideration which are made by producers in the country of exportation, in the usual wholesale quantities and in the ordinary course of trade, except (i) the amount for general expenses shall not be less than 10 percent of the cost as defined in subparagraph (A), and (ii) the amount for profit shall not be less than 8 percent of the sum of such general expenses and cost; and (C) the cost of all containers and coverings of whatever nature, and all other expenses incidental to placing the merchandise under consideration in condition, packed ready for shipment to the United States.[58]

In practice, however, this definition does not help very much to clarify the matter.

The determination of the time period for calculating costs is equally important. A study shows that, in their history, the Treasury and Commerce Departments have usually collected cost data for an annual period, generally the accounting period of the company under investigation.[59]

The purpose of adopting the constructed value concept is clear, whatever administrative difficulties the statute may carry. In its report on the 1974 amendment of adding the new Subsection (b) (constructed value) to Section 205, the Senate Finance Committee stated that "the Committee is concerned that, in the absence of such a provision, sales uniformly made at less than cost of production could escape the purview of the Act, and thereby cause injury to United States industry with impunity."[60]

Nonmarket Fair Value

Despite the evolution of the international economic structure and the increasing interdependence of the international community, the basic principle of antidumping law has remained unchanged. Western countries treat the pricing and costs of only the market economy as valid, while disregarding those of a state-controlled or centrally planned economy. In other words, Western countries accept only market-determined prices as valid costs, while they refuse to recognize costs defined in some other way. In the context of market prices, there is believed to be a constraint of some kind. "There is a game that a producer has to play, against market forces he cannot control. He can win or he can lose."[61]

Neither home market value nor constructed value is applicable to merchandise from Communist countries. The theory behind this nonapplication is that in market economies, "production costs reflect price competition between suppliers," and "merchandise prices are set in the market place,"[62] whereas prices in state-controlled economies or nonmarket countries are determined artificially without regarding market forces, and therefore home market prices and costs are not indicators of "fair value."

In order to deal with the situation, Congress in the Trade Act of 1974 added a new Subsection (c) to Section 205 of the 1921 Act.[63] This amendment codified the Treasury's previous practice of disregarding home market or third country prices of products from state-controlled economy countries in antidumping cases.[64] Prices of the same or similar merchandise manufactured in a market economy have been adopted as prices of merchandise from a state-controlled economy country. The reasoning for the substituted value test was derived from the theory mentioned earlier. The Senate Finance Committee stated, "The Committee is concerned that the technical rules contained in the Act are insufficient to counteract dumping from state-controlled-economy countries where the supply and demand forces do not operate to produce prices, either in the home market or in third countries, which can be relied upon for comparison purposes."[65] So the statute, as amended, was "designed to continue, and, in fact, improve, the effective and vigorous enforcement of this antiprice discrimination statute."[66]

Right after the adoption of the Trade Act of 1974, the Treasury Department had the opportunity to apply the new law in deciding the famous case of Polish Golf Cars.[67] Since Poland was considered a state-controlled economy country for that product, Pezetel's home market and third country prices were both disregarded as fair value in the case. During the investigatory phase of the proceedings, the fair value of the Polish golf cars was based on the price of a golf car produced in Canada by Marathon, Ltd.[68] After various adjustments were made to the Marathon price, Pezetel was found to be selling its golf cars at less than fair value.[69] The Pezetel case revealed the insufficiency of Treasury regulations concerning dumping by non-market countries;[70] that is, simple price comparison was not sufficient in deciding actual cases.

Having realized the problem, the Administering Authority made modifications to Section 153.7 of the Customs Regulations in 1978. This section provides that the prices of merchandise from state-controlled economy countries "should be determined, to the extent possible, from the prices or costs in a non-state-controlled economy country or countries at a stage of economic development comparable to the state-controlled economy country from which the merchandise is exported."[71] This provision has virtually excluded the use of home market prices of merchandise manufactured in a state-controlled economy country. The traditional price-to-price comparison was therefore abolished with regard to merchandise from state-controlled economy countries, except in cases in which the Commerce Department determines that the market economy where the merchandise is produced is comparable in terms of economic development with the state-controlled economy. If such or similar merchandise is not produced in a non-state-controlled economy country of comparable economic development, a constructed value of the merchandise shall be conducted by the Commerce Department.[72] This value should be based on the cost of production in a market economy country where such merchandise is produced. If no such market economy country, which is comparable in terms of economic development with the state-controlled economy country, exists, the constructed value should be based on the "costs of specific objective components or factors of production incurred in producing the merchandise in question," such as hours of labor required, quantity of raw materials employed, amount of energy consumed, and so on.[73]

The key issue of this provision seems to be how to determine "comparable economic development." Generally speaking, GNP per capita is considered to be the primary criterion in determining a country's stage of economic development. A different result may come about, however, when one uses different factors in the determination.[74] Even in cases where the determination of comparable economic development is made without difficulty, the determination of value may not be without problems. In determining the value, reference must be made to information from the industries of countries other than the state-controlled economy country whose merchandise is under investigation. Since those foreign industries are likely to be competitors of the state-controlled industry in question, there are few, if any, incentives for them to provide accurate data. Not surprisingly, the wisdom of this comparable development concept has been questioned.[75]

Causation Requirement

The ITC enjoys considerable discretion in its determination of the causal linkage between import and injury. The antidumping law does not require the injury to the domestic industry to be attributable solely to the allegedly dumped import. Congress has upheld the prior standard that the importation of the dumped goods need only be an identifiable cause of the injury. If a more stringent causation requirement were enacted, domestic industry would find it difficult to secure relief for injury.

This loose causation requirement has caused suspicion. Bruce A. Ortwine expressed great doubt about the criteria employed. He said, "Therefore, when a domestic industry is facing a slump in sales or loses because of domestic phenomena, whether a prolonged strike, outdated or otherwise inefficient plant and machinery, poor management, or changing consumer preferences, it is nonetheless possible for the additional presence of dumped imports to be considered a sufficient causal link for the Commission to make an affirmative determination."[76]

ESCAPE CLAUSE

The Escape Clause Law, which refers to Sections 201-203 of the Trade Act of 1974,[77] enacted by Congress in 1974, provides controls over the imports of merchandise from foreign countries. This law, which is free of the complex procedural and calculation problems of antidumping law, does not deal with the unfair value of imported goods. It is instead concerned with fair competition, which may cause injury to domestic industries. The advantage of this law is that it does not require foreign data. Its disadvantage seems to be that "if the test for response (e.g., for import restraints) is soft or easy to find, this approach will protect domestic industry from helpful foreign competition even when that foreign competition is achieved by the same market-oriented economic systems as in the United States."[78]

A proceeding under the escape clause may be commended upon petition "by an entity . . . which is representative of an industry,"[79] "upon the request of the President or the United States Trade Representatives, upon resolution of either the Committee on Ways and Means of the House of Representatives or the Committee on Finance of the Senate . . ." or upon the initiative of the ITC.[80]

The ITC is empowered to conduct fact finding and make recommendations to the president. These are supposed to be completed within a six-month period starting from the date the petition is filed.[81] Upon ITC recommendation, the president of the United States is to make a final decision.

The ITC Investigation

Section 201(b)(1) of the Trade Act of 1974 provides that the ITC, upon petition or request, "shall determine whether an article is being imported into the United States in such increased quantities as to be a substantial cause of serious injury, or the threat thereof, to the domestic industry producing an article like or directly competitive with the imported article."[82] The first issue frequently encountered by the commission is what constitutes "an article like or directly competitive." The Senate Finance Committee Report on the Trade Act of 1974 stated that "the terms 'like' [and] 'directly competitive' used . . . in this bill are not to be regarded as synonymous or explanatory of each other, but rather to distinguish between 'like' articles and articles which although not 'like', are nevertheless 'directly competitive'. . . . In such context, 'like' articles are those which are substantially identical in inherent or intrinsic characteristics . . . and 'directly competitive' articles are those which, although not substantially equivalent for commercial purposes, that is, are adapted to the same uses and are essentially interchangeable therefore."[83] Despite congressional guidance, the determination is in fact largely at the discretion of the ITC.

Relief requires the satisfaction of three tests: an increase of imports; a serious injury or a threat thereof to the domestic industry that produces like or directly competitive merchandise; and a showing that the increased imports are the substantial cause of the injury. In practice, the ITC has considerable discretion in its determination of escape clause cases.

In order to grant relief, the ITC must find that there exists serious injury or a threat thereof to a domestic industry. The statute does not define the term "serious injury" or "the threat thereof." Nevertheless, it directs the ITC to take into account all factors that it considers relevant, including the significant number of firms that operate at a reasonable level of profit, and significant unemployment or underemployment within the industry. Over the years, the ITC has defined the term one way or the other in its determinations. As one of the commissioners once stated, "Over the years since 1962 a number of Commissioners have established or accepted the definition of 'serious injury' to be 'an important, crippling, or mortal injury; one having permanent or lasting consequences'. Such injuries are to be distinguished from the less important and temporary injuries which domestic concerns are expected to absorb without Government assistance."[84] In the same manner, Commissioner Leonard described "serious injury" as a "damage or a hurt of grave or important proportions." He further maintained that the threat of serious injury occurs "when serious injury, although not yet existing, is imminent."[85]

The "substantial cause" is further defined by the law as "a cause which is important and not less than any other cause."[86] When reaching a conclusion, the ITC should take into account "all economic factors which it considers relevant . . . with respect to substantial cause and increase in imports (either actual or relative to domestic production) and a decline in the proportion of the domestic market supplied by the domestic producer."[87] The legislative history shows that a two-part test must be met in order to determine the existence of a substantial cause. In other words, the increased imports must be both an important cause of the serious injury and one that is not less important than any other single cause.[88] According to ITC practice, when a cause of injury is found to be more important than the increase of imports, the latter should not be regarded as a substantial cause. In the Wrapper Tobacco case, the ITC found that the decrease of domestic production and the reduction of large cigars were more important than the increased imports in the injury to this domestic industry. Therefore a negative determination was made.[89]

Presidential Determination

As mentioned earlier, upon receiving a report from the ITC regarding findings, the president must come to a decision within 60 days.[90] Owing to the complex nature of commercial activities today, the president is unable to make an effective decision in the national interest without the advice of experts. As a result, Congress and the president have established an interagency committee to assist in the decision making.[91]

The interagency structure is composed of three committees, namely, the Trade Policy Committee, the Trade Policy Review Group, and the Trade Policy Staff Committee. The Trade Policy Committee is a cabinet-level committee chaired by the US Trade Representative. It "usually becomes directly and actively involved in escape clause proceedings only when foreign and domestic political considerations have been raised to such a level that subcabinet officials or the professional trade staff bureaucracy are unable to reach consensus."[92] The Trade Policy Review Group is a sub-cabinet-level organization that is responsible for somewhat less significant issues. The Trade Policy Staff Committee is essentially for the day-to-day work. It is composed of experts from various agencies. They are the people who assess and evaluate different factors relating to the issue, including the ITC findings.

Indispensable assistance for the president also comes from the White House Office. Officials from the office frequently review interagency advice and give the president their own comments. At the same time, White House officials influence the decision making of the Commerce Department and other governmental agencies by personal contacts.

Congressional Review

The president can decide to provide relief, such as the increase of the ad valorem rate of customs duties on imports of the products in question or the setting up of quantitative restrictions or a tariff-rate quota.[93] At the same time, the president may decide to deny relief or to take a position different from that of the ITC. When it is decided that the relief proposed is not in the national interest, an ITC decision may be vetoed. President Carter's veto in the case of Certain Stainless Steel Flatware gave the following reasons as the basis of the denial of relief:[94] (1) The dominant US firm would remain profitable without import relief. (2) A tariff rate quota benefiting the domestic industry had been in effect for 13 of the previous 20 years, so any further extension would be inconsistent with the temporary nature of import relief. (3) Import relief would increase the cost to consumers, adversely affect demand, and discriminate against low-income purchasers. (4) Domestic production in the affected industry was on the upswing and employment losses had been small.[95]

Once the president decides not to provide relief, this decision can be overridden only by a concurrent resolution of both the House and the Senate "disapproving the action by the President or his determination not to provide import relief."[96] In practice, Congress has never overridden a decision of the president regarding this sort of matter.

CHINESE MUSHROOMS UNDER SECTION 406

Over the last few years, mushrooms have become an issue in US foreign trade relations with China. While a few petitions have been brought against mushrooms before the agencies concerned with foreign trade,[97] the petition against Chinese mushrooms was the first one under Section 406 of the Trade Act of 1974. The American Mushroom Institute of Kennett Square, Pennsylvania, on behalf of 16 domestic mushroom canners, filed a petition with the ITC on June 30, 1982, alleging that the canned mushrooms imported from the People's Republic of China had caused "market disruption" in the United States within the meaning of Section 406 of the Trade Act of 1974.

Scope of the Statute

Although the procedure of petition under Section 406 is the same as that under Section 201,[98] Section 406 was enacted for different purposes. It requires the ITC, upon petition or request, to "promptly make an investigation to determine, with respect to imports of an article which is the product of a Communist country, whether market disruption exists with respect to an article produced by a domestic industry."[99] It further provides that "market disruption exists within a domestic industry whenever imports of an article like or directly competitive with an article produced by such domestic industry, are increasing rapidly, either absolutely or relatively, so as to be a significant cause of material injury, or threat thereof, to such domestic industry."[100]

When introducing the bill (Section 406), the Senate Committee reported:

> However, the market disruption test is intended to be more easily met than the serious injury test in section 201. While section 201(b) would require that increased imports of the article be a "substantial cause" of the requisite injury, or the threat thereof, to a domestic industry, section 406 would require that the article is being, or is likely to be, imported in such increased quantities as to be a "significant cause" of material injury, or the threat thereof. The term "significant cause" is intended to be an easier standard to satisfy than that of "substantial cause." On the other hand, "significant cause" is meant to require a more direct cause relationship between increased imports and injury than the standard used in the case of worker, firm, and community adjustment assistance, i.e., "contribute importantly." In addition, the term "material injury" in section 406 is intended to request a lesser degree of injury than the "serious injury" standard employed in section 201.[101]

The purpose of the statute is to impose restrictions on imports from Communist countries, regarding market disruption. In determining the existence of market disruption, the ITC should be sure that it "occurred during a recent period of time . . . taking into account any historical trade levels which may have existed."[102]

The reason behind the enactment of the statute, revealed by the Senate Finance Committee, is that Congress "recognizes that a Communist country, through control of the distribution process and the price at which articles are sold, could disrupt the domestic markets of its trading partners and thereby injure producers in those countries. In particular, exports from Communist countries could be directed so as to flood domestic markets within a shorter time period than could occur under free market condition[s] . . . . In the face of such imports, traditional unfair trade remedies, such as under the Antidumping Act, have proved inappropriate or ineffective because of the difficulty of their application to products from state-controlled economies."[103]

Whatever the theoretical reasoning of the statute, it is applicable solely to imports from Communist countries. The same criteria for Section 201 cases are used in granting relief, except instead of requiring a "substantial cause," this statute requires that the importation of the products have a "significant cause of material injury" – a lower standard.

Rapidly Increasing Imports of Chinese Mushrooms

The production of canned mushrooms in China dates back many years. Fresh mushrooms are grown throughout the country. The oldest firms currently engaged in canning mushrooms began production in 1908, whereas the newest ones started their operation in 1974. The majority of the firms, however, started after 1956.[104] China's production of canned mushrooms accounted for about 36 percent of the world trade in the product in 1980, whereas it constituted 18 percent in 1978.[105] At the same time, China ships fresh mushrooms to Hong Kong and Macao for canning. If this kind of trade is included, China's share of the world canned mushroom trade in 1980 would have been 46 percent.[106]

Despite the fact that China is a substantial world supplier of canned mushrooms, its share in US imports was less than 1 percent before the year 1980, when China secured the MFN status.[107] Prior to this, imports of canned mushrooms from China were dutiable at the rate of 10 cents per pound plus 45 percent ad valorem. Since February 1980 (when the MFN treatment began), imports have been dutiable at the rate of 3.2 cents per pound plus 10 percent ad valorem.[108] In 1981, imports of canned mushrooms increased to 27.4 million pounds, valued at $23.0 million, from 14.8 million pounds, valued at $13.5 million, in the previous year.

The increase of China's imports was 85 percent over that of the previous year.[109] The findings of the ITC show that the increase in canned mushroom imports from China occurred concurrently with a decrease in imports from other foreign sources, with total imports declining in 1981.[110] Imports from China, however, constituted 31 percent of the canned mushrooms imported by the United States in 1981.[111] The imports from China rose to 15.5 million pounds in January-June 1982 from 9.4 million pounds in January-June 1981.[112]

The ratio of imports from China to domestic production increased from 0.3 percent in 1979 to 13.3 percent in 1980.[113] In 1981, this ratio was increased to 25.8 percent, whereas it was up to 33.3 percent in January-June 1982.[114] The ratio of imports from China to domestic canned mushroom consumption accordingly represented an increase in this period. It rose from less than 1 percent in 1979 to 6.8 percent in 1980, then to 15.6 percent in 1981, and finally to 16 percent in 1982.[115]

Based upon the above findings, the ITC concluded that there existed a rapidly increasing import of an article from the Communist country of China, both in terms of absolute and relative increase.

The China National Cereals, Oil, and Foodstuffs Import and Export Corporation (CEROILS), the respondent, nevertheless argued that "in order for market disruption to exist, overall imports of the article involved must be 'increasing rapidly, either absolutely or relatively'."[116] CEROILS contended that since China was not a factor in the US market before 1980, and since there was no increase in total imports, market disruption should not be assumed to exist; and that if the statute were interpreted in such a manner, it would have the effect of protecting foreign exporters who were not to be protected by the law. To back up its argument, it invoked the legislative history in which the Conference Committee "made clear that only domestic industries, and not foreign suppliers, were to be protected by the measure."[117] The Conference Committee stated that the Senate had made a number of substantial revisions to the House bill, and that "the Conferees understand that foreign entities would not be eligible to petition for relief under either section 201 or section 406."[118]

Nevertheless, in rejecting CEROILS' view, Commissioners Eugene Frank and Veronica Haggart stated that "section 406 is to be utilized only where market disruption exists with respect to imports from a Communist country."[119] They concluded that as long as exportation from a Communist country was increasing rapidly, market disruption might be assumed without regard to the total imports by the United States from all foreign sources. It seems that they are "particularly concerned about the ability of Communist countries to direct their exports so as to flood domestic markets within a shorter time period than could occur under free market conditions."[120] Both commissioners agreed with CEROILS' opinion that Congress assumed, when adopting the Trade Act of 1974, that imports from Communist countries would increase. They nevertheless believed that the import from China increased rapidly and had met the statutory requirement.

Significant Cause of Material Injury

The ITC was split on the issue of significant cause of material injury. Commissioners Eugene Frank and Veronica Haggart found that there was a link between the import of mushrooms from China and the difficulties suffered by the domestic industry. Chairperson Alfred Eckes and Commissioner Paula Stern, however, determined that although it seemed that there was suffering on the part of the domestic industry, the imports from China were not the significant cause.[121]

The ITC investigation concluded that domestic and imported canned mushrooms were "like" products and acknowledged that fresh mushrooms were "directly competitive" with the imported canned and other processed mushrooms. It determined that "the domestic industry is comprised of the US facilities canning mushrooms."[122] CEROILS, however, contended that the domestic industry included "sellers in both the fresh and canned markets."[123] The CEROILS' approach seems more consistent with the White House Task Force report which concluded the "mushroom industry [is] a single entity including both fresh and processed mushrooms. . . ."[124]

Frank and Haggart believed that the decline of the industry's capacity utilization and the net sale of canned mushrooms in the first half of 1982 represented material injury suffered by the domestic industry.[125] The irregular decline of the number of persons involved in mushroom canning operations presented, they stated, further evidence of material injury.[126] The linkage of the above injuries and the imports of Chinese mushrooms, Frank and Haggart concluded, was that "imports of low-priced canned mushrooms from China have underpriced and thus displaced the 'more traditional suppliers', whose exports to the US market cause the serious injury which the President is trying to remedy."[127] The logic of their conclusion is that domestic canners have been forced to "cut prices in order to maintain their market share," when competing with low-priced mushrooms from China.[128]

On the other hand, Eckes and Stern concluded that "although canned mushroom production declined in 1981 . . . it was unusually high in 1980."[129] They determined that domestic production increased in 1981 despite the imports from China increasing rapidly.[130] "Although domestic production decreased in the first half of 1982," they concluded, "domestic producers' sales increased."[131] They attributed the capacity utilization decline primarily to an "increase in domestic industry capacity."[132] Both Eckes and Stern found that "it was the increase in productivity, rather than import competition, which caused employment to decline slightly."[133]

With regard to the low profit margins of the domestic industry, Eckes and Stern found that China's exports were not a significant cause, for "when US canners' profit margins improved most significantly (1982), import from China gained their share of apparent US consumption."[134] The counsel for CEROILS argued vigorously about this issue. Part of his argument was that the decline of the profit margins was due to recalls of domestic products and indictments for health violations.[135]

Finally, Eckes and Stern concluded that the increase in imports from China appeared to be "largely at the expense of other foreign sources rather than US canners."[136] The effect of this finding is that since the total import of canned mushrooms has declined, a relaxation of the "serious injury" to the domestic industry the president worried most about in 1980 may exist.[137]

Threat of Material Injury

In addition to their finding of no significant cause of material injury, Eckes and Stern also found that there existed no significant cause of the threat of material injury. Following the Senate Finance Committee report that the threat of injury exists when injury, "although not yet existing, is clearly imminent if import trends continued unabated," they determined that "information available to the Commission does not indicate that imports of canned mushrooms from China are a significant cause of the threat of material injury."[138]

Analysis of the threat of material injury is twofold. On the one hand, in determining the threat, the capacity of production of domestic industry should be examined. On the other, the ability of the foreign exporter is also a decisive factor. The Eckes and Stern opinion seems to follow this analytical pattern. It first determined that although China's share of the US market grew rapidly, the US domestic industry had "either maintained or improved its performance."[139]

Examining China's production capacity, the commission found that production increased from 1979 to 1980 and 1981, but declined by 13 percent in 1981. China's exports of canned mushrooms increased in the successive years of 1979, 1980, and 1981, but the rate of increase declined significantly in 1981. Therefore, the commission decided that it was unlikely that "the trends of the last 3 years [would] continue unabated."[140]

The commission's analysis was apparently based on the facts submitted by China. Counsel for CEROILS carefully analyzed the economic limitations on increasing canning facilities in China.[141] Counsel argued that after the imposition of a quota on China's exports of canned mushrooms in 1981, the European Economic Community (EEC) invited CEROILS to increase its 1981 canned mushroom exports to the EEC by 2,000 to 3,000 metric tons in addition to the 25,000 metric tons already allocated to the country.[142] Nevertheless, owing to its limited capacity, China did not increase its export to the EEC. Accordingly, the counsel said that there would "be no significant increase in canned mushroom production in the next three years."[143]

Relief

Since the commission was equally divided with regard to the significant cause of material injury of the imports from China, the remedies recommended were different. While Eckes and Stern preferred not to recommend any relief for the domestic industry, Frank and Haggart advised the president to impose a quota of 21 million pounds per year for a three-year period. Anticipating that the proposed quota on imports from China would create opportunities for other foreign suppliers, they believed that the "general price level of imports [was] expected to increase as a result of the quota."[144]

The president, upon receiving the commission report, decided that the imports of canned mushrooms from China did not disrupt the domestic market and that therefore additional restrictions would not be imposed on the imports from China.[145]

Appraisal

Section 406 is discriminatory in nature regarding imports from Communist countries. It sets a lesser standard for domestic industries to secure relief against imports from these countries. But the statute fails to answer some important questions. For instance, when deciding about an import "increasing rapidly," shouldn't the administrative agencies take into consideration the exporter's starting point? In the Chinese mushroom case, as in other cases, China was a late- and newcomer to the US market. China's export of mushrooms to the United States was almost zero before 1980. At the same time, it produced about 46 percent of the total world production of canned mushrooms. Under such circumstances, the increase must have been rapid, because it started from zero. The statute also fails to take into account a country's share of a product in world trade. It seems that it would be fair for a larger producer to have a larger share in the US market. The statute does not mention whether a foreign producer can increase its exports to the United States at the expense of foreign rather than US domestic producers.

As a practical matter, Section 406 is vulnerable to political pressures and is subject to administrative discretion. Usually, while filing a petition, the domestic industry, often through lobbies, pressures the government. It may go directly to the executive agencies handling the case; it may at the same time go to Congress. Since congressional support is very important to the executive branch's actions, the president must treat Congress members' reactions very seriously when deciding the case. Other administrative agencies may face the same question, for congressional support is also crucial for the operation of their functions. In this regard, domestic industries seem to have quite a lot to rely on. The only resort foreign producers may have is diplomatic pressure, which has proved not very effective. Also, domestic industries have better sources of information concerning related factors of a case. Foreign producers may not even know the definition of a certain term in the statute, for it may be entirely subject to administrative interpretation. For example, whether canned mushrooms constituted an industry or both canned and fresh mushrooms belonged to the same industry in the Chinese mushroom case was a mystery to the Chinese.

The Chinese mushroom case was not decided under much political pressure, for the mushroom industry in the United States is comparatively small. It does not have a strong voice in Congress. Thus, both the administrative agencies, such as ITC, and the president could have a free hand to make decisions.

EFFORTS TO REFORM TRADE LAW

Currently, efforts are being made to reform US foreign trade laws. The feeling is that the remedy under present laws is too unpredictable because of the many political pressures to offer domestic industries any protection.

The proposed reform (The proposed bill was numbered S. 1351) would amend Title VII of the Tariff Act of 1930, as amended by the

Trade Agreements Act of 1979. Under S. 1351, an interested party could file a complaint against a "nonmarket economy" producer alleging artificial pricing. Procedures and time limits for the investigation would be the same as in a countervailing or antidumping investigation. In other words, it works as a parallel mechanism to normal countervailing or antidumping measures presently under Title VII. Although there were no countervailing duty cases against nonmarket economy countries before September 1983, S. 1351 is trying to deal with nonmarket economy producers in the context of both antidumping and countervailing duty lawsuits.

The Commerce Department is responsible for soliciting information from the "nonmarket economy" concerned. If the department believes that sufficient, verifiable information is provided to permit the case to be treated as a normal antidumping or countervailing duty case, the department has the power to do so, moving the investigation to the appropriate track at the same time. In such a case, an injury test would be applied if the nonmarket economy country in question had signed the relevant code,[146] that is, the GATT.

In cases where the nonmarket economy will not or cannot provide the necessary information, a different standard is employed. Under this standard, if a nonmarket producer sells a product at a price lower than the lowest average price of free market producers in the United States, this product is considered to be sold at an artificial price, and therefore a countervailing or antidumping duty must be imposed.

Although the concept of the "lowest average price" is new, S. 1351 does follow certain patterns of the existing laws, such as the differential treatment of "nonmarket economy" countries. It distinguishes nonmarket economy countries from other countries by applying a different standard. Under S. 1351, as Frank C. Conahan, director of the international division of the General Accounting Office, pointed out, "even when nonmarket economy enterprises' actual prices or costs are used in a dumping investigation, that investigation will not require a test of injury to domestic industry unless the nonmarket economy in question is a party to the Agreement on Implementation of Article VI of the GATT (relating to antidumping measures). This is not consistent with the way other countries are treated. Market economy countries receive an injury test whether or not they are signatories of the Antidumping Code. . . . This change could encourage the initiation of investigations involving products from nonmarket countries and adversely affect trade with countries with which the United States wishes to trade for economic and foreign policy reasons."[147] In fact, S. 1351 is designed to be another relief for US domestic industries. When dealing with nonmarket economies, the industries can either use section 406 of the Trade Act of 1974, if they believe that executive support may be secured, or file a petition under S. 1351, which is exclusive of executive interference.

The logic of S. 1351 is that any nonmarket economy product that is the subject of an investigation would be considered unfairly priced if priced below the lowest average price of equivalent market economy products. The difficulty, however, is how the Commerce Department is going to know "what the lowest average price is."[148] It is more difficult for a nonmarket exporter to find out the lowest average price of a certain manufactured product in the free market in order to avoid potential dumping, taking into consideration the fixed price system of nonmarket economies and the frequently changing prices in US markets. Especially when the nonmarket economy producer in question is from a country far away from the United States and with an inefficient information system, it may take forever to find out the lowest average price before selling the product.

This "lowest free market price" is by definition the lowest "fair value," so that a lower price from a nonmarket economy is defined as artificial. "That is not logical," commented Sholom D. Comay. "A more efficient producer of light bulbs, say, in Hungary, may well offer those items fairly at a lower price than less efficient producers in a market economy. In such a case, it is the 'lowest free market price' which would, in global terms, be artificial."[149] Of course, one may argue that there is no way to measure efficiency in nonmarket economies. This argument does not carry much force, because in every economic system, the rule of cost and benefit plays an important role, No one could afford to sell a product continuously in the international markets at a price lower than the actual cost.

It is difficult today to categorize an economic system one way or the other. In the traditional market economy countries, government intervention into economic activities has become more frequent than ever before. It affects marketing and production within and without the country. Changes have taken place in state-controlled economy countries, too. For instance, today, there are in China state-owned and -run entities, collectively owned companies, joint ventures, and foreign and Chinese privately owned entities. Neither the traditional approach of the state-control formula nor the one proposed by S. 1351 seems sufficient to determine which or to what extent an economy is state controlled.

One possible way to deal with imports from so-called nonmarket economies is to use the injury test for all countries without the distinction of GATT members. In other words, unless a domestic industry concerned is injured, no duty should be imposed on the merchandise in question. In case injuries are determined, the dumping margin can be measured by the lowest average price in the United States.

An injury test is essential for the concept of free trade and effective competition. Without the injury test, the US domestic industries may well undersell their competitors from nonmarket economy countries, for imported products from the latter will have to be priced above their own. It would at the same time "prevent American industry and consumers from obtaining the lowest priced merchandise on the world market even when the importation of that merchandise would not cause or threaten [to cause] injury to any domestic interests."[150] It is also inconsistent with the GATT obligations that are applicable to the United States, for the GATT itself requires that an injury test be provided to all GATT members in antidumping cases.

If this noninjury test were enacted, it would have a significant effect on trade relations between the United States and nonmarket economy countries. All merchandise from nonmarket economy countries would be under the strict scrutiny of the operation of law, despite the fact that some countries, for instance, China, are enjoying the MFN treatment in the United States. In addition, numerous antidumping cases would arise. Harry Kopp, deputy assistant secretary of state, having suggested to keep the injury test, stated: "An injury test will minimize the number of determinations which must be made by those administering a new law in this area, enhancing the predictability and speed of each case."[151]

Upon the above analysis, one may conclude that the US antidumping laws are protective in general and discriminatory against imports from nonmarket economy countries in particular. The discrimination is reflected in the adoption of Section 406 and the nonrecognition of the pricing systems of nonmarket economies. In practice, these laws offer quite adequate relief to domestic industries. Especially the establishment of the ITC has provided domestic industries with good opportunity for remedies. The ITC decisions are usually not vetoed by the president, although the veto power has been used in some cases. In addition, despite the fact that the president is given great discretion in deciding trade disputes involving foreign countries, in effect, domestic politics are always taken seriously into consideration when using this power.

While making efforts to amend current laws, the proposed amendment should not contain any discriminatory provisions against Communist countries. Instead, it should recognize the pricing systems of those nonmarket economies that have a mixed economic system, such as China. Also, GATT members should be treated equally, regardless of whether they are market or nonmarket economies. It may serve as an encouragement to bring all countries into the international economic system. The basic principle in antidumping and countervailing duty cases should be an injury test. Without a genuine injury test, neither foreign exporters nor domestic consumers benefit. It is also inconsistent with the notion of free trade, a policy that the US government officially supports.

NOTES

1. See Agreement on Implementation of Article Six of the General Agreement on Tariffs and Trade, Article 2(a), 19 USC 4348, TIAS No. 6431, 32 *Federal Register* 14,962 (1967).
2. J. Viner, *Dumping: A Problem in International Trade* (Chicago, The University of Chicago Press, 1923), pp. 374-375.
3. The Revenue Act of 1916, which was designed to prevent predatory European cartels from destroying small US competitors, was enacted in 1916 [15 USC Section 72 (1976)]. The statute was proved ineffective and was supplemented by the Antidumping Act of 1921 [Ch. 14, Section 201, 42 Stat. 11 (repealed 1979), new version 19 USC Section 1673 (Supp. III, 1979)].
4. See FTC v. Anheuser-Busch, Inc., 363 US 536, 549 (1960).
5. Public Law No. 96-618, Section 301, 88 Stat., 1978 [codified as amended 19 USC Section 2411 (Supp. III, 1979)].
6. Public Law No. 96-39, 93 Stat. 144 (1979).
7. The Antidumping Act of 1916 in the Revenue Act of 1916, Public Law No. 64-271, Section 801, 39 Stat. 798.
8. Ibid.
9. Ibid.
10. The federal government has never brought a 1916 Antidumping Act lawsuit. Even private actions have been rare. See A. Paul Victor, "United States Antidumping Rules," 10 *St. Mary's Law Journal* 216, 218 (1978).
11. S. Rep. No. 93-1298, 93rd Congress, 2nd Sess. 179, reprinted (1974) US Code Cong. & Ad. News 7186, 7317.
12. The secretary of the treasury was empowered to decide whether dumping existed and an injury thereof occurred or not.
13. Under the Customs Simplification Act of 1954, the function of determining the injurious impact on the US domestic industry was transferred to the US Tariff Commission, which was renamed, in 1974, the International Trade Commission [Chs. 12 and 13, Section 302, 68 Stat. 1138 (repealed 1979)].
14. Tariff Act of 1930, Ch. 497, Section 337, 46 Stat. 590 [codified as amended at 19 USC Section 1337 (1976 and Supp. III, 1979)].

15. Ibid.

16. 19 USC Section 1337 (1976). In 1969, the president for the first time in history issued an exclusion order on the recommendation of the Tariff Commission. See Furazolidore Inv. No. 337-21, TC Pub. 299 (November 1969).

17. Even at present, patent violations are still the main use of the law. For instance, Thermometer Sheath Packages, Inv. No. 337-TA-56, USITC, Pub. No. 992 (July 1979); Solder Removal Wicks, Inv. No. 337-TA-26, USITC, Pub. No. 823 (July 1977); and Above Ground Swimming Pools, Inv. No. 337-TA-25, USITC, Pub. No. 815 (April 1977).

18. The USITC is an independent agency created by an act of Congress, approved September 8, 1916, as the US Tariff Commission. The name was changed to the International Trade Commission by Section 171 of the Trade Act of 1974. The commission's present powers and duties are provided for largely by the Tariff Act of 1930, the Agricultural Adjustment Act, the Trade Expansion Act of 1962, the Trade Act of 1974, and the Trade Agreements Act of 1979. Commissioners appointed after January 3, 1975, are appointed for a term of nine years, unless designated to fill an unexpired term, and are not eligible for reappointment. The chairperson and vice-chairpersons are designated by the president for two-year terms, and succeeding chairpersons may not be of the same political party. The chairperson is generally responsible for the administration of the commission. Prior to January 3, 1975, the chairperson and the vice-chairperson were designated annually by the president. Not more than three commissioners may be members of the same political party (there are six commissioners altogether). See *The US Government Manual 1981-82* (Washington, DC), p. 641.

19. See *Federal Register* 43 Reg.8,304, Inv. No. 337-TA-29, USITC Pub. No. 863 (1978).

20. Ibid.

21. The Trade Agreements Act of 1979, Public Law No. 96-39, 93 Stat. 144 [codified in 19 USC Section 1673 (supp. III, 1979)].

22. Ibid., Section (a).

23. Ibid., Section 101.

24. Ibid., Section 1673d(b).

25. The ITC structure is very important under US laws, for it permits individual companies to initiate proceedings.

26. Trade Agreements Act of 1979, Section 771(7)(b).

27. Ibid., Section 771(7)(c).

28. Ibid.

29. Ibid., Section 771, (4)(a).

30. S. Rep. No. 249, 96th Congress, 1st Sess. 87, reprinted in (1979) US Code Cong. & Ad. News, pt. 6A, p. 91.

31. Trade Agreements Act of 1979, Public Law No. 96-39, Section 106(a), 93 Stat. 144, Section 771(4)(b).

32. Ibid., Section 771(4)(c).

33. Ibid., Section 771(4)(d).

34. The 1979 Act authorizes the "administering authority" or "authority" to determine whether there is an injury to domestic industry by reason of an import of merchandise and to initiate a dumping investigation. Section 771(1) of the act defines the "authority" to mean the "Secretary of the Treasury, or any

other officer of the United States to whom the responsibility for carrying out the duties of the administering authority under this title [is] transferred by law." Pursuant to the Presidential Reorganization Plan of 1979, after congressional approval, the responsibility for enforcing antidumping and countervailing duty laws was transferred from the Department of Treasury to the Department of Commerce. See "Reorganization Plan No. 3 of 1979," 44 *Federal Register* 69, 273 (December 3, 1979).

35. Trade Agreements Act of 1979, Section 723(c).

36. Ibid.

37. Ibid., Section 773(a).

38. Ibid., Section 773(b).

39. Ibid., Section 773(d).

40. Ibid., Section 735(c).

41. Ibid., Section 735(b).

42. Ibid., Section 773(c).

43. Ibid.

44. Ibid., Section 734(b).

45. Ibid., Section 751.

46. Prior to November 1, 1980, the initial forum was the Customs Court. The Customs Court Act of 1980 abolished the Customs Court and replaced it with the Court of International Trade. See Public Law No. 96-417, 94 Stat. 1727.

47. 28 USC Section 1541(a) (Supp. III, 1979), as amended by the Customs Court Act of 1980, Section 401(a)(1), 94 Stat. 1727.

48. Kleberg & Co. v. United States, 71 F. 2d 332, 21 CCPA, TD 46, 446 110(1933).

49. 19 CFR Section 353.1(1980).

50. Section 772(b) of the Trade Agreements Act of 1979 defines purchase price as the "price at which merchandise is purchased or agreed to be purchased, prior to the date of importation from the manufacturer or producer of the merchandise for exportation to the United States."

51. Section 772(c) of the Trade Agreements Act of 1979 defines exporter's sales price as the "price at which merchandise is sold in the United States, before or after the time of exportation, by or for the account of the exporter. . . ."

52. See S. Rep. No. 249, 96th Congress, 1st Sess. 38 (1979) reprinted in (1979) US Code Cong. & Ad. News, p. 381.

53. See Trade Agreements Act of 1979, Section 772(e).

54. 19 CFR Section 353.3(a) (1980).

55. Trade Agreements Act of 1979, Section 773(a).

56. Ibid.

57. 19 CFR Section 355.5 (1981).

58. Trade Agreements Act of 1979, Section 773.

59. Ibid.

60. S. Rep. No. 1298, 93rd Congress, 2nd Sess. 173 (1974).

61. See Robert E. Hudec in *Interface One* edited by Don Wallace, Jr., George C. Spina, Richard M. Rawson, and Brian McGill (Washington, DC, Georgetown Univ. Law Center, 1979), p. 31.

62. See Charles Owen Verrill in Wallace et al. (eds.) *Interface One*, p. 162.

63. Public Law No. 93-618, Section 321, 88 Stat. 2047 (1975).

64. The amendment provides: "If available information indicates to the Secretary that the economy of the country from which the merchandise is exported is state-controlled to an extent that sales or offers of sales of such or similar merchandise in that country or to countries other than the United States do not permit a determination of foreign market value under subsection (a), the Secretary shall determine the foreign market value of the merchandise on the basis of the normal costs, expenses, and profits as reflected by either (1) the prices . . . at which such or similar merchandise of a non-state-controlled-economy country or countries is sold either (A) for consumption in the home market of that country or countries, or (B) to other countries, including the United States; or (2) the constructed value of such or similar merchandise in a non-state-controlled-economy country or countries." Ibid.

65. S. Rep. No. 1298, 93rd Congress, 2nd Sess. 176 (1974).

66. Ibid., p. 169.

67. On May 6, 1974, Outboard Marine Corporation, the US manufacturer of Cushman golf cars, submitted a complaint alleging that Pezetel, a Polish electric golf car exporter, was selling its products on the US market at less than fair value and thereby injuring the domestic industry. See USITC Pub. No. 740 (1975).

68. See US Department of the Treasury, Office of the Secretary, Confrontation Conference on Electric Golf Cars from Poland 15 (April 21, 1975) (transcript of proceedings). (Available from Commissioner of Customs, Customs Service, US Treasury, now ITC, Washington, DC.)

69. Pezetel claimed itself to be a large and sophisticated manufacturer of golf cars. It urged the Customs Service to reduce by approximately 40 percent the fair value calculated from Marathon prices to adjust for relative economies of scale. Marathon produced 250 cars per year, whereas Pezetel manufactured between 5,400 and 6,600. Ibid.

70. The decision was severely criticized by Stanislaw Soltysinski. See "US Antidumping Laws and State-Controlled Economies," 15 *Journal of World Trade Law* 251-265 (1981). A few other scholars and practioners have shown displeasure with the finding of Polish Cars, too. See, in general, Wallace et al. (eds.), *Interface One*.

71. 19 CFR Section 153.7 (1980).

72. Ibid.

73. Ibid.

74. Stanislaw Soltysinski vigorously argued the case and questioned the criterion. He said, "Thus, for instance, using the criterion of industrialization, Poland, whose industrial production accounts for 59 percent of her gross domestic product, is ahead of such countries as Japan (37 percent), West Germany (43 percent), and even the United States (28 percent). On the other hand, if one assumes that it is not industry but services that determine the level of development, Poland would find itself at the bottom of the list with 8 percent way behind the United States (57 percent) and West Germany (43 percent)." See Soltysinski, "US Antidumping Laws," p. 253.

75. Professor Stanislaw Wasowski severely criticized the concept in his "Comparisons With Domestic Prices in Poland," in Wallace et al. (eds), *Interface One*, Appendix E. For others' critiques, see *Interface One* in general.

76. Bruce A. Ortwine, "Injury Determination Under United States Antidumping Laws Before and After the Trade Agreements Act of 1979," 33 *Rutgers Law Review* 1103 (1981).

77. The Trade Act of 1974, Public Law 93-618, 88 Stat. 20119 (1975).

78. See John H. Jackson, "Scope Paper," in Wallace et al. (eds), *Interface One*, p. 12.

79. 19 USC Section 2251(a)(1) (1976).

80. Ibid.

81. Ibid., Section 2251(d)(2).

82. Trade Act of 1974, Section (201)(b)(1).

83. S. Rep. No. 93-1298, 93th Congress, 2nd Sess. 121-22 (1974). The House Ways and Means Committee's report addressed the question with virtually identical language. See H. R. Rep. No. 93-571, 93rd Congress, 1st Sess. 45 (1974).

84. See Commissioner Moore's opinion in *Bolts, Nuts, and Screws of Iron or Steel*, USITC Pub. No. 747 (1975), p. 19.

85. Ibid., pp. 11, 12.

86. Trade Act of 1974, Section 201(b)(4).

87. Ibid., Section 201(b)(2).

88. See Report of the House Ways and Means Committee on the Trade Reform Act of 1973, H.R. Rep. No. 571, 93rd Congress, 1st Sess. 46 (1973).

89. See, generally, Wrapper Tobacco, USITC Pub. No. 746 (1975).

90. Section 202(c) requires the president, in making a decision, to take into consideration, in addition to such other considerations as deemed relevant, information and advice from the secretaries of labor and commerce, the probable effectiveness of import relief, the effect of import relief on consumers and US international economic interests, and so on.

91. See Reorganization Plan No. 3 of 1979, 3 CFR 513 9(1979) and Executive Order 12188 of January 2, 1980, 3 CFR 131 (1980).

92. See Christian R. Berg, "Petitioning and Responding Under the Escape Clause: One Practitioner's View on How to Do It," 6(3) *North Carolina Journal of International Law and Commercial Regulation* 422 (1981).

93. Trade Act of 1974, Section 203(c).

94. Certain Stainless Steel Flatware, USITC Pub. No. 884 (1978).

95. See *Federal Register* 29,259 (1978).

96. Trade Act of 1974, Section 203(c) Public Law 93-618 (1975).

97. During 1964-82, the ITC conducted eight investigations concerning mushrooms. The most recent investigation was conducted under Section 203 of the Trade Act of 1974 and was completed in April 1982. For detailed descriptions, see Canned Mushrooms from the People's Republic of China: Report to the President on Investigation No. TA-406-9, Appendix C.

98. The president, as required by law, should treat the determination of the ITC under Section 406 the same as that under Section 201, except that action can be taken only with regard to imports from a Communist country.

99. Trade Act of 1974, Section 406(a).

100. Ibid.

101. See S. Rep. No. 1298, 93rd Congress, 2nd Sess. 212 (1974).

102. Ibid.

103. Ibid., p. 210.

104. "Canned Mushrooms," p. A13.
105. Ibid.
106. Ibid.
107. Ibid., p. A14.
108. Ibid., p. 31.
109. Ibid., p. A14.
110. Ibid. The decline in total US imports in 1981 seems to have resulted from the additional duty imposed on mushroom imports pursuant to the presidential action in October 1980 and a generally depressed market.
111. Ibid.
112. Ibid., p. 11.
113. Ibid.
114. Ibid.
115. Ibid.
116. See Brief on the CEROILS, p. 7.
117. Ibid., p. 9.
118. See H. Rep. No. 93-1644, 93rd Congress, 2nd Sess. (1973), pp. 48-49.
119. See "Canned Mushrooms," p. 12.
120. Ibid., p. 10.
121. Ibid., in general.
122. Ibid., p. 9.
123. See Brief on CEROILS, p. 14.
124. The Mushroom Industry, USDA Marketing Research Report No. 1131 (July 1982), p. 8.
125. The commission agreed that material injury is a lesser standard than serious injury in the escape clause.
126. See "Canned Mushrooms," p. 14.
127. Ibid., p. 17.
128. Ibid., p. 18.
129. Ibid., p. 27.
130. Ibid. Data show that the production in 1981 was 22 percent higher than in 1979, a year when China was not a factor in the US market.
131. Ibid.
132. Ibid.
133. Ibid.
134. Ibid., p. 28.
135. The counsel invoked, as evidence of the effect of recalls, the New York State Health Commission's comment on its order not to sell or use any canned food produced by the Lerch Company: "We cannot allow continued distribution of food products within New York State manufactured by a company which has exhibited such *blatant disregard* for the health and safety of consumers." See Brief on CEROILS.
136. See "Canned Mushrooms." The combined imports from China, Taiwan, and South Korea, which accounted for 44.3 percent of US consumption in 1979, declined to 34.9 percent in 1981. At the same time, China's share in the combined imports increased dramatically.
137. In that year (1980), the president increased the tariff rate on imports of mushrooms from all suppliers, despite the ITC recommendation that an imposition

of a quota might be more effective. This adjusted tariff rate was to expire on October 30, 1983. See 45(214) *Federal Register* 72617-8 (1980).

138. See "Canned Mushrooms," p. 29.

139. Ibid., p. 30.

140. Ibid., p. 31.

141. See Brief on CEROILS, pp. 30-33.

142. Ibid., p. 42.

143. Ibid., p. 31.

144. See "Canned Mushrooms," p. 21.

145. See *People's Daily*, December 4, 1982, and *China Daily News*, December 6, 1982. The mushroom issue, however, has not yet come to an end. On October 13, 1982, one of the mushroom producers started a new petition under US anti-dumping law. See *China Daily News*, December 6, 1982.

146. See Hearing Before the Subcommittee on International Trade of the Committee on Finance, US Senate, 97th Congress, 2nd Sess., January 29, 1982.

147. Statement of Frank C. Conahan, Subcommittee on International Trade of Senate Committee on Finance, 97th Congress, 2nd Sess., January 29, 1982.

148. See Statement of Charles Owen Verrill, Jr., Senate Finance Committee, 97th Congress, 2nd Sess., January 29, 1982.

149. Testimony of Sholom D. Comay, Senate Committee on Finance, 97th Congress, 2nd Sess., January 29, 1982.

150. See the letter from the American Association of Exporters and Importers dated February 1, 1982, to the Senate Finance Committee.

151. Statement of Harry Kopp, Senate Committee on Finance, 97th Congress, 2nd Sess., January 29, 1982.

Chapter 7 Textile Trade

Every time [the Chinese] begin to develop a market here, they're threatened with quotas or dumping charges.*

– **Christopher Phillips**

On August 19, 1983, Chinese Vice-Minister of Foreign Economic Relations and Trade Zheng Tuobin and the US Ambassador to China Arthur W. Hummel, Jr., signed the second China-US textile trade agreement on behalf of their respective governments.[1] Notes were also signed at the occasion that officially put the agreement into effect. This agreement was initialed by chief Chinese and US negotiators on July 30, 1983, in Geneva. Negotiations on the second textile agreement started in August 1982. After seven arduous rounds of talks, the parties came to an agreement.

The textile trade, which includes wearing apparel, has both international and domestic dimensions. The textile industry is an important sector in both industrialized and industrializing countries. It serves as an indispensable transition for industrialization. A study shows that the international textile trade accounts for approximately 5 percent of the total world trade and about 9 percent of the world trade in manufactures.[2] It constitutes nearly 27 percent of the total export of manufactures from the non-oil-developing countries and 29 percent of their manufactures export to industrialized countries.[3] As far as developed countries are concerned, the United States remains

*See *Far Eastern Economic Review*, February 3, 1983, p. 40. Christopher Phillips is now the chairperson of the National Council on US-China Trade.

a leading producer of textiles in the world. The EEC, on the other hand, is one of the largest world importers and exporters of textile and clothing products, covering over four-fifths ($80 billion) of the world trade in these areas.[4]

For over three decades, the tension in the international textile trade has become more and more severe. Exports from developing to developed countries have been strictly restrained. On the other hand, the textile industry in industrialized countries has been adversely affected by factors both domestic and international; for example, the growth of imports from developing countries, the development of technology, the advent of new fibers, etc. The widespread geographical locations of these textile producers and the traditional high level of employment in the textile industry make this industry socially, economically, and politically sensitive in these countries.[5] The closure of textile firms and the fall of employment are often attributed to imports, particularly imports from sources that are emerging as sturdy competitors.

Textile trade is a sensitive sector in the bilateral trade relations between China and the United States, too. It is affected by the overall bilateral relationship. At the same time, it has a great impact on bilateral ties. This chapter studies the basic difficulties in bilateral textile trade and its possible impact on the overall bilateral relationship. Since textile trade has an international dimension, the study will be conducted in the context of the overall trade relationship, economic and political, between China and the United States. Owing to the complicated nature of textile trade at the domestic, bilateral, and multilateral levels, this study is perforce a survey of the matter.

HISTORICAL BACKGROUND

The development of a textile industry is an important stage of industrialization. The textile industry, which utilizes technology at various levels, is a comparatively labor-intensive industry. The textile product is easy to package, ship, and market, and has a high ratio of value to weight. Since most of the developing countries do not have sufficient high technology, development of a textile industry may fill the gap by utilizing the existing equipment and technology of the country in question, which may in turn lay a basis for further industrialization. It at the same time helps to resolve employment problems and generates foreign exchange by exports. As a developing rural country, China's textile industry plays an important part in its economy, both internally and externally. As far as foreign trade is concerned, a considerable amount of China's exports is textile products. Accounting for about 39 percent of the total Chinese sales to the United States in the last two years,[6] textile exports are a particularly important ingredient in China's foreign trade with the United States.

In 1971, China began to export a small amount of textile products to the United States. This situation continued until 1977, when the value of Chinese textile exports rose to $69 million (the equivalent of 88 million square yards).[7]

China's textile products came to the US market, however, at a critical and unfavorable time. Prior to 1971, the United States had limited cotton textile and apparel imports on a unilateral basis. But in 1971, the United States started signing comprehensive bilateral agreements that placed limits on all cotton, synthetic fiber, and wool textile imports from major suppliers. These agreements, which were designed to satisfy US textile producers, set growth rates for the imports of each supplier based on the 1971 figures. They were basically governed by rules set forth in the Arrangement Regarding International Trade in Textiles [known as the Multi-Fiber Arrangement (MFA)],[8] first concluded in 1973 and renewed in 1977 and 1981.

The forerunner of the MFA was the Long-Term Arrangement of Cotton Textiles,[9] which was concluded in 1962, after three-year discussions within the frame of the GATT. In 1972, the GATT Council set up a Working Party on Textiles to study the economic, technical, social, and commercial elements influential to international trade. This working party was converted into a negotiating group in 1973. After five months of negotiations, the MFA was adopted by the negotiating group, composed of about 50 exporting and importing countries.[10]

The MFA provides for restrictions on the import of textiles through unilateral restraints by importing countries and through bilateral agreements to eliminate the real risks of market disruption.[11] Under the MFA institution, the annual export level of 1977 was set as the base level for textile exporters. In other words, although importing countries may restrict textile imports, the level of the first year of the restraint cannot be lower than the annual level that an exporter had achieved in 1977. If the said restraint is to continue beyond one year, a growth rate of 6 percent is granted under the MFA.

Despite the fact that restraint on the importation of textiles is allowed, textile suppliers may use the flexibilities provided for in the MFA, for example, swing, carry forward, and carryover. Swing is an adjustment of the different textile products of an exporter in a particular year. Under this type of flexibility, certain products may exceed the level set up during a year, provided there is a decrease in other products, so that the total export may not exceed the aggregate level. The carry forward allows a textile exporter to borrow from the quota of the same product in the next year, if its exports are likely to exceed the level of the year. Carryover, on the other hand, enables an exporter to make use of the unused quota for the previous year. The MFA allows 7 percent swing, 5 percent carry forward, and 5 percent carryover.

The MFA, which was to expire at the end of 1977, was renewed by a protocol adopted by the negotiating group on December 14, 1977.[12] Making reference to the ongoing negotiations by the EEC with other countries, this protocol provided for reasonable departures from the original MFA if mutual agreements could be concluded between importing and exporting members. Since the word "reasonable" was not defined in the document, the protocol gave textile-importing countries leeway to impose more restrictive limits, that is, less than 6 percent growth, through bilateral agreements.

On December 22, 1981, a new protocol was adopted by the negotiating group.[13] Replacing the protocol of 1977, it entered into effect on January 1, 1982, and will continue to be effective until July 31, 1986, along with the MFA adopted in 1973. In addition to the creation of a new mechanism for monitoring structural adjustment in the form of a subcommittee of the Textiles Committee, this protocol has more built-in objectivity and specificity, which may make the operation of the multilateral surveillance and discipline more effective.[14]

Although the MFA (as amended and extended) calls for developed countries to increase textile quotas from and give favorable treatment to developing countries, most of the US bilateral textile agreements have been more restrictive, straying further and further from the MFA goals.

During the last few years, the United States increased its restrictions on textile imports. One of the well-known restrictions is the quota system. There are at present 108 textile categories, including 72 cotton, synthetic fiber, and wool apparel categories, any of which may be subjected to quota restrictions if the US government decides that the category in question increases rapidly.[15]

It was under this restrictive and increasingly comprehensive system that the Chinese textiles started coming to the US market.

No attempt was made to restrict Chinese textile exports to the United States before 1978, when the value of such exports was less than $133 million and its share of US textile and apparel imports was less than 3.5 percent (US Commerce Department statistics).[16] In 1978, however, the US textile industry began to impose pressure on the government to restrict the Chinese exports. As a result, former Special Trade Representative Robert Strauss went to China in May 1979 with the intention of negotiating a textile agreement to restrict textile imports from China.

Failing to negotiate a bilateral textile agreement, Strauss placed unilateral quotas on Chinese cotton gloves, knit shirts and blouses, woven shirts, trousers, and synthetic fiber sweaters. Over strong Chinese protest, the US government imposed additional unilateral quotas on blouses and synthetic fiber coats in October 1979. It embargoed a large quantity of Chinese shipments in bonded warehouses.

On September 17, 1980, a China-US textile agreement was signed, covering cotton, wool, and synthetic fiber textile and apparel products exported from China to the United States.[17] This agreement, which lasted for three years, from January 1, 1980, through December 31, 1982, set quotas or specific limits on eight categories of textile imports from China. An annual growth rate of approximately 4 percent was agreed on, in contrast to a 1 percent growth for other major suppliers such as Taiwan, Hong Kong, and South Korea.

The agreement was, as usual, a compromise between the two countries. On the US side, the key was a consultation clause providing that "in the event that the imports from the People's Republic of China classified in any category or categories not covered by Specific Limits are, due to market disruption, threatening to impede the orderly development of trade between the two countries, the Government of the United States may request consultations with the Government of the People's Republic of China with a view to avoiding such market disruption."[18] Thus, it gave the United States leeway to impose further restrictions on Chinese textile exports if necessary.

Although the agreement was more in line with the position of the United States, the Chinese agreed because of an informal commitment the United States had made to them. The promise in main part stated that the US government "would not call any category for consultations until China's exports were comparable to the principal suppliers."[19]

The conclusion of the textile agreement, however, failed to ease the tension in the bilateral trade. As soon as the pact went into effect, the US government frequently called for consultations. In the 20 months after the signing of the Textile Agreement, the United States initiated consultations four times.[20] Eighteen more categories were restricted,[21] and as a result, the import restraints applied to 26 categories of the total Chinese textile exports.[22]

Before the two countries were able to solve these problems in textile trade, a new and more serious crisis broke out. On December 31, 1982, the Textile Agreement of 1980 expired.[23] Although negotiations for a completely new agreement had started in August 1982, one was not reached because of the wide gap between the two countries.

On August 30, 1982, immediately following the first round of negotiations, calls were made with regard to four more categories of Chinese textile exports.[24] They included cotton sweater, suit-type coats, wool suits, and women's synthetic fiber coats. In October 1982, immediately after the second round of negotiations had broken down, four additional calls were effected, namely, cotton nightwear, cotton terry cloth towels, and men's synthetic fiber coats and trousers.[25] These new calls demonstrated that the United States had decided not to honor its promise with the Chinese government, for in some of the called categories, the Chinese imports to the United States were far below those of other substantial suppliers.[26]

In addition, the procedure for making the decision for calls was changed quietly. Ordinarily, a call must be approved at the assistant secretary level in a number of agencies. But many observers noticed that the 1982 calls of Chinese textiles appeared to be the "actions of lower-level bureaucrats. Particularly worrisome [was] the apparent shunting aside of the State Department, the agency with the most sensitivity to political issues at stake."[27] Whatever the reasons and motivations were, these actions coupled with the dumping petitions of various domestic industries created a hostile atmosphere for continued negotiations.[28]

At the beginning of 1983 after three rounds of failed talks, the situation reached a climax. The United States set January 15, 1983, as the deadline for the fourth round of negotiations. It threatened that if no agreement were worked out by that time, restrictions on Chinese textile exports, which had been outlined in late 1982, would be imposed. As China loudly denounced the United States for failing to reach an accord, the United States imposed unilateral quotas on Chinese textile exports, setting limits on about three dozen categories of textiles and clothing.[29] Most categories were held to 1982 import levels, while a reduction was mandated for print cloth.[30] Limits were set for the first time on cotton skirts, women's and girls' wool trousers and shorts, and synthetic fiber gloves and bras.

Although the unilateral quotas were said to aim at freezing Chinese textile exports in those categories at existing import levels,[31] "quotas on the categories restricted by past agreement were reduced by nearly 30%."[32] The quotas on the major categories of Chinese textile exports were cut by 45 percent.[33] It was estimated that "in at least one major category, the Chinese exports fell short of the quota level."[34] Under the old agreement, China was allowed to ship 742,000 dozen men's and boy's knotted shirts per year. The new limit was 601,929 dozen.[35] For cotton trousers, the new admissible volume was 1,414,672 dozen, compared with 1,730,000 dozen under the old quota.[36]

In January 1983, the Chinese government responded by deciding not to approve contracts for the purchase of cotton, synthetic fibers, and soybeans from the United States.[37] The Ministry of Foreign Economic Relations and Trade announced that China would also "reduce its planned imports of other US agricultural products."[38] In the first 11 months of 1982, China had bought $176.2 million worth of US cotton, $63.2 million worth of soybeans, and $124.5 million worth of yarns and fabrics.[39]

The US officials, however, assumed that the ban on these three items would be no more than a paper tiger. According to the officials from the Agriculture Department, they did not expect "the import ban on soybeans and cotton to have a significant effect on US producers."[40] The United States did fear, however, that the Chinese might cut back on imports of other agricultural products, such as lumber and wheat. These items accounted for about 65 percent of all US exports to China. In the market year July 1981 to June 1982, US exports of logs and lumber to China were valued at $204 million in the first 10 months of 1982,[41] with China being the number one importer of US wheat, purchasing 8.4 million metric tons of wheat, valued at more than $1.1 billion.[42] The total US exports to China in the first nine months of 1983 amounted to $1.43 billion, down 40 percent from the first nine months of 1982. In the same nine-month period of 1983, US agriculture exports fell by 73 percent from the same period of 1982 to $348.1 million.

This tense trade relationship was eased when the Chinese government lifted its curbs on US imports after the conclusion of the new textile agreement. Farm spokepersons in the United States said that "the Chinese cutback on wheat purchases had cost US farmers more than $500 million."[43]

The new textile agreement sets growth limits on 34 categories of Chinese textile exports to the United States.[44] The annual growth rate was set at about 3 percent.[45] Although the signing of the new textile agreement has not put an end to the textile dispute, it may help to stabilize the bilateral trade.

DIFFICULTIES OF THE TEXTILE TRADE

In order to understand the difficulties of the textile trade, it is necessary to study the political and economic context. The textile trade is affected by domestic and international forces.

The textile industry is one of China's older industries. By 1952, after the three years of rehabilitation following the establishment of the People's Republic of China, China was producing 680,000 tons of cotton yarn and 3.8 billion meters of cotton cloth. The textile industry accounted for over 25 percent of the total industrial output value of the country.[46] By 1979, annual production of cotton yarn was 2.63 million tons and cotton cloth was 12.1 billion meters, taking first place in the world.[47] According to an economic survey of world cotton and wool products conducted by US agencies, world cotton consumption rose by about 2 percent in recent years; 60 percent of the rise was in China. China's textile industry now has a relatively complete range of varieties. Production techniques have reached quite advanced levels.

As a consequence of the rapid development of the textile industry, China's export of textiles has boomed. In 1979, it topped $2.8 billion,[48] becoming one of the key export categories of Chinese foreign trade. In 1982, textiles accounted for 20.9 percent of China's total worldwide exports.[49]

Owing to the importance of the textile industry in China's national economy and foreign trade, it is understandable that China takes a hard-line position in its negotiations of textile agreements with foreign countries. Unless China can sell its textile products abroad successfully, it may not be able to earn enough foreign currency to buy advanced technology and equipment from industrialized countries. Besides textiles, China does not have much to sell abroad. This situation will continue in the near future; it is unlikely that China will be able to convert its textile industry into something different or that it will be able to export other products in substantial quantity.

Sino-American trade has been growing fairly rapidly in recent years. Bilateral trade was $2.4 billion after the establishment of normal relations in 1979.[50] The value of the trade in 1981 was $5.9 billion, compared with $4.8 billion in 1980.[51] Light industrial and agricultural products constitute the large majority of the bilateral trade. The main US exports to China are agricultural,[52] whereas Chinese textiles accounted for 39 percent of the total Chinese exports to the United States, valued at $800 million.[53] According to a study, China's non-agricultural exports, excluding textiles, to the United States in the first four months of 1983 were mainly gasoline ($101 million), crude oil ($10 million), tin, fireworks, wool rugs, baskets, and other light manufactures.[54]

With the growth of bilateral trade, China's trade deficit with the United States has been increased. It was estimated to be $2.8 billion in 1980 and $2.9 billion in 1981.[55] Although the gap narrowed in 1982, it was still $0.6 billion.[56]

Owing to this chronic trade deficit with the United States, China is very sensitive to US import restraints on light manufactures that so directly inhibit the expansion of Chinese exports. Chinese officials have pointed out that decreased sales of Chinese goods in US markets will limit China's foreign exchange earnings and subsequently China's ability to purchase US products. This trade deficit was one of the major obstacles in the textile agreement negotiations.

Another central issue is determining what share of the US market China should have. Commenting on the US proposals to enlarge the scope of restriction on China's textile exports to the United States, cut the quotas, delete some flexible clauses from the old agreement, and reduce the average annual growth rate, Li Dengshan, the Chinese chief negotiator of the textile agreement, recalled that China's textile exports to the United States started from almost zero. In 1981, he said, it reached only $420 million according to Chinese statistics, or less than $600 million according to US statistics (discrepancy resulting from different accounting methods), falling far behind other major textile exporters to the United States.[57] China's export of garments to the United States makes up 3.1 percent of the total US textile imports.[58] Even in the area of Chinese apparel exports, which aroused the most controversy in the United States, China accounted for only 9.3 percent of US imports (by volume) in the year ending July 1982, compared with 18 to 20 percent for Hong Kong, Taiwan, and South Korea.[59] It is reported that in 1981, US textile imports totaled about $10 billion, while the imports from China amounted to only $590 million, less than 6 percent of the US total.[60] The Chinese textile exports to the United States accounted for only about 0.7 percent of US consumption.[61] In addition, in 1981, China even suffered a textile trade deficit of $450 million with the United States.[62]

It was maintained that unlike other major textile exports, Chinese exports include semifinished cloth as well as garments. Chinese officials pointed out that a considerable proportion of China's textile exports consisted of gray cloth. They were made of cotton imported from the United States, and had been used as raw material by the US printing and dyeing and garments industries; therefore, it was beneficial to the US industries.[63] "It is ridiculous and unfair for the United States to restrict Chinese textile products which are made of raw materials from the United States," said a Chinese official.[64]

China's textile exports are at a competitive disadvantage compared with the exports of Taiwan, Hong Kong, and South Korea, because China can compete only in the low-price, less-fashion-sensitive market. The Chinese negotiators argued that, in terms of value, China accounts for only 6 percent of US imports, for Chinese textiles had tended to be of lower quality and value. Based on the above-mentioned factors, the Chinese argue that they should be entitled to more favorable treatment than the exporters who can compete in a broader sector of the market and earn more foreign exchange by commanding higher prices. China exported 54 categories of textiles to the United States in 1981, which accounted for only half of the total categories the United States imported.[65]

Taking into account its geographical size, its textile industry's total output, and its uncompetitiveness in fashion and quality, China thinks it is unfair for the United States to impose the same restraints on Chinese textile imports. "China's textile exports to the United States have not been allowed to develop in line with the actual needs and possibilities," said Li Dengshan, "but are subjected to strict and unfair control."[66] He pointed out that after the first Sino-American textile agreement went into effect, the US government unrestrainedly used the consultation clauses to enlarge the scope of restrictions and arbitrarily cut the quotas.[67] He accused the United States of delaying consultations and unilaterally restricting imports, thus seriously restraining China's export of textiles to the United States and impairing China's economic interests.[68]

In addition to the economic consideration, there are political issues that are very sensitive to China. Since the United States recognizes that there is only one China and that Taiwan is part of China, the Chinese government deems that it is illogical for a small part of the country to dominate in foreign trade with the United States. According to Department of Commerce statistics, in the year ending July 1982, mainland China captured a 10.6 percent share of total US textile imports (in quantity terms), compared with 17.9 percent for Taiwan.[69] The reason why China is not pleased seems to be that the continuation of this situation will hamper its efforts to reunify the nation.

The relationship between China and other foreign countries also has an impact on its relationship with the United States. China has economic and trade relations with more than 170 countries and areas.[70] It has concluded trade agreements with more than 80 countries.[71] The trade relationship between China and those countries and areas, especially Western Europe and Japan, has not come across the same difficulties and problems as with the United States, such as export controls and import restraints. Chinese textile exports as well as other light manufactures are being sold in those foreign markets without being dumped or severely restricted. In addition, China enjoys a trade surplus with those trading partners. In contrast to those partners, the United States does not appear to be the most favorable trading partner to China.

In addition to political and economic issues, technical matters, such as tradition and custom, may cause problems, too. For instance, the manner in which the United States treats China itself has made it difficult for the two countries to come into agreement. Before the fourth round of talks started, the United States announced the details of restraints on Chinese textiles and set a deadline for the negotiation. This certainly hurt China's self-respect and made the negotiations more difficult. A few sensitive US officials are aware of this problem. As one said: "It was less the textile quotas themselves than the way we handled the negotiations that bothered the Chinese."[72]

Hearing of the conclusion of the new textile agreement between China and the United States, foreign circles in Peking pointed out that it was for domestic reasons in the United States that the signing of this agreement had been delayed.[73] Domestically, the US government is under considerable pressure from the textile industry, which is widespread and involves intensive employment. Thus, any action concerning textile imports will draw immediate attention and concern from both the producers and the workers in the industry. Being a large and labor-intensive industry, the textile lobby in the government is very powerful. Representing both manufacturers and unions, it has a very strong voice in Congress. More than one-half of the members of the House of Representatives belong to the textile caucus. The caucus is the watchdog for the textile industry and sees to it that the administration will not give up its interest. The key is the administration's need for congressional support on other issues. If the textile industry is not happy with the administrative decisions in the textile trade, it may persuade the withholding of congressional support on governmental actions. Thus, it can be extremely difficult for the president to have any bill passed.

Because of its great lobbying power, the textile industry has been able to negotiate deals with the government. For instance, in 1979, when the US government needed legislative support to waive countervailing duties on imports that have been subsidized by foreign countries, it was embargoed by the House Ways and Means Committee pending arrival between the textile makers and the White House of an arrangement satisfactory to both.[74] On February 15, the administration reached agreement with the textile and apparel industry on import controls, which was said to clear the way for the waiver bill.[75] The textile industry is still one of the most powerful trade lobbies in Congress, and can seek to use Congress to force the administration to do its bidding.

The policy of the United States to balance textile imports from China and other suppliers makes the administration reluctant to give China too favorable treatment. This foreign policy consideration hampers the economic relations between the two countries.

Legal actions are another option for US textile producers. Textile makers use legal action as an alternative to bargaining with the administration and to imposing pressure on foreign countries for satisfactory agreements. Whenever the textile producers fail in getting a satisfactory agreement with the foreign country in question, they resort to legal actions.

Such actions are detrimental to a friendly relationship in bilateral trade. They create a hostile atmosphere for the negotiations, as demonstrated by the second Sino-American textile agreement.

Almost simultaneously with the start of the negotiations for the second agreement, two complaints were filed against Chinese textiles. On August 5, 1982, the American Textile Manufacturers Institute filed a petition alleging that greige polyester/cotton print cloth from China was being sold in the United States at less than fair market value, and that such sales were materially injuring, or were threatening to materially injure, the US textile industry. In July 1983, the Commerce Department ruled that print cloth made in China was being sold in the United States at an unfairly low price. The decision cleared the way for a final ruling by the ITC, which had to determine if the low pricing would injure US manufacturers.[76]

Another petition was filed by Milliken & Company on behalf of the US industry producing shop towels on August 24, 1982. The case rested on the dubious logic that since US factories are the most mechanized in the world, anything coming in under US producer prices is ipso facto dumped.[77] Although private industries, rather than the US government, are behind these cases, they still make the already difficult textile issue a more difficult and complicated one.

In addition to legal action problems, technical matters, such as categorization, cause difficulty. Most recently, the Commerce Department was involved in a controversy with the Customs Department over whether Chinese-made and New Zealand-refined sweaters should be placed under the Chinese or New Zealand quota.[78]

In the view of the Customs Department, these products should be treated as New Zealand-manufactured goods, because after shrinkage and other processes, including refining, conspicuous change has been done to these sweaters. The Customs Department maintained that they should be regarded as such.[79] The Commerce Department, however, held a different view. A deputy assistant secretary said that those New Zealand-processed sweaters did not change conspicuously and that they should be treated as products from China.[80] He advised Customs to change its view for the sake of the domestic industry. He stated that if the Customs view prevailed, the injured US textile industry would be further threatened by such imports from New Zealand and other countries.[81] The Customs Department's view finally prevailed in this case, but the Commerce Department has decided to amend the existing rules relating to the determination of the source of products.[82]

Cases like the sweater issue discussed above have a tremendous effect on bilateral textile trade between China and the United States, because the administration's decisions perforce become one aspect of the foreign trade policy of the United States.

PROSPECTS OF THE TEXTILE TRADE

Although the second Sino-American textile agreement has come into effect, the textile controversy between China and the United

States will continue in the future: first, because of the implementation of the existing textile agreement, and second, because of the economic structures and foreign trade policies of the two countries.

Within three months after the signing of the new textile agreement, three consultations were called by the US government, which caused serious concern on the part of the Chinese government.[83] If more restraints are imposed on Chinese textile exports to the United States, the tension in the bilateral trade, especially in textile trade, may continue or even increase.

As discussed earlier, it is unlikely that China can afford to make major changes in its economic structure and convert the textile industry into something else. Also, the Chinese government may not be willing to tolerate the chronic trade deficit with the United States. Since China is interested in purchasing US technology and equipment, Chinese textiles will continue to come in to pay for them. The Chinese government has repeatedly stated that its textile products are primarily for the domestic market and that its policy of using textile exports to earn foreign currency is only for the short run. The current trend of exporting textiles, however, may persist for some time.

Recently, the United States announced that it would ease restraints on the transfer of technology to China. This decision will undoubtedly improve the overall bilateral relationship. At the same time, it may have a negative impact on the bilateral textile trade. When China starts buying US technology in large quantities, it, in all likelihood, will need more foreign exchange to pay for the purchases. Since textile export will remain a major source of China's foreign exchange earnings for some time, there will be more short-term pressure to export Chinese textiles to the United States.

The US government, on the other hand, will be restricted by its foreign trade policies and regulations and the power of the domestic textile industry. The US textile producers are unhappy about the second Sino-American textile agreement, for, in their view, the United States has given away too much.

Before the textile negotiators had time to take a breath after the signing of the agreement in August 1983, the American Textile Manufacturers Institute, the Amalgamated Clothing and Textile Workers Union, and the International Ladies' Garmet Workers Union filed a countervailing duty petition with the Commerce Department on September 12, 1983.[84] The petition alleged that Chinese textile exports to the United States were being subsidized by the government of China. It was stated that on January 1, 1981, China introduced an internal settlement rate system under which the Bank of China gives a more favorable exchange rate than the official exchange rate of Chinese yuan to foreign currency to Chinese enterprises engaged in foreign trade.[85] According to the petition, under the current Chinese policy, national enterprises engaged in foreign trade are allowed to retain 10 to 15 percent of their foreign exchange earnings, which can be traded at the internal settlement rate to other national enterprises. In the end, enterprises that have foreign currencies will benefit from the favorable exchange rate.[86]

It was maintained that because of this internal settlement rate system, China's foreign trade "deficit was balanced."[87] The petitioners regard China's foreign trade surplus as a contributive result of the internal settlement rate system, despite the fact that China is suffering a trade deficit with the United States. It was also maintained that the unemployment in the US textile industry is a logical consequence of the subsidized Chinese textile exports to the United States.[88]

In response, the Chinese Ministry of Foreign Economic Relations and Trade issued two statements on October 27 and November 30, 1983. Pointing to the fact that China and the United States have fundamentally different social and economic systems, the first statement said, "The trial use of foreign exchange price for internal settlement of trade transactions is an economic measure adopted by China to meet the needs of opening to the outside world economically and of reforming its foreign trade management system."[89] In the second statement, the Chinese government explained that Chinese import and export trade follows the state plan for the entire economy. Export commodities are purchased at domestic prices and sold at prices prevailing on the international market. Import goods are bought at international prices and sold at domestic prices. There is no direct relation between the domestic and international prices of import and export commodities. Foreign exchange rates, it said, do not depend on the purchase and sale of import and export commodities abroad.[90]

Countervailing duties have, in the past, been imposed on dual-currency schemes. This is the first countervailing duty case against so-called nonmarket economy countries in the history of US foreign trade law, representing the US textile industry's displeasure with the second Sino-American textile agreement. If this case is decided in the US producers' favor, other Chinese exports to the United States will be regarded as government-subsidized products as well.[91]

Cases like this one have far-reaching implications for Sino-American trade as well as the trade relationships between the United

States and other countries. Although the case was brought as a legal issue, it is, as the petitioners have realized,[92] a very politically sensitive issue.

In sum, textile trade constitutes a very important part of Sino-American economic exchanges, amounting to approximately 40 percent of Chinese exports to the United States. Since it is a major source of foreign exchange, China has to continue the exportation of textile products to support its modernization program. On the other hand, the US textile industry is throughout all 50 states. Already being besieged with the problem of textile imports from foreign producers, the United States is very much concerned with textile imports from China. As a result, both countries have had difficulties in textile trade in the last few years. The crucial issue of the textile problem is China's share in the US market. Being a new- and latecomer to this market, and a large world producer, China insists on a bigger increase than other exporters. The United States, on the other hand, is reluctant to meet China's demands.

As discussed earlier, textile trade is political in nature, subject to both domestic and international political pressures. It seems that the textile issue may not ease soon, because of the economic structures of both countries. In shaping new trade policy, however, measures may be taken by both countries toward solving the problem. For instance, China may shift its foreign trade to other less competitive areas, such as electronics and small- and medium-sized machinery. It may also strengthen its competitiveness by producing fashionable textile products that are not directly competing with those in the US domestic industry. The United States should recognize the fact that China is a new- and latecomer to its market and the international market. Thus, certain preferential treatment may be allowed to Chinese exports. This may be accomplished by rescheduling shares of the US market among foreign producers. In deciding the increase of imports from each foreign producer, the United States should take into consideration foreign producers' size of territory, size of population, and level of industrialization.[93] Also, the bilateral trade situation, for example, whether the United States has a trade deficit or surplus with the trading partner in question, should be another consideration. Hence, those less-developed, large world producers having deficits in trade with the United States may be given a larger share of the US market. They may be allowed a bigger increase than other foreign producers, while the overall increase of foreign imports to the United States remains the same.

NOTES

1. FBIS-CHI-83-163, August 22, 1983, p. B1.

2. Bhagirath L. Das, "The GATT Multi-Fibre Arrangement," 17 *Journal of World Trade Law* 95 (1983).

3. Ibid.

4. "GATT: Third Multifibre Arrangement," 16 *Journal of World Trade Law* 178 (1982).

5. There were 1.8 million textile workers scattered across all 50 states in 1984. See "To Favor Concessions For US Textile Makers," *Wall Street Journal*, January 6, 1984, p. 1.

6. *New York Times*, January 3, 1983, p. 1.

7. The statistics are based on a US Commerce Department report. See *China Business Review*, November-December 1982, pp. 32-33.

8. GATT, Basic Instruments and Selected Documents, 21st Supp. (1975), p. 3.

9. Ibid., 11th Supp. (1963), p. 25.

10. Das, "GATT Multi-Fibre Arrangement."

11. See Multi-Fiber Arrangement, Articles 3 and 4.

12. GATT, Basic Instruments, 24th Supp. (1978), p. 5.

13. Ibid., 28th Supp. (1982), p. 3.

14. For a detailed discussion of this protocol, see Das "GATT Multi-Fibre Arrangement."

15. *China Business Review*, November-December 1982, p. 31.

16. Ibid., p. 32.

17. See Agreement Relating to Trade in Cotton, Wool, and Man-Made Fiber Textiles and Textile Products Between the Government of the United States of America and the Government of the People's Republic of China (Washington, DC, US Government Printing Office, 1983).

18. See Textile Agreement of 1980, Article 8(a).

19. See Martin Weil, "The Textiles Deadlock," *China Business Review*, November-December 1982, p. 32.

20. The information was secured through an interview by the author with officials from the Chinese Embassy who are involved in bilateral trade with the United States.

21. Eduardo Lachica, "US, China Resume Textile Talks Under Time Pressure," *Asian Wall Street Journal*, January 10, 1983.

22. Lachica, "US, China Resume Textile Talks."

23. See Textile Agreement of 1980.

24. *China Business Review*, November-December 1982, p. 34.

25. Ibid.

26. See Weil, "Textiles Deadlock," p. 32.

27. Ibid.

28. Two petitions were filed in August 1982 on print cloth and shop towels by the American Textile Manufacturers Institute and US shop towel producers, respectively.

29. See *Asian Wall Street Journal*, January 17, 1983, p. 6.

30. Ibid.

31. State Department officials commented that "with one or two exceptions, the effect of quotas would be to maintain imports this year from China at 1982 levels." *New York Times*, January 13, 1983, p. A1.

32. See "China Bars American Cotton, Soybeans, Synthetic Fibers to Protest Textile Curb," *Asian Wall Street Journal*, January 24, 1983.

33. Ibid.

34. Ibid.

35. Lachica, "US, China Resume Textile Talks."

36. Ibid.

37. "China Bars American Cotton."

38. Ibid.

39. See "The Tiger's Roar Is Real," *Far Eastern Economic Review*, February 3, 1983, p. 40.

40. Ibid. In fact, as soon as the Chinese announced their bans on imports, prices for the future delivery of soybeans and cotton fell on US markets. The wheat price declined, too, although it was not banned by China.

41. Ibid., p. 41.

42. "China Bars American Cotton."

43. *Asian Wall Street Journal*, September 12, 1983, p. 12.

44. Ibid.

45. Ibid.

46. Fang Yan, "China's Developing Textile Industry," *China's Foreign Trade*, March-April 1981, p. 2.

47. Ibid.

48. Ibid.

49. See *Business China*, August 10, 1983, p. 119.

50. *China Daily News*, January 18, 1983, p. 12.

51. Ibid.

52. Nonagricultural exports to China increased during the first four months of 1983 by 15 percent. See *China Business Review*, July-August 1983, p. 5.

53. See *Business China*, August 10, 1983, p. 119.

54. *China Business Review*, July-August 1983, p. 5.

55. *China Daily News*, January 18, 1983, p. 12.

56. *Business China*, January 19, 1983, p. 12.

57. See "China Rejects US Proposal to Restrict Textile Exports," *Beijing Review*, September 6, 1982, p. 9. A study shows that in 1982, China exported $834 million worth of textiles, while exports by Hong Kong, Taiwan, and South Korea were $1.907, $1.707, and $1.370 billion respectively. See *China Business Review*, November-December 1982, p. 32.

58. *China Business Review*, November-December 1982, p. 33.

59. Ibid.

60. *People's Daily*, August 12, 1982.

61. This information was given at an interview with an official of the Chinese Embassy in Washington, DC.

62. Ibid.

63. Ibid.

64. *China Daily News*, January 19, 1983.

65. "China Rejects US Proposal," p. 9

66. Ibid.
67. Ibid.
68. Ibid.
69. *China Business Review*, November-December 1982, p. 33.
70. *China Daily News*, January 18, 1983, p. 12.
71. Ibid.
72. See "Tiger's Roar Is Real," p. 40.
73. FBIS-CHI-83-163, August 22, 1982, p. B1.
74. *China Business Review*, January-February 1979, p. 63.
75. Ibid.
76. See *Asian Wall Street Journal*, August 1, 1983.
77. In September 1983, the ITC determined that the imports of shop towels from China were injuring domestic textile producers. It ruled that penalty duties must be imposed on imports of such products from China. See *Asian Wall Street Journal*, September 19, 1983, p. 10.
78. *Peimei News*, September 20, 1983, p. 4.
79. Ibid.
80. Ibid.
81. Ibid.
82. This information was provided by a Chinese official of the Chinese Embassy in Washington, DC, who is in charge of textile trade with the United States.
83. This information was provided by a Chinese official of the Chinese Embassy in Washington, DC.
84. *Asian Wall Street Journal*, September 19, 1983, p. 10.
85. See page 4 of the petition against Chinese textile products, filed on September 12, 1983. The material can be acquired at the Commerce Department.
86. Ibid.
87. Ibid., p. 5.
88. Ibid., p. 15.
89. *Beijing Review*, November 7, 1983, p. 8.
90. *Beijing Review*, December 12, 1983, p. 8.
91. On December 6, 1983, the textile industry withdrew its complaint under an agreement with the US government that the administration would take some measures regarding textile imports. On December 16, the government issued new rules on the imports of textiles. Under these rules, it is said, some imports of textiles from many countries, especially the low-wage Asian and Caribbean countries, would be kept out of the US market. See *New York Times*, December 17, 1983, p. 1.
92. See *Peimei News*, September 20, 1983, p. 4.
93. It is easier for more industrialized producers to shift their textile production to other areas and develop new industries for export.

Chapter 8 Alternatives

The United States is the largest developed country, and China the largest developing country. With their economies being complementary to each other, it is up to the two sides to seize every opportunity to expand their cooperation, and turn every possibility into reality.

– Zhang Wenjin, Chinese Ambassador to the United States

China has a population equivalent to one-quarter of humanity. It is increasingly interested in international economic exchanges. In addition to encouraging the establishment of direct economic relations between Chinese entities and foreign companies, the Chinese government encourages its domestic enterprises to learn the strong points of the growing number of foreign enterprises operating in the country. Since 1979, when the Chinese government first permitted foreign joint ventures in China, many compensation trade, processing, and joint ventures between Chinese enterprises have been established. The United States, on the other hand, is the biggest trader in the world. It seeks additional resources for raw material and foreign markets. Logically and practically, the two countries cannot avoid doing business with one another, though their social, politicolegal, and economic systems are dissimilar.

In recent years, despite occasional setbacks and tensions, economic exchanges between China and the United States have consistently increased. The development of Sino-American economic relations is not only in the best interests of both countries, but also conducive to world peace and stability. The future improvement of economic relations between the two countries, however, depends on joint efforts by both sides and the solution of the problems inhibiting progress.

These problems, in addition to the continuing impasse of Taiwan,[1] include the lack of an adequate understanding of each other's politico-legal system, decision-making process, and laws and bilateral trade issues. This chapter will offer some proposals as alternative long-, medium-, and short-term measures to aid in strengthening this bilateral relationship.

Owing to political and economic dissimilarities, China and the United States have long been suspicious of each other; in turn, the bilateral relationship has suffered from this lack of mutual trust. This absence of such understanding constitutes a major obstacle in negotiations both at governmental and company levels. A number of measures need to be taken to solve the problem. A greater exchange of views between various top and intermediate officials in executive, legislative, and other sectors is essential. This kind of exchange will provide opportunities for them to become acquainted with one another's customs and styles.

The establishment of institutions might also improve each country's understanding of the other's economic and politicolegal systems. In addition to existing institutions, such as the American Study Institute of the Social Science Academy of China, a national committee might be set up in both countries. The function of this committee would be to study the effects of Sino-American bilateral economic exchange on the social, political, and economic development of both countries, as well as on the world economy as a whole. Existing and potential problems in the bilateral economic exchange would be major concerns of this committee. In addition, the political, economic, and legal structures, customs, and changing situations of both countries would be analyzed. This committee would serve, on the one hand, as an information pool and, on the other, as an agency submitting proposals to its own government for decision making.

The committee members might include intermediate-level government officials and political leaders, practitioners of both economic and legal sectors, and those in the academic fields. Membership may be divided into full- and parttime. With a diversified membership, new issues arising in practice would be brought up promptly and be studied immediately; above all, proposals made by the committee would be more realistic and useful.

A nongovernmental relationship could be established between different Chinese and US associations, universities, and law schools. Through this kind of tie, economic and legal issues of both countries could be discussed. Materials might also be exchanged at this working group level. In addition, the exchange of visiting professors could be conducted. Professors from one country may offer courses for one semester or a year in the other country. They would teach economic and legal process and laws of their own country, while bringing up economic and legal issues widely discussed at both the domestic and international level. This would help a better understanding of, and a "refresher course" on, what is going on in the other country.

In addition, consultation regarding legislation may be conducted within the framework of these nongovernmental institutions, the purpose of which is to make known to one another the legislative histories, the meaning of certain ambiguous provisions, and the possible effects of the implementation of statutes in question.

In order to understand each other's decision-making processes, government officials from one country could spend some time in less-sensitive departments of the other. In case there is difficulty in making such arrangements, they might establish a direct relationship with their foreign counterparts through their own embassy. In fact, members of each embassy themselves could take the initiative toward this end. For instance, Chinese officials in Washington, DC, may spend some time and get to know someone in the executive branch and on Capitol Hill. They may discuss trade issues, legal and economic, and the reform of the foreign trade laws of the United States.

Unofficial exchanges, such as reciprocal visits of scholars, scheduled meetings, and the exchange of scholars and students, would be beneficial for resolving the problem of misunderstanding, too. Although the number of exchange students is growing fast, such students in the social sciences are still quite rare. In the coming years, more students in the fields of social science, such as law, economics, etc., may be exchanged. Also, reciprocal training and education in enterprise management, trade, and finance should be conducted among Chinese and US enterprises.

In order to resolve economic and legal issues arising from bilateral economic exchange, a few concrete measures can be taken at unilateral, bilateral, and multilateral levels. What China can do perhaps is first to perfect its laws and legal systems. With the development of its modernization program and the experience gained from it, China is now able to adopt more concrete and clear-cut rules, which are urgently needed, and supplemental laws and regulations to implement the existing ones. The publication of authoritative interpretations of current laws and court decisions would help implement existing laws correctly. It would also serve as a measure of education, for promulgated laws and regulations are still too new for both foreigners and most Chinese to know how they have been applied. Publicity of the actual application of laws, functioning as a guide, would help increase the legal sensitivity of the society as a whole.

The development of economic exchanges with foreign countries has posed to China's lawmakers the new question of the transfer of wholly foreign-owned companies' stocks.[2] Although the Chinese law on joint ventures with foreign countries stipulates that the foreign partner must seek the consent of the Chinese partner before transferring shares to third parties, those concerning wholly foreign-owned enterprises do not have provisions concerning the transfer of stocks. Issues like this may require China to make careful studies and to adopt relevant rules promptly.

China has no tradition of judicial review of administrative acts, although recent legislation establishes the courts as the forum of last resort – after friendly consultations have been exhausted to remedy disputes between foreigners and tax and labor authorities. In order to apply laws and policy coordinately, rules governing bureaucracy must be adopted. In addition, a statute regarding coordination among different agencies that are within the purview of the state bureaucracy could be adopted to avoid conflicting administrative regulations and policies.

In financing its ambitious economic development plan, China may introduce a stock market to its economy, allowing certain companies to issue stocks. Stock issues could benefit the Chinese economy in many ways. Having more investment opportunities, the Chinese would spend less on consumer goods, which in turn would help ease inflation. Efficiency and cost-effectiveness would also improve, because the managers of the enterprises going public would have to be responsible to shareholders. Small foreign investors would also welcome the opportunity to establish business relations with China by buying shares in Chinese enterprises. They might be able to give advice on how the plant should be run as well.

Another measure for developing bilateral relations taken by China is direct Chinese investment in US enterprises. To play the game of the stock market, however, requires a well-established information system, because of the risky nature of stocks. At present, China is by no means familiar with the sophisticated international stock market. Although this situation may change with China's increasing interest in international economic activities and especially with the establishment of an information system, large-scale measures may not be recommended at the moment. Nevertheless, this measure of investment would, at the very least, provide the Chinese with a close look at the management and operations of US companies.

The United States, on the other hand, can take some unilateral measures, too, at both the presidential and congressional levels. One of the actions the president can take is to expedite the process of transfer of technology to China. Although a set of new rules has been drafted, the effect of the new policy in individual cases is still waiting to be seen. The president could issue a policy guideline stipulating that in actual transactions China should be treated on the same basis with Western countries and that review of export applications by the Defense Department is not necessary unless the case in question is extraordinarily important.

China is a new- and latecomer to the US market, and it has trade deficits with the United States. Also, it is a less-developed and large country. Taking these factors into consideration, the US government should give China larger quotas and a bigger increase in some trade sectors in which China is disadvantaged compared with other foreign exporters, for example, in textile products. This may be achieved by balancing shares of the US market among foreign exporters in accordance with each exporter's domestic economic situation and bilateral trade circumstances with the United States, such as the balance of payment of the bilateral trade.

At the same time, flexibility might be allowed for certain Chinese exports. Because of the dissimilarity between the two countries, in social structure, habits and customs, and diet, traditional Chinese exports may not be familiar to US citizens and may not meet certain requirements. For instance, when China's special local products, such as edible fungus, fermented bean curd, and herbal medicine, first came into the US market, they were immediately subject to the Food and Drug Administration's standard of the US government. Under this standard, they were not qualified for import. Owing to the special and local nature of these products, the Chinese find it difficult to process them with modern facilities. If cases of such nature are treated with some flexibility, tension in the bilateral trade would ease to some extent.

Another step that may be taken at the presidential level is to make China qualified for access to US grain grants, under the Agricultural Trade and Development Assistance Act of 1954 (Public Law 480), which currently are not available to it. This can be accomplished by a presidential determination that China is not a country dominated by international Communism and is friendly to the United States.

At the congressional level, concurrent with the efforts to reform US trade laws, Congress can single China out from other nonmarket economy countries. The fact of putting China on the same footing with other friendly countries would have a tremendous effect on the bilateral relationship. It might not hurt US domestic industry either, since import regulations would be still applicable to China's products.

The separation of China from nonmarket economy countries has a material and logical basis, taking into consideration China's economic structure and policies. Although its economy is mainly state owned and centrally planned, it is becoming an increasingly diversified economy that may eventually lose its original face. Private enterprises and joint venures as well as wholly foreign-owned firms have been growing rapidly. In 1978, there were only 150,000 licensed private businesses. This number surged to 2.6 million by the end of 1982.[3] With the full endorsement of the Central Party Committee and State Council, more private enterprises, which include restaurants, tailors, specialized retailers, repair services, etc., will be set up.

A tax system is being introduced to China's economic system. It will be applicable to state-owned, collectively owned, and private enterprises. With these changes taking place, the market has become an important force in the economy. Under such circumstances, it seems necessary for the United States to treat China differently.

Another action that Congress can take is to amend the Foreign Assistance Act of 1961 to allow assistance to China. This proposed amendment could either remove the existing barriers to aid to China or allow the president with discretion to lift the restrictions on aid to China imposed by the statute.

There are several bilateral steps that can be taken to promote better China-US economic relations. In terms of legal institutions, although some have been established, more effective specific actions can be taken, such as the signing of detailed tax arrangements, an investment cooperation agreement,[4] and a long-term loan agreement. The tax arrangements should include provisions covering business earnings, individual income, and income from international transportation and investment. They should also include the definition of various terms, the accounting system to be employed in calculation, and nondiscrimination clauses.

In addition, more concrete provisions may be included, concerning the determination of natural and legal persons, personal and real property, deduction or exemption, applicability of tax credit, and procedures for dispute settlement. Of these, the determination of natural persons should be adopted so that a person living in the foreign country for a certain period of time, such as six months or one year, should be treated as a resident and taxed as its national. Those who live in the said foreign country for less than the said period should not be treated as its national and should therefore be taxed at a different tax rate. The effect of tax deductions or examptions by one country's tax law on the other country's law should be specified. China and the United States should also stipulate in the tax arrangements that taxes paid under one country's tax laws can be credited under the other's.

An investment cooperation agreement between China and the United States would facilitate US companies' participation in China's development projects. The question of negotiating such an agreement was brought up at the first session of the China-US Joint Commission on Commerce and Trade cochaired by Chen Muhua and Malcolm Baldridge in May 1983 in Peking. The proposed agreement should include provisions of protection and guarantee by the government for compensation for expropriation of foreign property and for convertibility of local currency. Another important provision should be consultation. It should specify that the two governments should consult with each other respecting projects and activities and their contribution to the economic and social development of each other. This consultation clause would better coordinate economic exchanges between the two countries. Other provisions might concern the transfer of capital and earnings, compensation for expropriation and war damages, and settlement of disputes.

A long-term loan agreement would serve US private sectors investing in China by being a further guarantee of China's capability to cooperate in joint programs. The difficulty is the interest rate. As discussed in Chapter 4, the US Ex-Im Bank does not have enough funds to provide large-amount preferential loans to foreign governments. Nor is it able to make discount loans on a large scale to domestic commercial banks. In order to sign a competitive loan agreement with China, the United States may have to allocate additional funds to the Ex-Im Bank.

At the multilateral level, GATT membership for China would accelerate China-US economic exchanges. China now enjoys the MFN status under the Trade Relations Agreement between China and the United States. Still more preferential tariffs would be gained if China became a member of the GATT. On December 15, 1983, China's application to become a party to the MFA, including the protocols adopted in the previous years, was enthusiastically approved by all other treaty nations with no rejections.[5] China had enjoyed an observer status in the negotiations of the arrangement since 1981. It is reported that a Chinese delegation conducted informal negotiations with officials of the GATT in September 1983,[6] with a view toward becoming a member. The GATT membership would place China on the same footing with other developing countries and make it eligible for Generalized System of Preferences duty treatment in bilateral trade. The Generalized System of Preferences allows for the dutyfree importation of certain nonsensitive items from beneficiary developing countries. It is estimated that from 13 to 19 percent of China's exports to the United States in 1980 would have been eligible for dutyfree tariffs, had it been granted this treatment.

NOTES

1. On many occasions, Chinese leaders have stated that the Taiwan issue is the major obstacle in Sino-American relations. At some points, the US policy toward Taiwan, especially its arms sales, caused serious problems in the bilateral relationship. Although the Taiwan issue is of great significance and interesting, it is not treated here.

2. In October 1983, creditors appointed Peat Marwick Mitchell & Co. as the receiver for LMK Nam Sang Dyeing Factory Ltd., which was unable to repay its debts. LMK Nam Sang, China's largest printing and dyeing factory, is a unit of the Lo's Mee Kwong Holdings Ltd., formerly part of the Lo's Mee Kwong group of Hong Kong. An earlier debt-rescheduling arrangement separated LMK Nam Sang from the Lo's Mee Kwong group, which was placed in receivership in September 1983. The group's creditors petitioned the Hong Kong Supreme Court to liquidate Lo's Mee Kwong Holdings so that some of its assets could be sold to an unidentified prospective buyer. LMK Nam Sang is in the Shenzhen special economic zone of China. About 70 percent of its shares are held by the Lo family.

3. *Asian Wall Street Journal*, October 10, 1983, p. 14.

4. Although an industrial cooperation agreement was initiated during Premier Zhao Ziyang's visit to the United States in early 1984, it has not yet been signed.

5. *China Daily News*, December 17, 1983, p. 2.

6. *Peimei News*, September 19, 1983, p. 2.

BIBLIOGRAPHY

PERIODICALS AND NEWSPAPERS

Asian Wall Street Journal, Hong Kong

Beijing Review, Beijing, China

Business America (biweekly), US Department of Commerce, Washington, DC

Business Asia, Business International Corp., New York, New York

Business China (biweekly), Business International Corp., New York, New York

Business International (weekly), Business International Corp., New York, New York

Business Lawyer, American Bar Association, Chicago, Illinois

Campaigns and Elections (Quarterly), Washington, DC, Stanley Foster Reed

China Business Review, National Council for US-China Trade, Washington, DC

China Daily News, New York, New York

China Law Reporter, Hong Kong

China's Foreign Trade, Beijing, China

China Trade Report, Far Eastern Economic Review Ltd., Hong Kong

Christian Science Monitor, Washington, DC

Faxue Yanjiu (法學研究 - Legal Studies), Beijing, China

Federal Register, Washington, DC

Hong Kong Standard, Hong Kong

International Trade Reporter's US Export Weekly, The Bureau of National Affairs, Inc., Washington, DC

Minzhu Yu Fazbi (民主與法制 - Democracy and Legal System), Beijing, China

New York Times, New York, New York

Peimei News, New York, New York

Public Citizen (Quarterly), Washington, DC

Quarterly Report to the Congress and the East-West Foreign Trade Board on Trade Between the United States and the Nonmarket Economy Countries, US International Trade Commission, Government Printing Office, Washington, DC

BOOKS AND ARTICLES

Abbott, Kenneth W., "Linking Trade to Political Goals: Foreign Policy Export Controls in the 1970s and 1980s," 65 *Minnesota Law Review* 739 (1981).

Adams, Walter, and Birlam, Joel B., "Import Competition and the Trade Act of 1974: A Case Study of Section 201 and Its Interpretation by the International Trade Commission," 52 *Indiana Law Journal* 535 (1977).

Alexander, Herbert E., *Financing the 1972 Election* (Lexington, DC Heath, 1976).

Anderson, William, *American Government* (New York, H. Holt and Company, 1938).

Anthony, Robert A., "The American Response to Dumping from Capitalist and Socialist Economies – Substantive Premises and Restructured Procedures After the 1967 GATT Code," 54 *Cornell Law Review* 159 (1969).

Arey, Hawthorne, *History of Operations and Policies of Export-Import Bank of Washington* (Washington, DC, 1953).

Aufricht, Hans, *The International Monetary Fund* (New York, International Monetary Fund 1964).

Babinski, David, "Trade – The Export Administration Act of 1979," 4 *Suffolk Transnational Law Journal* 361 (1980).

Barcelo, John J., III, "Subsidies, Countervailing Duties and Antidumping After the Tokyo Round," 13 *Cornell International Law Journal* 257 (1980).

Barnet, Richard, *The Roots of War* (Baltimore, Penguin Books, 1972).

Barnett, A. Doak, *China's Economy in Global Perspective* (Washington, DC, The Brookings Institution, 1981).

Barringer, William H., and Dunn, Christopher A., "Antidumping and Countervailing Duties Investigations Under the Trade Agreement Act of 1979," 14 *International Law and Economics* 1 (1980).

Beckhart, Benjamin Haggott, *Federal Reserve System* (New York, The American Bankers Association, 1972).

Berman, Harold J., and Garson, John R., "United States Export Controls – Past, Present, and Future," 67 *Columbia Law Review* 792 (1967).

Bertsch, Gary K., "US Export Controls: The 1970s and Beyond," 15 *Journal of World Trade Law* 67 (1981).

Bingham, Jonathan B., "The Export Administration Act of 1979: A Congressional Perspective," *American Society of International Law Proceedings* 88 (1980).

Black, Charles L., Jr., *Perspectives in Constitutional Law* (Englewood Cliffs, Prentice-Hall, 1963).

——*Structure and Relationship in Constitutional Law* (Baton Rouge, Louisiana State University Press, 1969).

Brandis, R. Buford, *The Making of Textile Trade Policy 1935-1981* (Washington, DC, American Textile Manufacturers Institute, Inc., 1982).

Branting, Luther Karl, "Reconciliation of Conflicting Goals in the Export Administration Act of 1979 – A Delicate Balance," 12 *Law and Policy in International Business* 415 (1980).

Brown, Peter R., "China's New Joint Venture Law: Analysis and Economic Overview," 4 *Boston College International and Comparative Law Review*, 115 (1981).

Bu, Ming, "China's Financial Relations with Foreign Countries," *Beijing Review*, No. 16, April 20, 1981, p. 21.

Burns, James MacGregor, Peltason, J.W., and Crowin, Thomas E., *Government by the People* (1978).

Buxbaum, David C., Cassondra, Joseph E. and Reynolds, Paul D., eds., *China Trade: Prospects and Perspectives* (New York, Praeger Publishers, 1982).

Buxbaum, David, and Reynolds, Paul, *Doing Business with China: An Export Perspective* (New York, Holt, Rinehart & Winston, 1980).

Castleman, Don R., "Taxation in the People's Republic of China: The System and Its Function," 46 *Albany Law Review* 776 (1982).

Childress, Steven Alan, "Executive Authority: Revocation of Executive Order Requiring Notification of Export of Hazardous Substances -Exec. Order No. 12, 290, 46 *Fed. Reg.* 12, 943 (1981)," 22 *Harvard International Law Journal* 683 (1981).

China – International Business: An Information and Research Series (New York, Pergamon Press, 1981).

Cohen, Jerome A., "A Look at China's Joint Venture Law," *Asian Wall Street Journal*, July 30, 1979, p. 10.

——, "Equity Joint Ventures," *China Business Review*, November-December 1982, p. 23.

Cohen, Richard A., "The Trade Agreement Act of 1979: Executive Agreements, Subsidies, and Countervailing Duties," 15 *Texas International Law Journal* 96 (1980).

Cox, Betsy C., and Shnerling, Gary, "Interagency Conflict: A Model for Analysis," 9 *Georgia Journal of International and Comparative Law* 241 (1979).

Crabb, Cecil V., Jr., *Invitation to Struggle: Congress, the President and Foreign Policy* (Washington, DC, Congressional Quarterly, 1980).

Cuneo, Donald L., and Manuel, Charles B., Jr., "Roadblock to Trade: The State Controlled Economy Issue in Antidumping Law Administration," 5 *Fordham International Law Journal* 277 (1982).

Dale, Richard, *Antidumping Law in a Liberal Trade Order* (New York, St. Martin's Press, 1980).

Das, Bohagirath L., "The GATT Multi-Fibre Arrangement," 17 *Journal of World Trade Law* 95 (1983).

Deferovich, Patrick B., "United States Export of Banned Products: Legal and Moral Implications," 10 *Denver Journal of International Law and Policy* 537 (1981).

Donovan, Christopher, "The Export Administration Act of 1879: Refining United States Export Control Machinery," 4 *Boston College International and Comparative Law Review* 77 (1981).

Duff, John M., Jr., "The Outlook for Official Export Credit," 13 *Law and Policy in International Business* 891 (1981).

Dvorin, Shirley Miller, "The Export Administration Act of 1979: An Examination of Foreign Availability of Controlled Goods and Technologies,"2NW *Journal of International Law and Business* 179 (1980).

Ecker, Janet E.B., "National Security Protection: The Critical Technologies Approach to US Export Control of High-Level Technology," 15 *Journal of International Law and Economy* 575 (1981).

Eckhardt, Bob, and Black, Charles L., Jr., *The Tides of Power* (New Haven, Yale University Press, 1976).

Edwards, W. David, "Legal and Economic Considerations on Doing Business in the People's Republic of China," 12 *California Western International Law Journal* 352 (1982).

Ehrenhaft, Peter D., "Holes in the Trade Agreements Act Becoming Evident," 3 *Legal Times Washington*, June 30, 1980, p. 11.

Elliott, Richard S., "The Export Administration Act of 1979: Latest Statutory Resolution of the Right to Export Versus National Security and Foreign Policy Controls," 19 *Columbia Journal of Transnational Law* 255 (1981).

Evrard, John T., "The Export Administration Act of 1979: Analysis of Its Major Provisions and Potential Impact on United States Exporters," 12 *California Western International Law Journal* 1 (1982).

Federal Reserve System (Washington, DC, Government Printing Office, 1974).

Flores, David A., "Export Controls and the US Effort to Combat International Terrorism," 13 *Law and Policy in International Business* 521 (1981).

Garson, G. David, *Power and Politics in the United States* (Lexington, Mass. D.C. Heath, 1977).

"GATT: Third Multifibre Arrangement," 16 *Journal of World Trade Law* 178 (1982).

Gellhorn, Ernest, and Boyer, Barry B., *Administrative Law and Process* (St. Paul, West Publishing Co., 1981).

Gold, Joseph, *Interpretation by the Fund* (Washington, DC, International Monetary Fund, 1968).

——, *Financial Assistance by the International Monetary Fund* (Washington, DC, International Monetary Fund, 1979).

——, *Legal and Institutional Aspects of the International Monetary System: Selected Essays* (Washington, DC, International Monetary Fund, 1979).

——, *The Legal Character of the Fund's Stand-By Arrangements and Why It Matters* (Washington, DC, International Monetary Fund, 1980).

Green, Mark J., *The Other Government* (New York, Norton, 1978).

Green, Mark J., Fallows, James M., and Zwick, David R., *Who Runs Congress?* (New York, Bantam Books, 1972).

Greenberg, Edward S., *The American Political System: A Radical Approach* (Cambridge, Winthrop Publishers, 1977).

Hemmendinger, Noel, and Barringer, William H., "The Defense of Antidumping and Countervailing Duty Investigations Under the Trade Agreements Act of 1979," 6 *North Carolina Journal of International Law and Commercial Regulations* 427 (1981).

Henkin, Louis, *Foreign Affairs and the Constitution* (New York, Foundation Press, 1972).

Hinman, George Burke, "China, Modernization, and Sino-United States Trade: Will China Submit to Arbitration?" 10 *California Western International Law Journal* 53 (1980).

Hsia, Tao Tai, "Sources of Law in the People's Republic of China: Recent Developments," 14 *International Lawyer* 25 (1980).

Hsia, Tao Tai, and Hahn, Elizabeth, "China's Joint Venture Law," 1 *China Law Reporter* 5 (1980).

Hsiao, Gene T., *The Foreign Trade of China: Policy, Law, and Practice* (Berkeley, University of California Press, 1977).

Inside Congress (Congressional Quarterly, Washington, DC, 1979).

Jehle, Eugene, *Investment and Taxation in the People's Republic of China*, 3rd ed. (Amsterdam, International Bureau of Fiscal Documentation, 1981).

Ji, Chongwei, "China's Utilization of Foreign Funds and Relevant Policies," *Beijing Review*, No. 16, April 20, 1981, p. 15.

Jones, William C., "Commentary Reflections on the Modern Chinese Legal System," 59 *Washington University Law Quarterly* 1121 (1981).

Kirby, James C., Jr., *Congress and the Public Trust* (New York, Atheneum, 1970).

Leigh, Monroe, "Dumping – Judicial Review of Negative Preliminary Injury Determination – Burden of Proof," 75 *American Journal of International Law* 660 (1981).

Lew, Luciana, "Recent Legal Developments in US-China Economic Relations," 36 *Business Lawyer* 1699 (1981)

Lewis, John Bruce, and Ottley, Bruce L., "China's Developing Labor Law," 59 *Washington University Law Quarterly* 1165 (1981).

Low, Patrick, "The Definition of 'Export Subsidies' in GATT," 16 *Journal of World Trade Law* 375 (1982).

Lowenfeld, Andreas F., 4 *International Economic Law* (1977).

Lubman, Stanley, "China Looks for Partners to Boost Output," *Boston Sunday Globe*, October 28, 1979, p. 4.

Lynch, Morris A., "Summary of Statutory Provisions Related to Import Relief," 94 *Federal Rules Decision* 503 (1982).

Marturano, Janice, "US Legislative Import Relief Options: A Compromise of Procedures," 13 *New York University Journal of International Law and Politics* 1049 (1981).

Meltsner, Arnold, *Politics and the Oval Office* (San Francisco Institute for Contemporary Studies, 1981).

Mills, C. Wright, *The Power Elite* (New York, Oxford University Press, 1956).

Moser, Michael J., "Documentation for Commercial Bank Loans to Chinese Borrowers: Some Legal and Practical Issues," in *Legal Aspects of Doing Business in China* (New York, Practicing Law Institute, 1983).

Murphy, John F., and Downey, Arthur T., "National Security, Foreign Policy and Individual Rights: The Quandary of United States Export Control," 30 *International and Comparative Law Quarterly* 791 (1981).

Murphy, Terrence Roche, "Antidumping and Countervailing Duties Under the Trade Agreements Act of 1979: A Preliminary Analysis," 14 *International Lawyer* 203 (1980).

National Council for US-China Trade, *The China Business Manual 1981* (Washington, DC, National Council for U.S. China Trade, 1981).

Neill, Denis M., "Export Legislation in 1982," 38 *Journal of the Missouri Bar* 127 (1982).

Nowaak, Nancy L., "The Trade Agreements Act of 1979: Countervailing Duties and Antidumping Duty Procedures," 14 *Journal of International Law and Economics* (1980).

Origins and Development of Congress (Congressional Quarterly, Washington, DC, 1976).

Ortwine, Bruce A., "Injury Determination Under United States Antidumping Laws Before and After the Trade Agreements Act of 1979," 33 *Rutgers Law Review* 1076 (1981).

Pattison, Joseph E., "China's Developing Legal Framework for Foreign Investment Experience and Expectations," 13 *Law and Policy in International Business* 89 (1981).

——, "Special Economic Zones in the People's Republic of China: The Provincial Experiment," 1 *China Law Reporter* 141 (1981).

Pious, Richard M., *The Power to Govern. Assessing Reform in the United States* (New York, Academy of Political Science, 1981).

Potts, Linda F., and Lyons, James M., "The Trade Agreements Act: Administrative Policy and Practice in Antidumping Investigations (Symposium: A Practitioner's Guide to International Trade Law)," 6 *North Carolina Journal of International Law and Commercial Regulations* 483 (1981).

Powers of Congress (Congressional Quarterly, Washington, DC, 1976).

Prensky, David N., el al., "International Trade Commission: Operations Under the Trade Act of 1974," 8 *Law and Policy in International Business* 310 (1976).

Propp, Kenneth, "Export Controls: Restrictions on the Export of Critical Technologies – Initial Militarily Critical Technologies List, 15 CFR 391.1 (1974), as amended by 45 *Fed. Reg.* 43010 (1980)," 22 *Harvard International Law Journal* 411 (1981).

Randt, Clark T., Jr., "China's Provisional Foreign Exchange Control Regulations," 1 *China Law Reporter* 117 (1981).

Reisman, W. Michael, *Folded Lies: Bribery, Crusades, and Reforms* (New York, Free Press, 1979).

Ren, Jianxin, "Some Legal Aspects of Our Import of Technology and Utilization of Foreign Investment," 1 *China Law Reporter* 85 (1980).

Rendell, Robert S., "Export Financing and the Role of the Export-Import Bank of the United States," 11 *Journal of International Law and Economics* 91 (1976).

Reynolds, Paul D., "Doing Business with the People's Republic of China: Tax Considerations," 14 *International Lawyer* 49 (1980).

—— "The Joint Venture Law of the People's Republic of China: Preliminary Observations," 14 *International Lawyer* 31 (1980).

Ribicoff, Abraham A., "The US Trade Agreement Act of 1979," 8 *Brooklyn Journal of International Law* 3 (1982).

Robinson, James A., *Congress and Foreign Policy Making* (Homewood, Greenwood; Princeton, Princeton University Press, 1976).

Rossiter, Clinton L., *Constitutional Dictatorship* (New York, 1948).

Rotberg, Eugene, *The World Bank: A Financial Appraisal* (Washington, DC, World Bank, 1981).

Saffell, David C., *The Politics of American National Government* (Cambridge, 1978).

Saye, Albert B., Allums, John F., and Pound, Merritt B., *Principles of American Government* (Englewood Cliffs, Prentice-Hall, 1962, 1978).

Schriftgiesser, Karl, *The Lobbyists* (Boston, Little, Brown, 1951).

Scott, Andrew M., and Wallace, Earle, eds., *Politics, USA Cases on the American Democratic Process* (New York, Macmillan, 1969).

Shannon, W. Wayne, *Party, Constituency and Congressional Voting* (Baton Rouge, Louisiana State University Press, 1968).

Siff, Ted, and Weil, Alan, *Ruling Congress* (Washington, DC, Congressman Publishers, 1975).

Skidmore, Max J., and Wanke, Marshall Carter, *American Government: A Brief Introduction*, 2nd ed. (New York, St. Martin's Press, 1977).

Slayton, John, "The Trade Agreements Act of 1979: Material Injury Standard," 14 *Journal of International Law and Economics* 87 (1980).

Solomon, Frederic, Cooper, Jeffrey, and Shapiro, Howard Roberts, eds., 4 *Banking Law* (New York, Matthew Bender, 1982).

Solomon, Richard H., ed. *The China Factor* (Englewood Cliffs, Prentice-Hall, 1981).

Staple, Peter D., "Subsidies and Countervailing Duties Under the Trade Agreement Act of 1979," 5 *North Carolina Journal of International Law and Commercial Regulations* 533 (1980).

Starr, John B., ed., *The Future of US-China Relations* (New York, NYU Press, 1981).

Stepanek, James B., "Direct Investment in China," *China Business Review* September-October 1982, p. 20.

Truman, David B., *The Governmental Process*, 2nd ed. (New York, Alfred A. Knopf, 1971).

Tung, Rosalie, *US-China Trade Negotiations* (New York, Pergamon Press, 1982).

US Department of Commerce, Industry and Trade Administration, *Doing Business With China* (Washington, DC, Government Printing Office 1979).

Vishny, Paul H., "Import and Export Financing," 3 *Banking and Commercial Lending Law* (1982).

Wallace, Don, Jr., Spina, George C., Rawson, Richard M., and McGill, Brian, eds., *Interface One* (Washington, DC, Georgetown University Law Center, 1980).

Wang, N.T., ed., *Business With China: An International Reassessment* (New York, Pergamon Press, 1980).

Wei, Yuming, "China's Policy on Absorption of Direct Investment from Foreign Countries," *Beijing Review*, July 26, 1982, p. 18.

—— "China's Absorption of Foreign Funds and Relevant Policies," *China's Economic News*, Supplement No. 3 (1981).

Welshans, Merle T., and Melicher, Ronald W., *Finance* (Cincinnati, South-Western Publishing Co., 1980).

Whitley, Sherry Castle, Schlichting, William H., and Cooper, Jeffrey, eds., *Banking Law* (New York, Matthew Bender, 1982).

Wildavsky, Aaron, *Perspectives on the Presidency* (Boston, Little, Brown, 1975).

Winter, Audrey S., and Garlson, Richard, *The World Bank* (Washington, DC, IBRD, 1957).

——"Export Licensing: Uncoordinated Trade Repression," 9 *Georgia Journal of International and Comparative Law* 333 (1979).

The World Bank Annual Report 1982 (Washington, DC, World Bank, 1982).

Yao, Zhuang, "The Positive Role of the Law on Joint Ventures Using Chinese and Foreign Investment," *Renmin Ribao*, July 24, 1979.

Young, Ralph A., *Instruments of Monetary Policy in the United States* (Washington, DC, International Monetary Fund, 1973).

Zhang, Enhua, "On Banking Reform," *Beijing Review*, No. 29, July 20, 1981, p. 24.

Zhao, Suzheng, "What Taxes Should Foreigners Pay in China?" *Beijing Review*, October 26, 1981, p. 43.

INDEX

A

Abourezk, James, 59
ACEP. *See* Advisory Committee for Export Policy
administrative agencies (US): cabinet, 65-66; decision-making functions, 67; economic relations with foreign countries, 66-67; judiciary functions, 67; power base of, 66; relation with interest groups, 68-69
Advisory Committee for Export Policy (ACEP), 126
Agricultural Bank of China, 91, 94
agricultural commodities: import ban by China, 180-181; United States exports to China, 3, 4, 9-10
Agricultural Trade Act of 1978, 3
Amalgamated Clothing and Textile Workers Union, 187
American Express Company, 89
American Mushroom Institute, 156
American Textile Manufacturers Institute, 185, 187
antidumping laws (US): Antidumping Act of 1916, 142-143; Antidumping Act of 1921, 143-144; Chinese mushrooms case, 156, 158-163; and comparable economic development, 151-152; constructed value determination, 149-150; Escape Clause Law, 152-153; fair value determination, 147-148; foreign market value determination, 148-149; and GATT, 164-167; like product provisions, 145-146, 153-154; material injury concept, 153-155, 160-162, 166; and nonmarket economies, 150-152, 163-167; Polish Golf Cars case, 151; presidential determination, 155-156; reform proposals, 163-167; significant cause, 152, 154-155, 160-162; Tariff Act of 1930, 144-145; Trade Agreements Act of 1979, 145-147
Arco China Inc., 12
assets, blocked, 5
Atlantic Richfield Co., 14

B

Baker Marine Corporation, 12
Ball, George, 122
Bank of China, 88, 89, 91, 92; export credits, providing of, 92, 96; participating in syndicated loans, 92-93
Bank of Tokyo, 93
Battle Act, 119-120
Beijing Economic Development Corporation, 96
bilateral economic relations: claims and assets settlement, 5; commercial exchanges, 9-13; emigration policies, 6, 7; institutional exchanges, proposed, 194-195; investment cooperation, proposed, 199; legal framework, 5-9; political factors, 13-17; pre-1971, 2; and Taiwan issue, 16; tax reforms, proposed, 198-199
bilateral trade relations: agricultural trade, 3, 4, 9-10; China's trade deficit, 4, 16, 182, 197; Chinese

mushrooms case, 156, 158-163; export control by United States, 118-119, 127-128; reforms, proposed, 197-198, 199-200; and technology transfer, 16-17, 132-137, 197. *See also* textile trade
Brady, Lawrence J., 133
Bu Ming, 90
bureaucracy, federal, *see* administrative agencies (US)

C

campaigns, election, *see* election campaigns
Carter, Jimmy, 1, 6, 98, 134, 156
CCC. *See* Commodity Credit Corporation
CCL. *See* commodity control list
CEROILS, 159-162
Certain Welded Stainless Steel Pipe and Tube case, 144
Chartered Bank, 93
Chen Muhua, 95
China: coal resources, 14; Election Law, 27-28; financial systems, history of, 90-91; five-year plan (1981-1985), 15; foreign economic relations, 22-23; foreign loans to, 88-90, 95-96; foreign trade, 184; as nonmarket economy, 198; oil resources, 13-14; taxation, 44-46, 100-101; textile industry, 181; trade deficit, 4, 16, 182, 197. *See also* bilateral economic relations; bilateral trade relations; foreign investments in China
China-Brown and Root Marine Engineering and Construction Company LTD, 13
China Commercial Shipping Corporation, 33
China Committee (CHINCOM), 118
China Council for Promotion of International Trade, 2
China International Travel Service, 102
China International Trust and Investment Corporation (CITIC), 89, 93
China Investment Bank, 94
China National Cereals, Oil, and Foodstuff Import and Export Corporation. *See* CEROILS
China National Offshore Oil Corporation, 12
China Ocean Shipping Company, 96
China Offshore Platform Engineering Corporation, 12
China-US Joint Committee on Scientific and Technological Cooperation, 8
CHINCOM. *See* China Committee
Chinese Communist Party, 31-32
Chinese mushrooms case, 156, 158-163
CITIC. *See* China International Trust and Investment Corporation
Claims and Assets Settlement Agreements, 5
coal industry: China, 14; economic exchanges, 11-12
COCOM. *See* Coordinating Committee
Commerce, US Department of: and dumping cases, 146-147; and export licensing, 125-126, 128-130; and fair value, 147-148; Office of Export Administration (OEA), 126, 131, 132
commercial banks: lending limit regulations, 98-100; loans to China, regulations for, 99-101; tax regulations in China, 100-101
commercial exchanges, 9-15
commodity control list (CCL), 130

Commodity Credit Corporation (CCC), 3; deferred payment programs, 4; export credit sales programs, 4
Communist countries, trade regulations by United States, 157-158
comparable economic development, 151-152
Congress (US): appropriation of funds power, 55; commerce power, 54-55; committee chairpersons, 60; conference committees, 59-60; filibuster rule, 58-59; joint committees, 59; legislative process, 61-63; select committees, 59; standing committees, 60; terms of office, 57; treaty power, 55
Congressional Quarterly, 57
constructed value, 149-150
contracts and agreements, 11-13, 14
Coordinating Committee (COCOM), 118-120
cotton, imports by China, 9-10

D

Daiwa Securities Company, 93
deferred payment program (US), 4
Deng Xiaoping, 1
Denysky, Bohdan, 133, 134, 135
Dolan, Terry, 77
dumping: Congressional review, 155-156; definition, 140; ITC investigation, 145-147, 153-155, 158-163. *See also* antidumping laws

E

economic relations, bilateral, *see* bilateral economic relations
economic zones in China: employment contracts, 37-38; regulations, 36-37; Shantou, 34; Shenzhen, 33-34; taxation, 36-37; Xiamen, 34-35; Zhuhai, 34
Eckes, Alfred, 160, 161, 162
EEC. *See* European Economic Community
Elcap Electronics Ltd., 134
election campaigns (US): expenditures, 70-71; fund raising, 71-72; laws regulating fund raising, 72-73; role of pressure groups, 77
Election Law (China), 27-28
emigration policy (China), 6, 7
ES Pacific hotel venture case, 40
Escape Clause Law, 152-153
European Economic Community (EEC): mushroom imports from China, 162; textile trade, 175
Ex-Im Bank of the United States: credit policy toward China, 97-98; establishment of, 96-97; problems, 103, programs, 97
export control policy of United States: administrative structure, 125-127; Battle Act, 119-120; country groups, 127-128; Export Administration Act of 1979, 122-125; Export Control Act of 1949, 116-118; Export Control Act of 1969, 120-122; on technical data, 130-132; toward China, 118-119, 127-128; toward Hong Kong, 133-135; and Western Europe cooperation, 118-120. *See also* export licenses; technology transfer
export credit sales program, 4
Export-Import (Ex-Im) Bank of the United States. *See* Ex-Im Bank of the United States
export licenses: application for validated license, 130; by Department of Commerce, 125-126, 128-130; general license, 128-129;

reviewing of, 128; validated license, 129; violations, 132. *See also* technology transfer
Export-Import Bank Act of 1945, 96

F

fair value, 147-148
Fairchild Test System Group, 133, 134
federal bureaucracy, *see* administrative agencies (US)
Federal Election Campaign Act of 1974, 72
Federal Register, 68
Federal Reserve Act, 78
Federal Reserve System (US): board of governors, 78-79; establishment, 78; Federal Advisory Council, 79-80; Federal Open-Market Committee, 79; member banks, 78; relations with Treasury, 80; role in financial decision making, 80
Feng Tienshun, 43
financial institutions in China, 90-94
First National Bank of Chicago, 93, 96
First National Boston Ltd., 96
Five-year plan (China), 15
Fluor Mining and Metals Inc., 12
Ford Motor Company, 75
Foreign Credit Insurance Association, 97, 103
Foreign Enterprise Tax Law (China), 45, 100
foreign exchange control (China), 46-47
foreign investments in China: economic zones, 33-38; employment contracts, 37-38; Foreign Enterprise Tax Law, 45; foreign exchange control, 46-47; international competition, 101-104; Joint Venture Law, 38-44; Regulations, on Special Economic Zones in Guangdong Province, 36-37; role of CITIC, 93; taxation 36, 44-46. *See also* foreign loans to China; joint ventures
foreign loans to China: borrowing practices, 95-96; by Ex-Im Bank of the United States, 98, 103; export credit agreements, 89, 92, 95, 96, 101; guarantee of, 96; by IMF, 106; interest rates, 101-103; international competition, 101-104; by Japan, 101-102; lines of credit, 95; syndicated loans, 92-93; by United States commercial banks, 99-101; utilization of, 88-90; by World Bank, 106-107. *See also* foreign investments in China
foreign market value, 148-149

G

GATT. *See* General Agreement on Trade and Tariffs
General Agreement on Trade and Tariffs (GATT): and antidumping, 164-167; and nonmarket economics, 164-167; Working Party on Textiles, 176
Grain Trade Agreement of 1980, 10
grains, *see* agricultural commodities

H

Hainan International Trust and Investment Corporation, 35
Hainan Island, 35
Han Yutong, 31
Hawley-Smoot Act, 7
high technology exports, *see* Technology transfer
Hitachi, Ltd., 119
Hong Kong, export control by United States, 133-135
Hong Kong & Shanghai Banking Corporation, 102
House of Representatives (US): debate, 59; Rules Committee, 59, 60, 62; Speaker of the House, 57-58; terms of office, 57
Hu Yaobang, 31
Hua Guofeng, 1
Hua Ko Electronic Company, 133
Hummel, Arthur W., Jr., 174

I

IBM Corporation, 119
IDA. *See* International Development Association
IMF. *See* International Monetary Fund
Import restrictions by US, on textile trade, 176-181
Industrial and Commercial Bank of China, 91
Industrial Bank of Japan, 93
industrial development (China), 15
International Development Association, 90; loans to China, 106-107
International Ladies' Garment Workers Union, 187
International Monetary Fund (IMF), 90; China's membership, 104-108; loans to China, 106; subscription rights of China, 104
International Trade Commission (ITC): Chinese mushrooms case, 158-163; and dumping investigation, 145-147, 153-155

J

Japan, loans to China, 101-102
Japanese Overseas Economic Cooperation Funds, 89, 101
Joint-Venture Law, 38-44; boards of directors, 40-41; contributions to equity, 39-40; foreign exchange, 46-47; ownership ratios, 39; profit sharing, 40-41; raw materials purchasing, 42; workers, 42
joint ventures: in coal development, 11-12; engineering firms, 11, 12; laws, 38-44; in marine engineering, 13; in offshore oil exploration, 12; role of CITIC, 93; taxation, 44-46
Joint-Venture Tax Law, 44-46

K

Kock-Weser, Caio, 107
Kravitz, Walter, 60

L

Law of Organization, 24
legal systems in China: establishment of, 22; reforms, proposed, 195-196
Li Dengshan, 182, 183
like products, 145-146, 153-154

Liu Shaoqi, 28
Liu Tianfu, 38
Li Xiannian, 39
lobbyists, 73-77; activities, 75-76; influence on legislative process, 74-75; for textile industry, 184-185
Long-Term Arrangement of Cotton Textiles, 176

M

McIntyre, Francis, 117
Manatt, Charles T., 71
Marathon, Ltd., 151
market disruption, 156-158, 159
Markley, Rod, 75
material injury concept, 153-155, 160-162, 166
Metzenbaum, Howard M., 59
MFA. *See* Multi-Fiber Arrangement
MFN. *See* most-favored-nation
Milliken & Company, 186
Ministry of Communications (China), 33
Mondale, Walter, 1, 98
Moore, John L., Jr., 97
most-favored-nation, 3, 6-7
Multi-Fiber Arrangement (MFA), 176-177
mushrooms, *see* Chinese mushrooms case

N

National Bank Act (US), 99
national deputies, 27-28
National People's Congress: election of deputies, 27-28; functions, 24; special committees, 26-27; Standing Committee, 25-26; terms of members, 24
NATO. *See* North Atlantic Treaty Organization
Nixon, Richard M., 2
Nomura Securities Company, 93
nonmarket economies: and antidumping laws, 150-152, 163-167; and GATT, 164-167
nonmarket fair value, 151-152
Nordic Bank, 92
North Atlantic Treaty Organization (NATO), 118
Norwegian Export Finance Authorities, 92
nuclear cooperation agreements, 9

O

Occidental Petroleum Corporation, 11
OEA. *See* Office of Export Administration
Office of Export Administration (OEA), 126, 131, 132
offshore oil exploration, China, 12, 13-14
OPIC. *See* Overseas Private Investment Corporation
Ortwine, Bruce A., 152
Otis Elevator Company, 11
Overseas Private Investment Corporation, 7-8, 99, 103

P

PACs. *See* political action committees
patent protection, 7, 144
Peng Zhen, 26
Penrose, Boies, 76
People's Bank of China, 90, 91, 100

People's Construction Bank, 93
People's Insurance Company of China, 91
Phillips Petroleum Company, 12
Polish Golf Cars case, 151
political action committees (PACs), 77
political parties (US), 69-70
political risk, OPIC role, 7-8
political systems in China: Chinese Communist Party, 31-32; National People's Congress, 24-28; State Council, 29-31; state power, 23-24
Powell, Jody, 71
president, of China, 28-29
president, of United States, 55-56; and dumping cases, 155-156; executive office, 64-65; executive power, 63-64; powers in foreign affairs, 55-56
Presidium (China), 25
Price, Robert, 71
Private Export Funding Corporation (US), 103

R

RCL Semiconductors Ltd., 134
Reagan, Ronald: on export control policy, 133-135; immigration policy, 7; visit to China, 8-9
Regulation of Lobbying Act, 74, 76
Ren Jianxin, 40
Rong Yiren, 41
Royal Bank of Canada, 93

S

San Jose, Inc., 133
Santa Fe Minerals, 12
scientific cooperation, 8
Section 406, 156-158, 159, 162-163
Senate (US): filibuster rule, 58-59; terms of office, 57; unlimited debate, 58-59
Shanghai joint communique, 2, 3
Shanghai Tractor & Automobile Corporation, 39
Shell Oil Company, 12
Shing Kwan Pte Ltd., (Singapore), 102
Sirnot, Nancy, 71
special economic zones, *see* economic zones in China
Standing Committee (China), 25-26
State Administration for Foreign Exchange Control (China), 91
State Council (China), 29-31; functions and powers, 30
Stern, Paula, 160, 161, 162
Strauss, Robert, 178

T

Taiwan issue, and bilateral relations, 16
tariff, 7, 199-200
Tariff Act of 1930, 144-145
tax treaty, 9
taxation (China), 44-46, 100-101; Foreign Enterprise Tax Law, 45; Joint-Venture Tax Law, 44-46
Taylor, John Thomas, 75
technological cooperation, 8
technology transfer, 127; to China, 16-17, 132-137, 197; role of Defense Department, 127; export categories, 135; types of, 130
Thermo Products Corporation, 133
textile trade: China's market share in US, 182-183; competitive

disadvantage of China, 183; countervailing duties, 187-188; difficulties, 181-186; exports by China, 182-183; historical background, 175-181; import restrictions by United States, 177-179; lobbying (US), 184-185; Multi-Fiber Arrangement (MFA), 176-177; prospects of, 186-189; Textile Agreement of 1980, 178-179; unilateral quotas by United States, 179-180

Tianjin Elevator Company, 11

Trade Act of 1974, 6; scope, 156; section 406, 156-158, 159, 162-163

Trade Agreements Act of 1979, 145-147

trade deficit (China), 4, 16, 182

trade delegations, 2-3

trade relations, bilateral, *see* bilateral trade relations

Trade Relations Agreement, 5-6

transfer of technology, *see* technology transfer

U

Union des Banques Arabes et Françaises, 89

United States: administrative agencies, 63-69; agricultural exports, 3, 4, 9-10; Congress, 57-63; export controls, 120-137; foreign economic policies, 3-4; joint ventures with China, 11-13; immigration policies, 7; import restrictions on Communist countries, 157-158; imports from China, 10; loans to China, 96-101; manufactured goods, exports of, 10; monetary policies, 78-81; political parties, 69-73; trade history with China, 2. *See also* bilateral economic relations; bilateral economic relations; bilateral trade relations

V

Varian Associates, 133

Volkswagenwerk AG, 39

W

Wardley Ltd., 102

Wei Yuming, 90

Western Europe, trade with China, 118-120

World Bank, 90, 94; and China, 104-108; loans to China, 106; subscription rights of China, 104

Y

Yan Shan Petrochemical General Corporation, 89, 95

Yuan, Stanley, 92

Z

Zhao Ziyang, 8-9

Zheng Tuobin, 174

ABOUT THE AUTHOR

GUIGUO WANG is currently working at Paul, Hastings, Janofsky & Walker, Los Angeles.

Dr. Wang received his Doctor of the Science of Law (J.S.D.) from Yale University in May, 1984. Dr. Wang also holds a LL.M. from Columbia University and a Diploma (B.A. equivalent; no degree system existent at that time) from Peking Foreign Languages Institute, China. Dr. Wang was also admitted to the LL.M. program in Peking University and finished all the course requirements. In addition, Dr. Wang was the first Chinese recipient, since the establishment of the People's Republic of China, of the United Nations Institute for Training and Research's Fellowship for International Law and participated in seminars offered by the justices of the International Court of Justice and courses offered by the Hague Academy of International Law.

From January 1979 to August 1980, Dr. Wang was a legal officer with the Chinese Ministry of Foreign Affairs. Dr. Wang also served as a translator with the United Nations Economic and Social Commission for Asia and the Pacific, and was an intern with the Office of Legal Affairs of the United Nations and the World Bank. During his stay in the United States, Dr. Wang also worked as a summer associate at Simpson, Thacher & Bartlett, Debevoise & Plimpton and O'Melveny & Myers.